D1334387

A COMPANION TO BEDE

The Venerable Bede (c.672–735) was a scholar of international standing from the early period of the Anglo-Saxon church. He not only wrote the well-known *Ecclesiastical History of the English People* but also scriptural commentaries, hagiographies, scientific works on time, admonitory letters, and poetry. Bede's life and writings provide more important information about the development of Christianity in England than any other source, and his influence extended far beyond his own time. This book provides an informative, comprehensive, and up-to-date guide to Bede and his writings, underlining in particular his importance in the development of European history and culture. It places Bede in his contemporary Northumbrian and early Anglo-Saxon England, dedicates individual chapters to his works, and includes a chapter on Bede's legacy for subsequent history.

Anglo-Saxon Studies

ISSN 1475–2468

GENERAL EDITORS
John Hines and Catherine Cubitt

'Anglo-Saxon Studies' aims to provide a forum for the best scholarship on the Anglo-Saxon peoples in the period from the end of Roman Britain to the Norman Conquest, including comparative studies involving adjacent populations and periods; both new research and major re-assessments of central topics are welcomed.

Books in the series may be based in any one of the principal disciplines of archaeology, art history, history, language and literature, and inter- or multi-disciplinary studies are encouraged.

Proposals or enquiries may be sent directly to the editors or the publisher at the addresses given below; all submissions will receive prompt and informed consideration.

Professor John Hines, School of History and Archaeology, Cardiff University, Colum Drive, Cardiff, Wales, UK CF10 3EU

Dr Catherine Cubitt, Centre for Medieval Studies, University of York, The King's Manor, York, England, UK YO1 7EP

Boydell & Brewer, PO Box 9, Woodbridge, Suffolk, England, UK IP12 3DF

Previously published volumes are listed at the back of this volume

A COMPANION TO
BEDE

George Hardin Brown

THE BOYDELL PRESS

First published 2009
The Boydell Press, Woodbridge

ISBN 978–1–84383–476–2

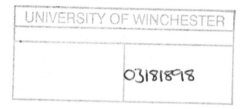

The Boydell Press is an imprint of Boydell & Brewer Ltd
PO Box 9, Woodbridge, Suffolk IP12 3DF, UK
and of Boydell & Brewer Inc.
668 Mt Hope Avenue, Rochester, NY 14620, USA
website: www.boydellandbrewer.com

The publisher has no responsibility for the continued existence or
accuracy of URLs for external or third-party internet websites
referred to in this book, and does not guarantee that any content on
such websites is, or will remain, accurate or appropriate.

A catalogue record of this publication is available
from the British Library

This publication is printed on acid-free paper

Printed in Great Britain by
CPI Antony Rowe, Chippenham and Eastbourne

Contents

Preface and Acknowledgments

From the eighth century to the present, the Venerable Bede has been honored as the father of English history; his contributions to every discipline of the early medieval curriculum have been established. During the past twenty years many new editions and translations of his works have appeared; some works thought lost have been rediscovered and wrongly attributed works have now been culled from his great repertory; numerous critical appraisals have been published emphasizing Bede's program of reform in his later works; and important studies of early Anglo-Saxon history have changed basic understandings of his life and times. Although excellent essays have examined Bede's contributions to individual disciplines, extensive analysis of all Bede's writings as related works are exceptionally rare. This new analysis of Bede's writings and influence synthesizes recent and older critical studies, especially of his less well-known writings, and reexamines his historical, exegetical, pedagogical, and epistolary writings from a unified perspective enriched by years of study.

Bede understood all his endeavors as related, and the thematic unity appears in various degrees and guises in every work; to see the unity of the whole, the entirety of his lifework must be encompassed. Historians have tried to detect Bede's motives in composing the *Ecclesiastical History of the English People* and his historically related works. Some think he was idealistically inspired to record the history that would go unrecognized if he did not do it; others suggest he had a more particular purpose, cleverly devised in execution, such as to counter Bishop Wilfrid's coterie and powerbase by holding up Cuthbert and his values as the true ideal. Without denying such special intentions, I contend that a complete survey of all Bede's writings reveals a larger consistent purpose and an overall design integral to his whole work. A review of Bede's exegesis and hagiography can elucidate his other writings, all sharing a single purpose: to express the working out of salvation history particularly among the English.

My research on the Venerable Bede and his works has greatly profited from numerous publications as well as shared insights and communications from Bedan scholars. Although I have tried to read all the available scholarship on Bede, I list only works I actually cite; so I apologize to all those whose works I have not formally noted.

I am particularly grateful for the resources, textual and electronic, of the Stanford University Libraries, and for my study in Green Library, a daily haven for research and writing. Michael Keller, University Librarian, and

Assunta Pisani, Associate University Librarian for Collections and Services, have been generous in their support. The reference librarians, especially Eric Heath, Rose Harrington, Miriam Palm, and Molly Molloy, have been unfailingly helpful; Mary-Louise Munill has efficiently provided interlibrary borrowing; R. T. Carr III has cheerfully searched for missing books in the stacks (and found them!); my former student in paleography and now assistant library director, David Jordan, has provided manuscript and bibliographic information; and John Mustain, rare book librarian, has enthusiastically assisted with numerous services and friendly counsel. I owe Kate Mustain special thanks for her meticulous proofreading of the manuscript and many suggestions for its improvement. I gratefully acknowledge the fine services of the expert copy editor Pam Cope and of the indexer *sans pareil*, Julia McVaugh.

In 1987 Twayne Publishers, now owned by CENGAGE Learning, published my *Bede the Venerable*, which received welcome reviews and has been widely cited. CENGAGE now generously permits me to use in this book the few portions of the earlier text that did not require revision; I am grateful for the permission. I am also grateful to the two readers of my manuscript for Boydell and Brewer who provided a number of helpful suggestions for improvement, which I have incorporated into my text. To Caroline Palmer, Editorial Director of Boydell & Brewer, I am particularly indebted for her encouragement, prudent advice, and always positive and thoroughly professional criticism.

To my wife Phyllis and sons Austin and Malcolm, and to Shannon Hogue, I give thanks for their loving support, and I dedicate this book to them with gratitude.

Abbreviations

ASE   *Anglo-Saxon England*. Ed. Malcolm Godden, Simon Keynes, et al. 35 vols. to date. Cambridge, 1972– .

CCCM   Corpus Christianorum, Continuatio Medievalis. c. 250 vols. to date. Turnhout, 1971.

CCSL   Corpus Christianorum, Series Latina. 251 vols. to date. Turnhout, 1953– .

CSEL   Corpus Scriptorum Ecclesiasticorum Latinorum. 95 vols. to date. Vienna, 1860– .

CSASE   Cambridge Studies in Anglo-Saxon England. Cambridge, 1990– .

DACL   *Dictionnaire d'archéologie chrétienne et de liturgie*, ed. F. Cabrol, H. Leclercq, and H. Marrou. 15 vols. Paris, 1907–53.

EHD   *English Historical Documents*, vol. 1: c. 500–1042, ed. Dorothy Whitelock. 2nd ed. Oxford, 1979.

HAA   *Historia abbatum auctore Baedae, in Baedae opera historica*, ed. Charles Plummer. Oxford, 1896; rpt. 1975. I: 384–87.

HE   *Bede's Ecclesiastical History of the English People*, ed. Bertram Colgrave and R. A. B. Mynors. Oxford, 1969.

JEGP   *Journal of English and Germanic Philology*. Bloomington, IN, 1897– .

MGH   Monumenta Germaniae Historica. Munich, 1826– .

PL   *Patrologia Latina*, ed. J-P. Migne. 221 vols. Paris, 1844–64.

RB   *Revue Bénédictine*. Maredsous, 1884– .

RSV   *The New Oxford Annotated Bible*, ed. Bruce M. Metzger and Roland E. Murphy. New Revised Standard Version. New York, 1994.

1

Bede's Life and Times

BEDE stands an eminence on the landscape of the eighth century; there is no other writer comparable. Gregory of Tours in the sixth century and Isidore of Seville and Aldhelm in the seventh century preceded him, and Alcuin of Tours followed at the end of the eighth century, but as a scholar Bede is supreme. In all Europe no contemporary matches his talents and influence. How do we account for Bede's erudition in a remote region of the North with its limited resources?[1] How is it that he is elevated so quickly to the high status of Father of the Church, the only monk to be granted that title, on a plane with Ambrose, Jerome, Augustine, and Gregory?[2] He spent his life far from urban centers of Europe, in a geographically isolated monastery. And who is responsible for his extraordinary erudition and mastery of Latin, of prose and poetry both? Of teachers besides his abbots Benedict Biscop and Ceolfrith, he mentions only one, Trumberht, "who taught me the Scriptures."[3] Although Bede was in fact an autodidact, he had great mentors, namely, the biblical texts and patristic authors found in his monastic library supplied by his provident superiors. With his energy and genius devouring and absorbing those works, he became master of every discipline in the monastic curriculum and "teacher of the whole Middle Ages."

Bede gained all that knowledge within the confines of the remote but well-endowed monastery established by his solicitous abbots, as the first words of his oft-quoted summary at the end of the *Ecclesiastical History* record:

---

[1] On the cultural shift to northern Europe during the age of Bede, see J. M. Wallace-Hadrill, *Bede's Europe*, Jarrow Lecture 1962, rpt. *Bede and his World*, ed. Michael Lapidge (Aldershot, 1992), I: 73–85 and in Wallace-Hadrill, *Early Medieval History* (Oxford, 1975), pp. 60–75: "A looking north, indeed, may be thought to characterize the age of Bede in Europe. It has been seen as a turning-away from the Mediterranean world of Late Antiquity, and as the beginning of the opening-up of a new, northern Europe, and Atlantic Europe, whether in compensation or through processes that were coincidental," p. 61.

[2] Pope Leo XIII, *Bulla Urbis et Orbis*, Acta Sanctae Sedis, 1897, pp. 338–39, declared Bede Doctor of the Universal Church, quoting Cardinal Bellarmine's words, "Beda Occidentem, Damascenus Orientem sapientia sua illustravit" ["Bede enlightened the West with his wisdom as John Damascene did for the East"], cited by Benedicta Ward, "Beda Venerabilis: *Doctor Anglorum*," in *Väter der Kirche: Ekklesiales Denken von den Anfängen bis in die Neuzeit*, ed. Johannes Arnold, Rainer Berndt, and Ralf M. W. Stammberger (Paderborn, 2004), pp. 533–42 at 533.

[3] "... sicut mihi frater quidam de his qui me in scripturis erudiebant," *Bede's Ecclesiastical History of the English People*, ed. Bertram Colgrave and R. A. B. Mynors (Oxford, 1969), p. 242. Hereafter abbreviated as *HE*.

I, Bede, servant of God and priest of the monastery of St. Peter and St. Paul which is at Wearmouth and Jarrow, have, with the help of God and to the best of my ability, put together this account of the history of the Church of Britain and of the English people in particular, gleaned either from ancient documents or from tradition or from my own knowledge. I was born in the territory of this monastery. When I was seven years of age I was, by the care of my kinsmen, put into the charge of the reverend Abbot Benedict and then Ceolfrith, to be educated. From then on I have spent all my life in this monastery, applying myself entirely to the study of the Scriptures; and, amid the observance of the discipline of the Rule and the daily task of singing in the church, it has always been my delight to learn or to teach or to write. At the age of nineteen I was ordained deacon and at the age of thirty, priest, both times through the ministration of the reverend Bishop John on the direction of Abbot Ceolfrith. From the time I became a priest until the fifty-ninth year of my life I have made it my business, for my own benefit and that of my brothers, to make brief comments from the works of the venerable fathers on the holy Scriptures, and also to add my contribution to their formulations of understanding and interpretation.[4]

From that serene autobiographical note we might be led to assume that Bede would be remote and disengaged from the world and public life, but his writings, both exegetical and historical, show an acute awareness of the extramural world.[5] He is aware of severe failures in both secular and religious realms. He addresses the problems of his church and society and expresses a sober and strong call for reform.[6] Because of his stability and support within an austere but humane monastic environment Bede could develop his brilliant powers of assimilation and production, and address contemporary issues in both the religious and secular spheres. Even though his monastery was under the direct protection of the papacy and exempt from episcopal control, and even though Wearmouth-Jarrow was an independent landhold, Bede and his community were seriously affected by events and policies of

---

4   *HE*, V. 24, p. 567; Latin on p. 566. Colgrave's translation of the last phrase is corrected to interpret Bede's Latin more accurately, as I explain in Ch. 3, p. 33 with n. 5. On the semantic significance of Bede's use of the term "brothers" especially in the *Ecclesiastical History* see Olivier Szerwiniack, "Frères et sœurs dans *l'Histoire ecclésiastique du peuple anglais* de Bède le Vénérable: De la fratrie biologique à la fratrie spirituelle," *RB* 118.2 (2008): 239–61.

5   Catherine Cubitt, "Monastic Memory and Identity in Early Anglo-Saxon England," in *Social Identity in Early Medieval Britain*, ed. William O. Frazer and Andrew Tyrell (London, 2000), pp. 253–76 at 256: "The image created by [Janet] Coleman [in *Ancient and Medieval Memories: Studies in the Reconstruction of the Past* (1992)] of the early medieval monastery as a placid collection of individuals, striving in unison for spiritual perfection, absorbed in the study of books, fits ill with what other texts tell us about it."

6   A number of scholars have emphasized Bede's call and commitment to reform; see, for instance, Alan Thacker, "Bede's Ideal of Reform," in *Ideal and Reality in Frankish and Anglo-Saxon Society*, ed. Patrick Wormald, Donald Bullough, and Roger Collins (Oxford, 1983), pp. 130–53; on Bede's strict moral stance and call for repentance, see, for instance, Sr. M. Thomas Aquinas Carroll, *The Venerable Bede: His Spiritual Teachings* (Washington, DC, 1946), esp. chs. 4 and Conclusion.

both secular and sacred realms. Bede dealt with various parties ecclesiastical and secular with diplomatic care.

The monastery, its founders, and its library

Almost all the information we have about the early history of the abbey, the founder and early superiors, and indeed much of the history of Northumbria comes from Bede himself – from his *Historia ecclesiastica*, *Historia abbatum*, and occasional comments in the prefaces and texts of his biblical commentaries. What other documentation we have, such as regnal and genealogical lists, archaeological remains, the *Anglo-Saxon Chronicle*, and some local histories, such as the anonymous *Life of Abbot Ceolfrith*, largely corroborates Bede's accounts.

The founder of the monastery, Benedict Biscop (d. 689), had been a member of the court of King Oswiu (ruled 655–70). Like a number of early Anglo-Saxon kings and nobles, Biscop left the precarious secular life of the warrior-class to become a religious pilgrim and then a monk: "He put behind him the things that perish so that he might gain those that last forever, despising earthly warfare with its corruptible rewards so that he might fight for the true king and win the crown in the heavenly city."[7] Monks, abbots and inmates such as Bede, though subject to contagious diseases within their enclosed communities, lived relatively long. By comparison, kings and athelings (nobles who in the Germanic clan society were all eligible for kingship) rarely survived middle age. Rulers and princes were subject to conspiracies, assassinations, feuds, and frequent warfare, and their kingdoms lasted but briefly and precariously. In the seventh century the rich and powerful Northumbrian kings of the joint kingdom of Deira and Bernicia usually died in battle; in the eighth century the multiple claimants to the thrones died by treachery. Barbara Yorke concludes the grim history of the later Northumbrian kingship thus:

> This bald summary does not do justice to the details of the many conspiracies of the period nor give the full flavour of the violence of the times. Violent attacks were not only made against the reigning kings, but also against æthelings, the sons and close relatives of kings who were potential candidates for the

---

[7] Bede, *The Lives of the Abbots of Wearmouth and Jarrow*, trans. D. H. Farmer in *The Age of Bede* (Harmondsworth, 1965, rpt. 1986), p. 185. The Latin original is printed as *Historia abbatum auctore Baeda* in Charles Plummer's excellent edition and commentary, *Baedae opera historica* (Oxford, 1896, rpt. 1975), I: 364–87 (hereafter abbreviated as *HAA*). Most information about Benedict comes from this biography, but see also Eric Fletcher, *Benedict Biscop*, Jarrow Lecture 1981, rpt. *Bede and his World*, ed. Michael Lapidge (Aldershot, 1994), II: 539–54; Patrick Wormald, "Bede and Benedict Biscop," in *Famulus Christi*, ed. Gerald Bonner (London, 1976), rpt. Patrick Wormald, *The Times of Bede*, ed. Stephen Baxter (Oxford, 2006), pp. 3–29; and the entry on Benedict with bibliography by Lapidge, *Blackwell Encylopedia of Anglo-Saxon England* (Oxford, 1999), p. 60. For an analysis of the secular and ecclesial social relationships in Anglo-Saxon society see my article, "Royal and Ecclesiastical Rivalries in Bede's *History*," *Renascence* 52.1 (1999): 19–34.

throne. King Eadbert, for instance, besieged the church of Lindisfarne in 750 in order to extract Offa, the last surviving son of King Aldfrith, and King Æthelred murdered Ælf and Ælfwine, the sons of King Æflwold, in 791 ... There were fourteen reigns between those of Osred and Eardwulf. The fate of two rulers, Cenred and Osric, is obscure but their reigns are suspiciously short; six rulers were deposed and forced into exile or into religious houses; four were murdered; and two apparently resigned voluntarily to enter religious houses and secure the succession of relatives.[8]

Of course, the warrior-class, disruptive as it was, was necessary for the life of the monastery: it formed the territorial state and provided political, albeit fragile, stability, furnished some protection against invaders, gave the land and endowment for the foundation and its continuance, and served as the source in large part for the major personnel of the community.

Benedict Biscop left the king's court and set off at age twenty-five on what would be the first of five trips to Rome with another young noble from court, Wilfrid, destined to become the great controversial abbot and bishop. After his second trip to Rome Biscop became a novice at the austere monastery of Lérins (off the coast of the French Riviera), which had been founded by St. Honoratus in 410; there during his two-year sojourn he exchanged his secular name of Biscop Baducing for Benedict Biscop. Returning to Rome, he was assigned by Pope Vitalian (ruled 657–72) to accompany Theodore (c. 602–90; like St. Paul, a native of Tarsus in Cilicia) to England as archbishop-elect of Canterbury (elected 667 or early 668, consecrated March 668). Benedict Biscop became the abbot of Saints Peter and Paul in Canterbury for two years, until the arrival of Theodore's colleague, the African Hadrian, in 670.[9] The following year Benedict Biscop was again on the Continent, collecting books for a monastic foundation, which he established in his native Northumbria at present-day Monkwearmouth (at the mouth of the Wear River, as the name indicates), with land given by King Ecgfrith (ruled 670–85).[10]

As was the custom for early monastic founders, Benedict Biscop created his own rule, which he said was selected from the best of those used in seventeen monasteries,[11] but from the writings of Bede and echoes of the

---

8   Barbara Yorke, *The Kings and Kingdoms of Early Anglo-Saxon England* (London, 1990, rpt. 1992), p. 89. Note the regnal list on p. 87 with annotations of "murdered," "deposed," "exiled," etc. See also David N. Dumville, "The Local Rulers of England to AD 927," in *Handbook of British Chronology*, ed. E. B. Fryde, D. F. Greenway, S. Porter, I. Roy (London, 1986), pp. 1–25.

9   On the careers of Theodore and Hadrian, see Bernhard Bischoff and Michael Lapidge, *Biblical Commentaries from the Canterbury School of Theodore and Hadrian* (Cambridge, 1994), chs. 2–3.

10 On this history of the territory, foundations, and institutions of Northumbria, Durham, and Wearmouth-Jarrow see William Page, ed., *The Victoria History of the Counties of England: Durham*, 3 vols. (London, 1905, rpt. 1968), and the earlier great *History and Antiquities of the County Palatine of Durham* by Robert Surtees, 4 vols. (London, 1816–40); also Frank Stenton, *Anglo-Saxon England*, 3rd ed. (Oxford, 1968, reissued 2001); and Rosemary Cramp, *Wearmouth and Jarrow Monastic Sites*, English Heritage (Swindon, 2005).

11 Bede, *Lives of the Abbots*, ch. 11, trans. Farmer, p. 196; *HAA*, I: 374; Bede, *Homilies on the Gospels*, Homily I. 13, trans. L .T. Martin and D. Hurst (Kalamazoo, 1991), I: 129. It is possible

Rule in his works, it is clear that the Rule of St. Benedict was an important part of that synthetic compilation.[12] Furthermore, Bede's description of the monastic life at Wearmouth-Jarrow in his history of his abbots seems to imply a considerate rule, similar to that of St. Benedict, rather than the austere *regulae* of the Irish foundations, such as Iona and Lindisfarne.

Although Benedict Biscop provided fine decoration for his abbey churches, the heart of his enterprise was the library he had assembled on his journeys. His dying request was that "the fine and extensive library of books which he had brought back from Rome ... should be kept preserved as a single collection and not allowed to decay through neglect or be split up piecemeal."[13] If the Wearmouth-Jarrow library was one of the best in Europe, with ca. 250 books (excluding biblical and liturgical texts),[14] it could not compare with the great libraries of classical antiquity or those of the later Middle Ages and after. Bede made remarkable use of the library which Benedict Biscop and Ceolfrith established for him and his fellows, even though, rich as it was for the time, it was lacking in many works from antiquity that we would consider essential. As Calvin Kendall points out,

> Bede's library did not contain any of the major philosophical, educational, or philological texts of classical Antiquity. It goes without saying that the Greek authors were missing. So also were Cicero and Quintilian and Varro. But the gaps extend to other works, which are often considered to have been instrumental in the molding of the curriculum of the early Middle Ages – the *Ad Herennium*, Martianus Capella, Fulgentius, Boethius, Macrobius.[15]

But Bede was grateful for what he did have for his use, and he speaks with great respect for Benedict Biscop in the *Ecclesiastical History*, the *History of the Abbots*, and the Homily on the Founder's Feast Day, in which he says:

---

that the "regulae" referred as much to individual customaries (local variants) as to integral rules. On the flexible nature of monasticism in Ango-Saxon England and how it differed from the later monasticism of the tenth-century Benedictine reform, see Sarah Foot's excellent history, *Monastic Life in Anglo-Saxon England, c. 600–900* (New York, 2006).

[12] The notion that the monasteries of Wearmouth-Jarrow followed the Rule of St. Benedict despite Bede's testimony to the contrary was widespread, especially among Benedictine historians of the last century. Charles Forbes, comte de Montalembert, for instance, in *The Monks of the West, from St. Benedict to St. Bernard* (London, 1896), 4: 179, claims that Benedict Biscop "took care to constitute his community upon the immovable basis of the rule of St. Benedict," and on pp. 239–71 he lauds Bede as an ideal Benedictine. Even more recently Bede is sometimes still called a Benedictine: Friedrich Stegmüller, *Repertorium biblicum medii aevi* (Madrid, 1950–80), II: 186, lists "Beda O.S.B." The fact that Benedict Biscop's early companion, Wilfrid, did adopt the Rule of Benedict for his foundations and Bede echoes phrases of the Rule may have contributed to the historical confusion. See Peter Hunter Blair, *The World of Bede* (Cambridge, 1970, rev. 1990), ch. 19, "The Regular Life," pp. 197–210.

[13] Bede, *Lives of the Abbots*, trans. Farmer, ch. 11, p. 196. Latin in *HAA*, I. 375.

[14] Michael Lapidge, *The Anglo-Saxon Library* (Oxford, 2006), p. 60. To compare the library holdings of Wearmouth-Jarrow to other Anglo-Saxon and ninth-century Carolingian libraries, see pp. 58–60. For Bede's individual works in the libraries see the General Index, pp. 385–86.

[15] Calvin B. Kendall, ed. and trans., *Libri II De arte metrica et De schematibus et tropis* (Saarbrücken, 1991), Introduction, p. 17.

Now we are his children, since as a pious provider he brought us into this monastic house. We are his children since he has made us to be gathered spiritually into one family of holy profession, though in terms of the flesh we were brought forth of different parents. We are his children if by imitating him we hold to the path of his virtues, if we are not turned aside by sluggishness from the narrow path of the rule that he taught.[16]

Towards the end of the homily Bede speaks to his community about their indebtedness to Benedict Biscop:

He worked so zealously that we are freed from the need to labor in this way; he journeyed so many times to places across the sea that we, abounding in all the resources of spiritual knowledge, can as a result be at peace within the cloisters of the monastery, with secure freedom to serve Christ.[17]

After Benedict Biscop, the second major personage to figure in the monastic foundation is Ceolfrith (c. 642–716), a noble fourteen years junior to Benedict, who had been a monk first in North Gilling (Yorkshire) and then at Ripon, where he was ordained by Bishop Wilfrid. He joined Benedict Biscop, to become first prior at St. Peter's but returned to Ripon after losing control over a group of noblemen who had entered the monastery unwilling to accept the discipline of the rule. Benedict Biscop persuaded Ceolfrith to return; and with order restored and community life thriving, he went with Benedict to acquire on the Continent, especially at Rome, books and other furnishings for the monastery.

The fourth trip of Benedict Biscop and Ceolfrith from England was of particular importance for the acquisition of more books as well as relics, paintings for the church, a papal letter of privilege providing exemption from episcopal and secular control, and the service of John, "chief cantor of St. Peter's [Rome] and abbot of the monastery of St. Martin," brought to teach the English monks proper liturgical chant.[18] Ceolfrith is credited by Bede with doubling the library's collection, already impressive because of Benedict's acquisitions.[19] On their return they received into their care the seven-year-old Bede. With a second endowment of land from King Ecgfrith, Benedict Biscop opened the second foundation, St. Paul's, at nearby Jarrow, but the two houses were constituted a single monastery. Benedict Biscop appointed his cousin Eosterwine as abbot to serve in his place during his extended travels. Eosterwine, though a noble, exemplified in his way of life (*conversatio*) egalitarian humility:

---

[16] Bede the Venerable, *Homilies on the Gospels*, trans. Lawrence Martin and David Hurst (Kalamazoo, 1991), I: 131; The Latin text is found in Bedae Venerabilis, *Homiliarium evangelii libri II*, ed. D. Hurst, CCSL 122 (Turnhout, 1955), *Homelia* I. 13, pp. 89–94, at 93.

[17] Translation by Benedicta Ward, *The Venerable Bede* (Harrisburg, PA, 1990), p. 6.

[18] Bede, *HAA*, ch. 6, and *HE*, IV. 18 (16).

[19] *HAA*, ch. 15, p. 201.

When Eosterwine entered the monastery it never occurred to him to use his birth or his relationship to the abbot to his own advantage; nor was he shown the slightest favour by Benedict. Realizing that monastic profession put him and his brethren on an equal footing, this young man resolved that his only pride should lie in striving to to keep the monastic rule in every detail. When he had turned his back once and for all on the life of the world and had ceased to be King Ecgfrith's thane by laying down his arms and girding himself for spiritual warfare, he kept himself so humble and identified himself so completely with the brethren that he took positive delight in sharing their ordinary work. He took his share of the winnowing and threshing, the milking of ewes and the cows; he laboured in bakehouse, garden and kitchen, taking part cheerfully and obediently in every monastery chore. He was no different when he attained to the rank and authority of abbot.[20]

Eosterwine lasted only a short time as abbot because he and many of his monks were struck down by the plague. Benedict Biscop replaced him with Sigfrid and had Ceolfrith, with a colony from the hive at St. Peter's at Wearmouth, establish the sister monastery of St. Paul's at nearby Jarrow; and, as abbot, Ceolfrith dedicated the new basilican church on 23 May 685 (the ancient dedicatory stone is still *in situ*).[21] The new house nearly failed when the plague struck, carrying off all the choir monks except Ceolfrith himself and one boy, who some speculate was Bede.[22] When Bede was seventeen the abbots Benedict Biscop and Sigfrid died, and Ceolfrith became at about forty-seven abbot of both houses of the monastery. Although Bede revered Benedict Biscop, he had a special love for Ceolfrith, so much so that at Ceolfrith's resignation from the abbacy and departure for Rome, Bede underwent a crisis, which he tells us about in the preface to the fourth book of his commentary on I Samuel:

Having completed the third book of the commentary on Samuel, I thought I would rest a while, and, after recovering in that way my delight in study and writing, proceed to take in hand the fourth. But that rest – if sudden anguish of mind can be called rest – has turned out much longer than I had intended owing to the sudden change of circumstances brought about by the departure of my most reverend Abbot; who, after long devotion to the care of his monastery, suddenly determined to go to Rome and to breathe his last breath amid the localities sanctified by the bodies of the blessed apostles and martyrs of Christ,

---

[20] Bede, *Lives of the Abbots*, trans. Farmer, ch. 8, pp. 192–93; Latin in *HAA*, I: 371–72.

[21] See Rosemary Cramp, *Wearmouth and Jarrow Monastic Sites* (Swindon, 2005), pp. 31–172 at 144.

[22] *Life of Ceolfrid*, trans. D. S. Boutflower (London, 1912; rpt. Llanerch, 1991), ch. 14, p. 65; the Latin original is printed by Plummer in *Baedae opera historica* as *Historia abbatum auctore anonymo*, I: 388–404 at 393. Plummer remarks, I: xii, "The little boy here mentioned can hardly be any other than Bede himself"; and a number of subsequent scholars agree. Dorothy Whitelock, however, in "Bede and his Teachers and Friends," in *Famulus Christi*, ed. Gerald Bonner (London, 1976), pp. 20–23, for a number of (inconclusive) reasons doubts that Bede was meant; possibly it was the anonymous author (Hwætberht?) of the *Life of Ceolfrid* himself. If so, that would perhaps mean that Bede was a monk not at St. Paul's but at St. Peter's at the time.

thus causing no little consternation to those committed to his charge, the greater because it was unexpected.[23]

The abbots who provided the books for the library assured the functioning of a well-ordered monastery in which Bede could pray and work.[24] Although limited in scope to religious texts, the library boasted a fine collection, including part-Bibles (that is, individual books of the Bible separately bound), and, unusual for the time, a complete Bible (pandect), the Codex Grandior from Cassiodorus's Vivarium, brought by Ceolfrith from Italy in c. 679–80.[25] With its spacious layout and formal script it served as a proper model for the three great Bibles created at Wearmouth-Jarrow, including the still-extant Codex Amiatinus (now in Florence, Biblioteca Medicea Laurenziana, as Amiatino 1), "the earliest surviving complete Vulgate Bible anywhere and our only complete pre-Conquest source for the Old Testament text in Anglo-Saxon England."[26] The scriptorium produced high-quality books, both Bibles and other texts.[27] The abbey, a haven of ascetic life, prayer, and study in the midst of the stormy world of Anglo-Saxon England, provided Bede the right home for his productive life and a base from which to observe critically his world.

Bede's career and works

Into this bleak world comes the brilliant Bede, without recorded parentage and traceable ancestry and with an unusual name, a name that appears only three or four times in all Anglo-Saxon records.[28] In the early manuscripts of the *Historia ecclesiastica* and in other contemporary sources his name appears as Bæda; in the Middle Ages he was Beda, but to the English-

---

23 Translation by Charles Plummer in Bede, *Opera historica*, I: xv; the Latin text is Bede, *In I Samuhelem*, ed. D. Hurst, CCSL 119, liber IV, *praefatio* (Turnhout, 1962), p. 213.

24 Richard Marsden, *The Text of the Old Testament in Anglo-Saxon England*, CSASE 15 (Cambridge, 1995), p. 86, calls attention to the fact that the anonymous chronicler in *Vita Ceolfrithi*, ch. 20, ed. C. Plummer, *Venerabilis Bedae opera historica*, I: 395, says that Ceolfrith augmented the texts in the monastery by having the Bible and other books copied, "et bibliothecam, quam de Roma uel ipse, uel Benedictus adtulerat, nobiliter ampliauit, ita ut inter alia tres Pandectes faceret describi ..." ["he splendidly enriched and enlarged the collection of books which he and Benedict had brought back from Rome, so that, among other things, he caused to be made three pandects ...].

25 *Historia abbatum*, ch. 15, in Plummer, ed., *HAA*, in *Bedae opera historica*, I: 379–80; Peter Hunter Blair, *World of Bede*, 2nd ed. (Cambridge, 1990), pp. 221–25; Meyvaert, "Bede, Cassiodorus, and Codex Amiatinus," p. 836; Marsden, *Text of the Old Testament*, pp. 6, 30, 86.

26 Marsden, *Text of the Old Testament*, p. 76.

27 Superior quality Bible production was a specialty of Wearmouth-Jarrow, as Julian Brown, Malcolm Parkes, and others have noted. Marsden, in *Text of the Old Testament*, adds, p. 80: "The fact that, under Ceolfrith (689–716), the house was able to produce three books of one thousand leaves each, the last of them, at least, written and illustrated to the finest standards, as well as undertake a programme of gospel-book, psalter and other copying, argues for a scriptorium with excellent human and material resources."

28 See the summation of the data regarding Bede's name in N. J. Higham, *(Re-)Reading Bede* (London, 2006), p. 9 and nn. 21–24.

speaking people he is known as Bede. Bede was fittingly born on the very property that in a year or two (674) would become the monastery's domain. He was totally dedicated to the religious life, subject to his surrogate parents in religion Benedict and Ceolfrith. Though he gives some bare essentials of his life, we would like to know much more.[29] Historians James Campbell and Alan Thacker have theorized that Bede was of noble even royal descent and related to Benedict Biscop and Ceolfrith, but there seems no evidence for this other than that he writes with secure authority. On the other hand, others have assumed Bede was probably not a member of the aristocracy, which may help explain why he was never, like the nobles Benedict and Ceolfrith, appointed prior or abbot.[30] Bede's autobiographical sketch quoted above, remarks in his writings, the report of his student and later abbot, Cuthbert, and the witness of his contemporaries all indicate that he lived the monastic life exemplarily. We know very little about his early education. Apart from his mentor-abbots Benedict Biscop and Ceolfrith, we have the name of only one instructor, Trumberht, whom Bede mentions in his *Ecclesiastical History* (IV, 3) as one of his teachers in the Scriptures.[31] Although Dorothy Whitelock asserts that "it is obvious that Bede's knowledge could not have been acquired only from books," the lack of a contemporary record of any comparable Latinist, historian, or theologian in Bede's circle argues for Bede's being largely an autodidact.[32] What models he followed to develop his admirable Latin style (or styles, as he varies his style according to genre – history, exegesis, poetry) is unknown, but he obviously learned a great deal from his perusal of the writings of the Fathers. Moreover, he was at the time one of the very few in the West besides the disciples of Theodore and Hadrian at Canterbury to acquire a working knowledge of Greek (the only other one who comes to

---

[29] Henry Mayr-Harting, *The Venerable Bede, the Rule of St Benedict, and Social Class*, Jarrow Lecture 1976, pp. 16–17, rpt. in *Bede and his World*, ed. Michael Lapidge (London, 1994), I: 422–23, suggests that Bede with his clerical ideal of a classless monastic society wished to be like the priest Melchisedech (Genesis 14: 18), who "had no beginning to his priesthood, no end, no predecessor, no successor." Cf. Bede, *In Genesim*, CCSL 118A, p. 192. He deliberately suppressed biographical data of family and parentage, linking himself closely only to his monastery.

[30] James Campbell in his entry on Bede for the *Oxford Dictionary of National Biography*, ed. H. C. G. Matthew and Brian Harrison (Oxford, 2004) 4: 758–65 at 758 (also online at http://www.oxforddnb.com/) wrote: "A coincidence of names in a list (c. 800) of the kings of Lindsey strengthens the considerable likelihood that he was of high birth: a Beda there appears in succession to a king called Biscop, the name of the noble founder and first abbot of Bede's monastery." However, the genealogical list makes Biscop Beding the successor to Beda Bubbing, not the other way around. Since the text is late ninth-century and the author is acquainted with Bede's work, the genealogy may be invented. For the list see David Dumville, "The Anglian Collection of Royal Genealogies and Regnal Lists," *ASE* 5 (1976): 31; also www.kmatthews.org.uk/history/anglian_collection.html. Alan Thacker, "Bede and the Ordering of Understanding," in *Innovation and Tradition in the Writings of the Venerable Bede*," ed. Scott DeGregorio (Morgantown, 2006), pp. 37–63 at 40, asserts that "Bede was not a humble or a modest figure. He was probably socially very grand ..." Although Bede writes with the voice of dignity, "socially very grand" seems excessive.

[31] See Plummer, ed., *Bedae opera historica*, I: 210 and II: 209.

[32] Dorothy Whitelock, "Bede and his Teachers and Friends," in *Famulus Christi*, ed. Gerald Bonner (London, 1976), 19–39 at 24.

mind is John Scottus Eriugena).[33] Though he had access to other information about Greek grammar and vocabulary, a Greek version of Acts parallel with the Latin aided his acquisition of the language.[34] Bede was able to read and draw from a Greek source for entries into his *Martyrologium*.[35] His knowledge of Hebrew seems confined to the explanation of Hebrew names and etymons by Jerome.

Although he was later to write admiringly of locations sacred to Christianity, such as the Holy Land (for which he wrote a guidebook based on Adomnán's report from a supposedly eyewitness account by a wandering bishop called Arculf), Rome – a pilgrimage to which "in those days was considered an act of great merit"[36] and Canterbury, and though he praised pilgrimages as acts of great merit undertaken by kings Oswiu and Cædwalla, and his abbots Benedict Biscop and Ceolfrith, nevertheless, except for a few short trips (we know of one to Lindisfarne and one to York), he never engaged in the pilgrimages so beloved by Irish-trained monks. He spent the rest of his life in his monastery practicing the virtue of stability.[37]

Bede had the exceptionally well-stocked library to draw upon; and, since his abbots procured choice books, which the scriptorium amplified, Bede was assured a supply of major texts for his research, writing, and teaching.[38] He immersed himself in his studies and, ordained deacon at the age of nineteen, six years before the canonical age, and priest at an early age, he took up his position of *magister*.[39] He prepared for that role by vast reading, deep study,

---

[33] Eriugena is also associated with Bede because he drew upon Bede's scientific works: see John J. Contreni, *History and Eschatology in John Scottus Eriugena and his Time* (Leuven, 2002), ch. 6: "John Scottus and Bede."

[34] Bede probably had use of the still-extant bilingual manuscript Oxford, Bodleian MS Laudianus Graecus 35. See M. L. W. Laistner, ed., *Bedae venerabilis expositio Actuum Apostolorum et retractatio* (Cambridge, MA, 1939), pp. xxxix–xl. Although W. F. Bolton expressed doubt about Bede's active knowledge of Greek in "An Aspect of Bede's Later Knowledge of Greek," *Classical Review*, n.s. 13:1 (1963): 17–18, Kevin M. Lynch, "The Venerable Bede's Knowledge of Greek," *Traditio* 39 (1983): 432–39, demonstrated by a number of convincing examples Bede's active and rather extensive knowledge of biblical Greek.

[35] See Michael Lapidge, "Acca of Hexham and the Origin of the Old English Martyrology," *Analecta Bollandiana* 123 (Brussels, 2005): 29–78 at 71.

[36] *HE*, IV. 23, pp. 408–9. On the putative Arculf, see Thomas O'Loughlin, *Adomnán and the Holy Places* (London and New York, 2007), pp. 61–63, 192.

[37] Cf. *RB 1980: The Rule of St. Benedict* (Collegeville, 1981), Rule 58.17 and Appendix 5, pp. 463–64.

[38] See Dorothy Whitelock, *After Bede*, Jarrow Lecture 1960, pp. 13–14; rpt. *Bede and his World*, ed. Michael Lapidge (Aldershot, 1994), I: 47–48. The library of Wearmouth-Jarrow, though respectably large, seems not to have equaled that of Canterbury under the masters Theodore and Hadrian. See Bede's own statement, *HE*, IV. 2, and Michael Lapidge, "The School of Theodore and Hadrian," *ASE* 15 (1986): 45–72; "The Study of Greek at the School of Canterbury in the Seventh Century," in *The Sacred Nectar of the Greeks: the Study of Greek in the West in the Early Middle Ages*, ed. Michael W. Herren, King's College London Medieval Studies 2 (London, 1988), pp. 169–94; Bernhard Bischoff and Michael Lapidge, *Biblical Commentaries from the Canterbury School of Theodore and Hadrian*, CSASE 10 (Cambridge, 1994), and Michael Lapidge, ed., *Archbishop Theodore: Commemorative Studies on his Life and Influence*, CSASE 11 (Cambridge 1995).

[39] *HE*, Historical Introduction, ed. Colgrave and Mynors, pp. xx–xxi.

and phenomenal familiarization with and memorization of patristic texts. As Max Laistner in *Thought and Letters in Western Europe AD 500–900* comments:

> No writer within the period covered by this book had read as widely as Bede. He had studied most of Jerome's works, much of Augustine, all of Gregory the Great, six or seven treatises by Ambrose and most of Isidore. But besides these standard authors, he cites from a surpisingly large and diversified number of other writings, so that the total number of titles with which he shows acquaintance is not far short of two hundred.[40]

As Michael Lapidge notes, "For more than a century Wearmouth-Jarrow outshone all other Northumbrian monasteries as a result of the learning and fame of its most celebrated monk, the Venerable Bede."[41] Using his capacious learning, he became the outstanding teacher of his monastery, and, drawing on his encyclopedic mastery of all the subjects in the monastic school curriculum, in each discipline he created works that served for the instruction of the whole Middle Ages.[42]

As the long list of works that Bede appends as his bibliography at the end of the *Ecclesiastical History* manifests, his life, if pious and meditative, was quietly energetic. In chapel he established, as Alcuin attests, a reputation as a devout monk who always participated in the chanting of the sacred Office.[43]

In the scriptorium his output was prodigious.[44] He not only composed the texts but at least for an extended period made the copies as well: he wrote to his patron bishop and intimate friend Acca, "I myself am at once my own dictator, stenographer, and copyist."[45] Having completed a draft ("edere")

---

[40] M. L. W. Laistner, *Thought and Letters in Western Europe AD 500–900* (Ithaca, 1957), p. 162. He continues, p. 63: "Yet, however great his debt to his predecessors may be, he does not copy uncritically. He is careful to select what will be useful and intelligible to his readers, he adds his own comments and observations, and he has knit the whole together in a way that raises his theological works well above the level of mere complilation of *catenae* and which bears clearly the impress of his own mind and personality."

[41] Michael Lapidge, *Anglo-Latin Literature, 600–899* (London and Rio Grande, 1996), p. 14. For a succinct survey of Bede's career and writings, see pp. 14–21. Lapidge has now done a detailed annotated list and dating of Bede's works in his introduction to the Italian edition of the *HE* (Milan, 2008), I: xlii–lvii.

[42] On Bede as teacher see my *Bede the Educator*, Jarrow Lecture 1996 (Jarrow, 1997).

[43] Alcuin writes in a Letter to the monks of Wearmouth translated by Plummer, *Baedae opera historica*, I: xii–xiii: "It is said that our master and your patron, the blessed Bede, said, 'I know that angels visit the canonical hours and the meetings of the brethren. What if they should not find me there among them? Will they not say, where is Bede? Why does he not come to the devotions prescribed for the brethren?'" The Latin of the text is in *Councils and Ecclesiastical Documents relating to Great Britain and Ireland*, ed. A. W. Haddan and W. Stubbs (Oxford, 1869–78), III: 470–71.

[44] To see Bede's works within the context of the whole history of Latin ecclesiastical writers, see Roger Gryson's great *Répertoire général des auteurs ecclésiastiques latins de l'antiquité et du haut Moyen Âge* (Freiburg, 2007), I: 327–34.

[45] Bede, *In Lucam*, prologus, ed. D. Hurst, CCSL 120, p. 7: "Ipse mihi dictator simul notarius et librarius existerem." In responses to Acca, Bede dedicated five of his commentaries to him. See Lapidge, "Acca of Hexham," *Analecta Bollandiana* 123 (2005): 66.

and sending it to one or more trusted readers for comment, he would then publish it ("transcribere") and let it be copied and circulated in a finished form.[46]

Bede taught and wrote school texts for the first two and probably all three basic disciplines of grammar, computus, and music: grammar, to understand the text of Scripture; computus, to reckon time for the liturgical calendar; and music, to sing in various chant modes for the *opus Dei* in choir. Although musical notation for chant was not to be devised until a century later, Bede did instruct his pupils in hymnology.[47] Bede wrote texts as part of grammatical instruction on metrics and figurative language, and organized a handbook on correct usage. He did a small piece on natural science, and two major works, one early and the other late and completely revised, on computus, the instruction in the complicated science of time reckoning. He wrote a book of hymns in various meters, a book (now lost) of poetic epigrams, and occasional poems. He composed a versified and a prose *Life of St. Cuthbert* as well as other saints' lives and a martyrology.

As a teacher-scholar Bede produced commentaries on books of the Old and New Testament, by far the largest section of his collected works. As the primary subject of monastic study is the Bible this emphasis is not surprising. Within the past forty years many new editions and translations have made his commentaries available and have brought a great deal of interest, once concentrated on Bede's historical writings, to these works. It is also not surprising that Bede, as a religious dedicated to spreading God's word, produced two books of homilies, containing fifty reflections on the gospels, many derived from his gospel commentaries. These homilies have also been translated. In the Middle Ages they found their way into homiletic collections for the use of preachers during the course of the ecclesiastical year, and parts of them are still used in the Roman Breviary. Readers of Bede's writings today are principally clerics and scholars, and that was also the case in his own day. He ardently espoused education for both clergy and laity, as his famous letter to Bishop Ecgbert witnesses, but though he produced some catechetical texts in English, his primary function was pastoral educator of religious, clergy, and of educated secular leaders; and for them he wrote in Latin, the language of educated Europeans.[48]

---

46 See Paul Meyvaert, "Medieval Notions of Publication," *Journal of Medieval Latin* 12 (2002): 78–89 at 80.

47 The editor of Bede's *Opera didascalia*, Charles Jones, CCSL 123A, pp. vi, viii–ix, thinks it likely that Bede was indeed the choirmaster in his monastery. Cuthbert in his Letter on the Death of Bede links Bede's daily instructing with chant performance, referring to "the lessons which we received from him daily and his chanting of the Psalter" (*HE*, pp. 582–83). If Bede instructed in music practice, he had no means of writing a practical text for it, since there was no system of writing notation until much later; Augustine's and Boethius's theoretical tracts *De musica* provided no instruction for the actual singing of chant.

48 Arthur G. Holder, trans., *Bede: On the Tabernacle* (Liverpool, 1994), p. xiv: "The primary audience of Bede's biblical commentaries was that select group of preachers and teachers which included the members of the ordained clergy as well as others holding some form of spiritual

Although Bede was honored in the Middle Ages mainly for his theological treatises, he is best known to our age as an historian. The accomplishment of the *Ecclesiastical History of the English People* gained Bede the accolade "father of English History," and the uniquely valuable information the *History* furnishes puts all English, medieval, and church historians greatly in his debt. It is also stylistically and structurally a masterpiece of literature, and its early translation into Old English (at the end of the ninth century) further enhances its worth for literary historians. Bede's *Lives of the Abbots of Wearmouth and Jarrow*, though limited in its scope and length, is also an important study, for it describes the lives and careers of the first abbots of Wearmouth-Jarrow, discussed above, under whom Bede served, and conveys the spirit of the monastery itself. Bede wrote some important letters on ecclesiastical subjects, which have been preserved. He lists five of them in his bibliography at the end of the *History*. Another two date from his last years: a brief letter to Albinus, abbot of the monastery of Sts. Peter and Paul at Canterbury, when Bede sent him a copy of the *History*; and the admonitory epistle to Ecgbert on the critical state of the Church in Northumbria.

Establishing the chronological order of Bede's works, especially the exegetical works, is difficult, for they rarely carry an indication of time of completion. However, a number include references to specific dates or contain references to other of his works, so a rough chronology can be inferred.[49]

Proximate dates of Bede's works

691 x 703: *De arte metrica* [*On the Art of Poetic Meter*]; *De schematibus et tropis* [*On Figures of Speech and Tropes*]
? 691 x 703: *De orthographia* [*On Orthography*] ("may well be the first book composed by Bede," Laistner, *Hand-List*, p. 137)
702–703: *De locis sanctis* [*On the Holy Places*]
c. 703: *De natura rerum* [*On the Nature of Things*]
703: *De temporibus Chronica minora* [*On Time, Shorter Book on Chronology*]
703 x 709: *Expositio Apocalypseos* [*Commentary on the Apocalypse*]

authority." This would have included abbesses and nuns, as his dedicatory preface of *In canticum Habacuc* to "dilectissima soror in Christo," shows (CCSL 119B, p. 381). Bede's dedicatory preface to the *HE* is directed to King Ceolwulf in Latin; and we know of some lay nobles literate in Latin. It is possible that at least some of them had to have the texts interpreted in Anglo-Saxon. See Higham's expressed doubts about lay literacy in *(Re-)Reading Bede* (London, 2006), pp. 42–43.

49 My list is an emended version of William Houghton's, http://home.mchsi.com/~numenor/medstud/chrono.htm, compiled from Plummer, *Baedae opera historica*, I: cxlv–clix ("On the Chronology of Bede's Writings"), M. L. W. Laistner and H. H. King, *A Hand-List of Bede Manuscripts* (Ithaca, 1943), and Jones, ed., *In Genesim*, Introduction, CCSL 118A, pp. vi–x, and modified according to the opinions of recent Bedan editors and scholars (DeGregorio, Holder, Kendall, Meyvaert, Thacker). For a detailed dating of Bede's works see also Michael Lapidge's extensive analysis in his introduction to Bede's *HE* (Milan, 2008), I: xlii–lvii.

703 x 709: First version of *Expositio Actuum Apostolorum* [*Commentary on the Acts of the Apostles*]

c. 705: *Vita metrica Cuthberti* [*Metrical Life of Cuthbert*] (705 x 716 according to Laistner, *Hand-Book*, p. 88)

708: *Epistola ad Pleguinum de sex aetatibus saeculi* [*Letter to Plegwin on the Six Ages of the World*]

708 x 716: Second version of *Expositio Actuum Apostolorum* (and *Nomina regionum*) [*Commentary on the Acts of the Apostles* and *Gazetteer*]

c. 709 x 716: *In epistolas catholicas* [*On the Catholic Epistles*] (*In 1 Joannem* [*On I John*] was sent to Acca along with *Expositio Actuum* [*Commentary on Acts*])

? *Collectaneum* [*Collected Excerpts from Augustine on the Pauline Epistles*]

709 x 716: *In Lucam* [*On Luke*]

c. 715: *In Regum librum quaestiones XXX* [*Thirty Questions on the Book of Kings*] (Meyvaert, 1997)

before 716: *In canticum canticorum* [*Commentary on the Song of Songs*]

716: *In primam partem Samuhelis* [*On the First Part of the Books of Samuel*]

716: *De mansionibus filiorum Israel; De eo quod ait Isaias "Et claudentur"* [*On the Resting-Places of the Children of Israel; Concerning what Isaiah says "And they will be shut up in prison"*] (In the form of Letters to Acca)

c. 716: *Historia abbatum* [*Lives of the Abbots of Wearmouth and Jarrow*]

c. 716: *In Marcum* [*On the Gospel of Mark*]

c. 717–718: First version of *In Genesim* [*On the Book of Genesis*] (Book 1a and b; Kendall, p. cxi)

c. 720: Second version of *In Genesim* [*On Genesis*] (Book 1 with Book 2; Kendall, p. cxxxi)

c. 720: *Vita sancti Cuthberti* [prose *Life of Saint Cuthbert*]

c. 721–725: *De Tabernaculo* [*On the Tabernacle*]

c. 722–725: Expanded edition of *In Genesim* [*On Genesis*] in four books (Kendall, pp. cxxxi–cxxxii)

c. 725: *De ratione bissexti* [*Letter to Helmwald on the Reckoning of Leap-Year*]

725: *De temporum ratione, Chronica maiora* [*On the Reckoning of Time, Longer Book on Chronology*] (see Jones, Introduction, CCSL 123B, p. 241)

725 x 731: *Epistola ad Wicthedum* [Letter to Wicthed] (see Jones, *Bedae opera de temporibus*, pp. 138–39)

725 x 731: *Martyrologium* [*Martyrology*]

c. 725 x 731: *Retractatio in Actus Apostolorum* [*Retraction on the Commentary on the Acts of the Apostles*]

? *In Proverbia* [*On the Book of Proverbs*]

729 x 731: *De Templo* [*On the Temple*]

729 x 731: *In Ezram et Neemiam* [*On the Books of Ezra and Nehemiah*] (DeGregorio [2006], pp. xli–xlii)

Before 731, but otherwise undated:

In canticum Habacuc [*On the Canticle of Habakkuk*]

14

Homeliae [*Collected Homilies*]
Hymni [*Hymns*]
In librum beati Tobiae [*On the book of Tobit*]
Octo quaestionum liber [*On Eight Questions*] (perhaps collected posthumously, Meyvaert [1997])
Passio sancti Anastasii [*The Martyrdom of St. Anastasius*]
Vita sancti Felicis [*Life of St. Felix*]
731: *Epistola ad Albinum* [*Letter to Albinus*]
731: *Historia ecclesiastica* [*The Ecclesiastical History of the English People*]
734, Nov. 5: *Epistola ad Ecgbertum* [*Letter to Egbert*]

Bede died as he lived, teaching and praying. Bede's disciple Cuthbert, afterwards abbot of Wearmouth-Jarrow, wrote a letter describing Bede's last days. He remarks, "I never saw or heard of any man so diligent in returning thanks to the living God" (*HE*, pp. 580–81). He did not languish: he continued to give lessons from his bed, to translate the Gospel of John (1: 1 – 6: 9) into English, and to make certain corrections in Isidore's book *On the Wonders of Nature* because, he said, "I cannot have my children learning a lie and losing labor on this after my passing" (*HE*, pp. 582–83). On the very day of his death he dictated a chapter of a book. That evening he disposed of a few token gifts to the brothers and expressed to them the sentiment, "My soul longs to see Christ my King in all his beauty." The young scribe Wilberht said:

> "There is still one sentence, dear master, not written down." And he said, "Write it." After a little the boy said: "There, now it is written." And he replied: "Good. It is finished [as in John 19: 30]; you have spoken the truth ..." And so upon the floor of his cell, singing "Glory be to the Father and to the Son and to the Holy Spirit" and the rest [of the doxology], he breathed his last.[50]

Although such texts indicate that Bede had devoted students, he produced but few disciples to carry on his work, certainly no one of his caliber. As William of Malmesbury scathingly remarked: "There was no English competitor in his field of study, no would-be rival of his fame to follow up the broken thread ... So, as each proved more idle than the last, zeal for these studies languished long in the whole island."[51]

Though a pragmatic realist and also an advocate of reform, Bede exemplified in his calm life, asceticism, and writings the ideals of the monastic life. His embodiment of those ideals has won the admiration of scholars of every age,

---

[50] *HE*, Cuthbert's Letter, pp. 584–85.
[51] William of Malmesbury, *Gesta regum Anglorum*, ed. R. A. B. Mynors, R. M. Thompson, and M. Winterbottom (Oxford, 1998), I: 62, pp. 94–95: "Adeo nullus Anglorum studiorum eius emulus, nullus gloriarum eius sequax fuit ... Ita, cum semper pigro succederet pigrior, multo tempore in tota insula studiorum detepuit fervor"; cited by Thacker, "Bede and the Ordering of Understanding," in *Innovations and Tradition in the Writings of the Venerable Bede* (Morgantown, 2006), pp. 37–63 at 41, who remarks that in fact we can name only two disciples of Bede, Cuthbert, the author of the letter on Bede's death, and Cuthwine, the addressee of the letter.

and critics have searched in vain to find in Bede the foibles and failings of even great later monks like Peter Abelard and Guibert de Nogent. Although scholars such as Gerald Bonner and Sr. Benedicta Ward have emphasized Bede's piety, a piety they find exemplifying Anglican spirituality, his acute personal and historical awareness of human failings and wickedness mark him as a realistic assessor of the poor and sometimes vicious human condition. He had no illusions about his society or his community. Although Bede's writings as a monk were directed to the spiritual life of the individual soul, in later life both his historical and exegetical writings emphasize the great need for societal and ecclesiastical reform.[52] He was deeply committed to the salvific power of Christianity and was actively engaged in the apostolate for the salvation of his people. He used his authoritative writings, as the previous Fathers of the Church did, as instruments of reform. He saw his apostolate and his monastery as institutions dedicated to helping fallen man to be lifted up by grace in this life for preparation for the better life of eternity.[53] While doing what he could to bring about the betterment of his world, his society and his church, he entertained no roseate expectations. He saw all mankind as being called from the exile of a lapsed world to the perfect world found only in God.[54] His early commentary on the Book of Revelation and his homilies, however, proclaim his faith in the ultimate mondial and cosmic victory of Christ.[55] The earthly residence was indeed fragile and transient.

Soon after Bede's lifetime, the glory of Northumbria disappeared under the Viking onslaught. Most of Bede's writings, however, and a few letters from his students and admirers, some beautiful manuscripts (such as the Bible codex Amiatinus) and manuscript fragments, and some archaeological remnants and shards have survived. And Bede's works lived on through the transmission of the Anglo-Saxon missionaries to the Continent and by the development of the school at York and the emergence of its illustrious pupil, Alcuin, who brought Bede's works to Francia to foster the Carolingian renaissance.[56]

---

[52] See especially Scott DeGregorio, "'Nostrorum socordiam temporum': The Reforming Impulse of Bede's Later Exegesis," *Early Medieval Europe* 11 (2002): 107–22; Alan Thacker, "Bede's Ideal of Reform," in *Ideal and Reality in Frankish and Anglo-Saxon Society*, ed. Patrick Wormald, Donald Bullough, and Roger Collins (Oxford, 1983), pp. 130–53, and the same author's "Bede and the Ordering of Understanding," pp. 37–63. See also Catherine Cubitt, "Images of St Peter: The Clergy and the Religious Life in Anglo-Saxon England," in *The Christian Tradition in Anglo-Saxon England*, ed. Paul Cavill (Woodbridge, 2004), pp. 41–54.

[53] On Bede's "monasticism of service," see William D. McCready, *Miracles and the Venerable Bede* (Toronto, 1994), pp. 125–32.

[54] The concept is brilliantly epitomized in Gerhard Ladner's "*Homo viator*: Medieval Ideas on Alienation and Order," *Speculum* 42 (1967): 233–59. He remarks, pp. 241–42, that the Benedictine Rule dictates that "no alien order must alienate the monk from his alienation from an alienated world."

[55] See Gerald Bonner, *Saint Bede in the Tradition of Western Apocalyptic Commentary*, Jarrow Lecture 1966 (Jarrow, 1967), p. 11, rpt. in *Bede and his World: The Jarrow Lectures*, ed. Michael Lapidge (London, 1994), I: 153–73, at 165.

[56] For the later vast proliferation of Bede's works see Ch. 6 below, and especially my monograph, *The Bedan Legacy*, publication of the *Journal of Medieval Latin* (in preparation).

2

Educational Works

BEDE's educational manuals tap into the collective heritage of the late Roman, patristic, and early medieval educational tradition.[1] The heritage involves complex issues and attitudes. Many early monastic ascetics were hostile to the educational system inherited from the Romans not only because pagan literature was deemed frequently immoral but also because the arts – such as literature and rhetoric – and the sciences lured the mind away from concentrating on the spiritual realm. Although each of the four great Fathers of the western Church, Ambrose, Augustine, Jerome, and Gregory, whose footsteps Bede strove to follow, had received an aristocratic Roman education before commencing their religious careers, each of these great men went on record as rejecting the pagan secular tradition and their training in it when they turned wholly to the Christian life.[2]

Nevertheless, the Fathers recognized that secular studies were necessary requisites for the reading of Scripture. Jerome asserted that profane literature could be a useful assistant just as the beautiful captive woman in Deuteronomy (21: 11–13) could become a good Jewish wife.[3] Similarly, Augustine tolerated

---

[1] For the late antique and early medieval instructional tradition see Pierre Riché, *Education and Culture in the Barbarian West, Sixth through Eighth Centuries*, trans. John J. Contreni (Columbia, 1976), intro. and pt. 1; H. I. Marrou, *A History of Education in Antiquity*, trans. George Lamb (Madison, 1982), pt. 3; Stanley F. Bonner, *Education in Ancient Rome* (Berkeley, 1977), esp. pt. 3; M. Roger, *L'enseignement des lettres classiques d'Ausone à Alcuin* (Paris, 1905), chs. 1 and 4.

[2] Jerome's own rhetorical and dialectical powers were extraordinary and his diatribes and controversial works potent. Yet he repudiated those very gifts in his famous Letter 22, in which he reports the numbing vision of Christ accusing him of being a Ciceronian and not a Christian (Jerome, *Selected Letters*, trans. F. A. Wright, Loeb edition [London, 1933]), p. 127). Augustine in the *Confessions* remarks how terrible it was that literary artifice could make him in his youth weep for Dido's dereliction by Aeneas but not for his own sins (Augustine, *Confessions*, trans. R. S. Pine-Coffin [Harmondsworth, 1961], p. 33). Gregory in a famous statement to Desiderius refused to submit to the rules of grammar because he thought it "highly improper to subject the words of the celestial oracle to the rules of Donatus". None of the interpreters have observed these rules in regard to the authority of sacred Scripture" (Gregorii I papae, MGH, *Registrum epistolarum* I, *Epistolae* V. 53a, p. 357). Ambrose had made the same point (Ambrosii, *Expositio Evangelii secundum Lucam*, II. 42, PL 15: 1568). Gregory was also scandalized by the report that Bishop Desiderius of Vienne was teaching grammar, since that entailed the teaching of profane literature; Gregory insisted that "the same mouth cannot utter the praises of both Jupiter and Christ" ("... quia in uno se ore cum Iouis laudibus Christi laudes non capiunt," Gregorii papae, *Epistola* XI. 34, in *Registrum epistolarum*, ed. Dag Norberg, CCSL 140A [Turnhout, 1982], p. 922). For more on the cultural debt owed by the Fathers, see Harald Hagendahl, *Latin Fathers and the Classics*, Göteborgs Universitets Årsskrift 64: 2 (Göteborg, 1958).

[3] Jerome, *Epistulae*, ed. I. Hilberg, CSEL 54 (Vienna, 1996), *Epistula* 70. 2, p. 702.

profane studies if appropriated to the study of the sacred text: "History helps us a great deal in the understanding of sacred books, even if we learn it outside of the Church as part of our childhood education." On the analogy of the Israelites despoiling the treasures of the Egyptians by divine command (Exodus 3: 22, 11: 2, 12: 55), he argued that Christians ought to feel free to expropriate from pagan literature "the liberal disciplines more suited to the uses of truth."[4] Gregory the Great was credited with saying, "In knowing the liberal arts we understand divine words better."[5] For that reason only, the study of profane literature was allowed. The Fathers distinguished, not always carefully, between the illegitimate indulgence in the reading and enjoyment of pagan literature and the pragmatic appreciation of pagan letters for educating the Christian to read and enjoy Scripture sophisticatedly and to defend the Christian position against the subtle attacks of erudite enemies. As to the actual use of classical literature and rhetoric in their works, Jerome is on one end of the spectrum with the fullest usage and Gregory on the other with the least; but all of the Fathers drew upon their classical training and repertoire. It is also important to remember that, whether rejected or not, the values and attitudes culled from Roman education pervaded the Fathers' thought, and as a result much that filtered through the system as Catholic doctrine about history, society, and morality was Roman and not specifically Christian.

Bede as a patristics scholar and exegete follows in the footsteps of these Fathers, but he is primarily a monk.[6] In the age of monasticism, education was directed to the needs and ideals of the religious life. The monastic rules of the West made but one scholastic demand: literacy. Grammar was therefore welcomed and fostered in the monastery because it helped provide this indispensable skill as well as the interpretative methods necessary for the communal and personal perusal of the Bible and holy books.[7] For the monk grammar supplied the desired knowledge for understanding the sacred text; as Augustine said in his *De ordine*, "Everything which does not deserve to

---

4   Augustine, *On Christian Doctrine*, trans. D. W. Robertson, Jr. (Indianapolis, 1958), Book II. ch. 28, p. 63; Book II. ch. 40, p. 75.

5   *In librum primum Regum expositionum libri sex/ Commentaire sur le premier livre des Rois*, ed. Adalbert de Vogüé (Paris, 2003), who says, V. 84. 3, p. 214: "Aperte quidem daemones sciunt quia, dum saecularibus litteris instruimur, in spiritalibus adiuuamur"; see also the following two paragraphs on pp. 214–16. Recent scholarship has revealed that it is not Pope Gregory I but pseudo-Gregory (Petrus/Pierre de Cava), who is the true author of this commentary.

6   Scott DeGregorio, "Bede, the Monk, as Exegete: Evidence from the Commentary on Ezra-Nehemiah," *RB* 115 (2005): 343–69, points out, pp. 344–45, that "As far as Bede himself goes, scholars have rightly emphasized that, however much he looked to the Fathers and viewed himself to be following in their footsteps, he was not of their world but the product of an early medieval monastic culture, making his intellectual formation, his motives as a scholar and writer, his views of classical antiquity and its learning, and even his Latinity different from theirs."

7   On the history of grammar from ancient to medieval times, see Martin Irvine, *The Making of Textual Culture: 'Grammatica' and Literary Theory 350–1100* (Cambridge, 1994), on Bede pp. 272–98; R. H. Robins, *Ancient and Medieval Grammatical Theory in Europe* (London, 1951). On Bede's sophisticated understanding of the role of grammar in monastic studies, see Janet Coleman, "Bede, Monastic *Grammatica* and Reminiscence," ch. 9 in her *Ancient and Medieval Memories* (Cambridge, 1992), pp. 137–54.

pass into oblivion and has been trusted to writing belongs necessarily to the province of grammar."[8] Rhetoric and dialectic, however, with their goals of artful argument and cunning suasion, could only be permitted, if at all, under considerable strictures. In later Benedictine tradition, classically described by Jean Leclercq, the more humane love of learning with studies in the arts would be coupled with the pursuit of virtue.[9] Wearmouth-Jarrow, however, under its first abbots was more restrictive.

Some English were imbued with Anglo-Saxon aristocratic secular values when they turned, like Benedict Biscop and Ceolfrith, to religion. Certain prelates who had lived at court in their youth, such as Aldhelm (c. 639–709/10), enjoyed reputations as native poets, scops, even though their education in letters was monastic and Latinate. Monks who like Bede and Abbot Hwætberht (d. 716) had entered the monastery as children had scarcely the opportunity to participate in the Anglo-Saxon secular code. There was no education in letters outside the Church; there was only the monastery or the episcopal school. The monk was to be trained in the service of the Lord, though some, like Benedict Biscop, were called upon for service to the state by the secular lord. There was no apparent reason why the monastic curriculum should provide anything more than the study of grammar (for the reading of the Bible and liturgy and composition of hagiography, history, and hymns, and for the correct writing of manuscripts), computus (for the reckoning of the church calendar and history), and the practical arts of music performance (for chanting the texts of Office and the Mass), as well as physical arts such as husbandry, agriculture, and domestic management.

As the science that teaches one how to persuade and sway an audience regardless of the truth or falsity of one's position (indeed, the shakier the case, the greater should be the rhetoric to compensate for its weakness), rhetoric was held suspect. However, Scripture often presents examples of rhetorical devices, and knowledge of those devices is needed to understand the pregnant meaning of the text. Because late antique grammar had already usurped large parts of what rhetoric comprised, such as rhythm, metrics, figures of speech, the curriculum at Wearmouth-Jarrow could safely dispense with a formal course in rhetoric and could teach the expanded discipline of grammar to cover the literary bases. There is no evidence that either a course in rhetoric was taught at Wearmouth-Jarrow or that rhetoric texts, such as Quintilian's or the anonymous *Ad Herennium*, were in the Wearmouth-Jarrow library.[10]

---

8   Augustine, *De ordine*, ed. W. M. Green, CCSL 29, II, xii, 37: "Poeterat iam perfecta esse grammatica sed … factum est, ut, quicquid dignum memoria litteris mandaretur, ad eam necessario pertinet"; quoted in English by Janet Coleman, *Ancient and Medieval Memories* (Cambridge, 1992), p. 145.

9   Jean Leclercq, *The Love of Learning and the Desire for God* (New York, 1961).

10   Although a number of works should now be added to Max Laistner's inventory in "The Library of the Venerable Bede," in *Bede: His Life, Times and Writings*, ed. A. Hamilton Thompson (Oxford,

Bede's own attitude towards Roman rhetoric was, from the evidence of his textbooks and commentaries, ambivalent and in some instances antagonistic. Like the Fathers he recognizes that rhetorical artifice can be very alluring, that in the hands of heretics or the devil it can lead one astray and entice one to evil. For example, speaking of the wanton woman in chapter seven of Proverbs as a figure of heresy, he remarks that the description of her bed's coverlet with its decorated Egyptian tapestry signifies "the adornment of eloquence and the trickery of dialectical art, which took its origin from the pagans."[11] Following Tertullian by way of Jerome, Bede identifies philosophers with heretics: "A certain one of ours nicely remarked that philosophers are the patriarchs of heretics."[12] Philosophers, of course, had been identified with sophists and dialecticians since antiquity. Elsewhere, explicating a text about the Samaritans' eating salted food in the palace of Artaxerxes (symbolic of their being salaried in his employ), Bede explains that they were thus corrupted "by the taste of worldly philosophy, by the charm of the art of rhetoric, and by the cunning of the art of dialectic."[13] He excoriates those contemporaries who should ascend to hearing the word of God but instead descend to listen to "secular fables and teachings of demons, reading the dialecticians, rhetoricians, and poets of the gentiles."[14] Indeed, Bede strongly discouraged the reading of pagan literature. In *De arte metrica* he mentions a volume by the poet Porphyry cited by Jerome that exemplifies various meters, but adds: "Because they were pagan, it was not permitted for us to touch them."[15] However, though he prefers to quote Christian poets whenever possible, Bede does plunder the pagans, particularly Vergil, and points out that there is precedent in Moses' learning all the wisdom of the Egyptians, Daniel learning the language and culture of the Chaldaeans, and St. Paul quoting Greek poets.

As a monastic educator, Bede expresses strong reservations about rhetoric and dialectic; but that does not mean that he did not know the basics of rhetoric nor believe that in the hands of a qualified, mature scholar it could

---

1935, rpt. 1969), pp. 237–66, I have found no evidence to contradict his findings about the lack of rhetorical texts in the Wearmouth-Jarrow library.

11 "... in tapetibus uero pictis ex Aegypto ornatus eloquentiae et dialecticae artis uersutia quae ab ethnicis originem sumpsit intelligitur per quam mens heretica sensum doctrinae pestilentis quasi meretrix thorum facinoris se texisse gloriatur," Bede, *In proverbia Salomonis*, I. vii. 16, ed. Hurst, CCSL 119B, p. 58; see also I. vii. 10, p. 57.

12 "Vnde pulchre quidam nostrorum ait: Philosphi patriarchae hereticorum ecclesiae puritatem peruersa maculauere doctrina," Bede, *In I Samuhelem*, IV. 31. 1, ed. Hurst, CCSL 119, p. 267; quoting directly Jerome, *Epistulae*, Letter 133, ed. I. Hilberg, CSEL 54, p. 243.

13 Bede, *In Ezram et Neemiam libri III*, I. lines 1883–94, ed. Hurst, CCSL 119A, pp. 285–86; trans. DeGregorio, *Bede: On Ezra and Nehemiah*, p. 75.

14 "Descendunt et hodie non nulli relicta altitudine uerbi Dei ad quod audiendum ascendere debuerant auscultantque fabulis saecularibus ac doctrinis daemoniorum et legendo dialecticos rhetores poetasque gentilium ad exercendum ingenium terrestre quas ad fabros Philisthiim pro exacuendis siluestris siue ruralis culturae ferramentis inermes, hoc est spiritali scientia priuati, conueniunt," Bede, *In I Samuhelem*, II. 13. 20, ed. Hurst, CCSL 119, p. 112.

15 Bede, *De arte metrica*, I. 24, ed. Kendall, CCSL 123A, p. 138: "Quae, quia pagana erat, nos tangere non libuit."

serve a useful purpose. A key text that reveals Bede's positive attitude towards the subject is in Book II of his commentary on I Samuel. After warning that Christians should neither love nor pursue too ardently the sweetness of secular eloquence, he discusses the meaning of Jonathan's nourishment from the forbidden honeycomb. Certain noble leaders of the Church enjoyed the books of the pagans too much, and one of them was severely chastised for being a Ciceronian rather than a Christian (here Bede means Jerome, of course). However, Jonathan's eyes were brightened by the honey, and so the properly careful wise one instructed in the doctrine of the Church and in letters can say: "I have become more effective, acute, and ready to speak what are fitting, in so far as I have tasted a little from the flower of the Tullian text."[16] The use of the phrase *Tullianae lectionis* implies some approbation of Ciceronian rhetoric. Texts such as these counterbalance those which, even in the same commentary, seem to deplore the use of classical sources and rhetoric. Nonetheless, in practice Bede seems to align himself more closely with Gregory's attitudes than with any of the other Fathers'; he prefers to cite Christian authors, except for Vergil, and leaves very few, if any, identifiable traces of classical rhetoric.

In the abbey school the two main disciplines were grammar and biblical exegesis, with some study of time reckoning and a bit of natural history and geography as a complement to the Bible. Bede made texts for each of these. As in all his work he aimed for a clear, easily understandable presentation of the principles and details of the curricular subjects. Unlike Boniface and Alcuin of the next generation, Bede did not compose a new type of grammar for teaching Latin to his Germanic learners.[17] Donatus was deemed generally adequate for his purposes, and the library of Wearmouth-Jarrow, like those of most other English monasteries, possessed such a text; it boasted an admirable collection of other grammatical treatises as well.[18]

THE EDUCATIONAL WORKS

Bede's educational manuals were designed to provide basic instruction for reading, interpreting, and expounding Scripture and history. The fact that they are intended to prepare for those subjects does not mean that Bede composed the treatises early in his career, before his undertaking theological

---

[16] "Videtis, inquit, quia efficacior sum factus et acutior promptiorque ad peroranda quae decent eo quod gustauerim paululum de flore Tullianae lectionis," Bede, *In I Samuhelem*, II. 14. 29–30, ed. Hurst, CCSL 119, pp. 121.

[17] For an excellent summary of the complex history of grammatical texts in Anglo-Saxon England, see Vivien Law, *The Insular Latin Grammarians* (Woodbridge, 1982), ch. 2. The grammars themselves are found in *Grammatici Latini*, ed. Heinrich Keil, 7 vols. and suppl. (Leipzig, 1857–70).

[18] On Donatus, see Louis Holtz, *Donat et la tradition de l'enseignement grammatical: étude sur l'Ars Donati et sa diffusion (IVe–IXe siècle) et édition critique* (Paris, 1981).

and historical works. This was once assumed but has now been completely disproved from internal evidence.[19]

On the Art of Poetic Meter

> *De arte metrica*, ed. C. B. Kendall CCSL 123A, pp. 81–141, 222. Translation by Kendall in Bede, *Libri II De arte metrica et de schematibus et tropis / The Art of Poetry and Rhetoric* (Saarbrücken 1991), pp. 36–167.[20]

Where Bede did find Donatus inadequate for his students was in the treatment of metrics. To remedy that, he composed the *De arte metrica* for them. As native speakers of a Germanic language, Bede's students had no sense of classical Latin vocalic quantity (long and short) or quantitative verse. These had to be learned, and Bede set about teaching them in this very logical, orderly text that differed considerably from Aldhelm's instructions on composing Latin dactylic hexameters.[21]

Bede's *De arte metrica* is a systematic exposition of Latin versification fortified by a judicious compilation of examples from Vergil and Christian poets together with selected grammarians' comments (principally from Servius's continuation, titled *De finalibus*, of Donatus's *De pedibus*, with excerpts from the late antique grammarians Pompeius, Sergius, Audax, and others). Because it contains a reasonably full account of most Latin classical and postclassical metrical usage, the little treatise could teach a pupil who had mastered the foundation of Latin grammar in his earlier studies how to recognize and read correctly the verse forms found in hymns, metrical saints' lives, epigrams, the liturgical chants, as well as in classical Latin poetry. Although the piece is mainly a compilation of extracts, Bede's careful arrangement and presentation of the material made it a standard text in the age of Charlemagne. A comparison with the texts of the grammarians he cites reveals Bede's excellence as a textbook writer, demonstrated by his order of selection, his omission of non-essential material and editing of the rest, by the accuracy, simplicity, and precision of his definitions, and by the formation of a new synthesis that maintains respect for the authority of his sources. He discusses without digression what the letters are, their classifications as vowels or consonants and their characteristics (ch. 1), syllables (chs. 2–8) and metrical feet (ch. 9), and then metrics (chs. 10–24). A unique contribution

---

[19] Carmela Vircillo Franklin presents and summarizes the evidence in "Grammar and Exegesis: Bede's *Liber de schematibus et tropis*," in *Latin Grammar and Rhetoric from Classical Theory to Medieval Practice*, ed. Carol Dana Lanham (New York, 2002), pp. 63–91.

[20] Bede's sources are noted in the footnotes, where M. H. King has also provided the commentaries and glosses of Remigius [Remy] of Auxerre. Despite the title of Kendall's translation, Bede considered his treatise a part of grammar, not rhetoric; see Gabriel Knappe, "Classical Rhetoric in Anglo-Saxon England," *ASE* 27 (1998): 5–29 at 17.

[21] See the excellent analysis by Carin Ruff, "The Place of Metrics in Anglo-Saxon Latin Education: Aldhelm and Bede," *JEGP* 104.2 (2005): 149–70; also Robert B. Palmer, "Bede as Textbook Writer: A Study of his *De arte metrica*," *Speculum* 34 (1959): 573–84; Holtz, *Donat*, p. 349.

to metrical history is the short description in chapter 24 of isosyllabic stress rhythm (that is, accentual meter), which largely superseded quantitative Latin verse in medieval poetry.[22] The work concludes with chapter 25, on three genres of poetry.

Unlike Aldhelm, who proposes mastery of metrical formulae (*schemata*), Bede emphasizes "the relationship of verse forms to semantic units, and accentual verse," with the integration of grammar and quantitative metrics. "He explains the bare essentials of the system in a splendidly logical manner, but he keeps the focus on examples and exhortations to careful reading."[23]

In an epilogue, Bede dedicates the *Metrics* to his "dulcissime fili at conlevita Cuthberte."[24] Although Bede is the master addressing his pupil as son, some had surmised that "conlevita," which usually means "deacon," indicates that Bede himself was still in the diaconal state when he dedicated the work. However, Arthur Holder has demonstrated that Bede, as ordained deacon as well as priest, was following Augustine's precedent in addressing Cuthbert as an ecclesiastical equal, even though he himself had advanced to higher status.[25]

On Figures of Speech and Tropes

Bede, *De schematibus et tropis*, ed. Kendall, CCSL 123A, pp. 142–71. Translation by Kendall in Bede, *Libri II de arte metrica et de schematibus et tropis* (Saarbrücken 1991), pp. 168–209.

Bede says that he is subjoining the little book, *De schematibus et tropis*, to the *De metris* in order to assist Cuthbert. In the *Ecclesiastical History* he describes it thus: "And to this [*On Metrics*] is added another small book on figures of speech or tropes, that is, concerning the figures and modes of speech with which the holy Scriptures are adorned" (*HE*, V. 24). As an expansion of Donatus's *De schematibus* and *De tropis* (the last two sections of the *Ars grammatica*), Bede clearly thought of the book with its companion piece as a grammatical work; but editors and critics have frequently, and even recently, called it a rhetorical treatise. This confusion arises from the fact that vocational grammarians at an early date arrogated such topics to grammar from rhetoric, because figures of speech obviously applied to the grammatical study of language and its literary interpretation. The goals of the two disciplines, while sharing some identical topics, are distinct. Isidore in the *Etymologiae* was therefore compelled to include the treatment of figural speech twice, once under grammar in Book I and again under rhetoric in Book II. As a sort of appendix to grammar, treatises on figures were often

---

[22] Dag Norberg, *An Introduction to the Study of Medieval Latin Versification*, trans. Grant C. Roti and Jacqueline de la Chapelle Skubly (Washington, DC, 2004), pp. 81–129 at 81–82 and n. 2.

[23] Ruff, "Place of Metrics," pp. 165, 170; see also p. 153.

[24] Bede, *De arte metrica*, I. xxv, ed. Kendall, CCSL 123A, p. 141.

[25] Arthur Holder, "(Un)Dating Bede's *De arte metrica*," in *Northumbria's Golden Age*, ed. Jane Hawkes and Susan Mills (Stroud, 1999), pp. 390–95.

treated as separate entities and circulated independently of other grammatical texts. Bede's wholesale inclusion of these figures within the pale of grammar allowed him to avoid espousing suspect rhetoric in the abbey school, while permitting a study of metrics and literary devices for interpretation of poetry in the Bible and Christian authors. Recent scholarship has determined that the work was composed in Bede's maturity (after 709) and is a sophisticated work.[26]

One remarkable thing about Bede's manual is that it is the first one to give not a single example from Roman pagan literature, not even Vergil, whom he included in the *De arte metrica*. Only three examples are not Scriptural, and those are from Christian poets. Earlier authors, such as Isidore in the *Etymologies*, Cassiodorus in his *Expositio psalmorum*, and Julian of Toledo in *De vitiis et figuris*, drawing on a lost work (a Christianized *ars* of Donatus) best represented by a text dubbed Isidorus Iunior, had included Scriptural references in their treatises;[27] but Bede is the first to exclude pagan examples entirely.[28] The effect of this bold approach of dispensing with the classics is to assert the priority and pre-eminence of the biblical text. As Bede states in the prologue:

> The Greeks pride themselves on having invented these figures or tropes. But, my beloved son, in order that you and all who wish to read this work may know that Holy Scripture surpasses all other writings not merely in authority because it is divine, or in usefulness because it leads to eternal life, but also for its age and artistic composition, I have chosen to demonstrate by means of examples collected from Holy Scripture that teachers of secular eloquence in any age have not been able to furnish us with any of these figures and tropes which did not appear first in Holy Scripture.[29]

A second remarkable thing about this treatise is that it is the first to attempt a synthesis of linguistic and theological symbolism within a grammatical treatise. Structured according to Donatus's system of seventeen *schemata* (figures, the artistic ordering of words) and thirteen *tropi* (tropes, transferred meanings), Bede goes through each, furnishing for each a definition and at least one example, usually explained, until he comes near the end. When he comes to allegory, he obviously felt that the treatments by Donatus and the

---

26 See especially Carmela Vircillo Franklin, "Grammar and Exegesis: Bede's *Liber de schematibus et tropis*," in *Latin Grammar and Rhetoric*, ed. Carol Dana Lanham (London, 2002), pp. 63–91, esp. 64.

27 Ulrich Schindel, *Die lateinischen Figurenlehren des 5. bis 7. Jahrhunderts und Donats Vergilkommentar (mit zwei Editionen)*, Abhandlungen der Akademie der Wissenschaften in Göttingen, Philosophisch-historische Klasse, dritte Folge (Göttingen, 1975).

28 Franklin, "Bede's *Liber de schematibus et tropis*," pp. 65–72.

29 Bede, *De schematibus et tropis*, ed. Kendall, CCSL 123A, pp. 142–43; trans. Gussie Hecht Tannenhaus, "The Venerable Bede, Concerning Figures and Tropes," in *Readings in Medieval Rhetoric*, ed. Joseph H. Miller, Michael H. Prosser, Thomas W. Benson (Bloomington, 1973), p. 97, slightly modified; also translated by Kendall, *Libri II*, p. 169. Franklin, "Bede's *Liber de schematibus et tropis*," p. 84 n. 5, pronounces these translations faulty.

Christian *ars,* though detailed, were inadequate to deal with even Christian hermeneutics common since the fourth century. In the light of the exegetical techniques of the Fathers and in view of Bede's own fondness for allegorical interpretation of Scripture, it is easy to understand why Bede adds to this section on allegory a Christ-centered typology. Donatus had a brief section on the trope of allegory, listing its seven species,[30] but Bede dilates the section by furnishing Scriptural examples for each of the seven types and then adds an important adjunct: the division between factual and verbal allegory.[31] Here he is attempting a general theory of symbol applied to Christian salvific history. The treatment is grounded on Augustine's doctrine of sign and symbol in Book II of *On Christian Doctrine* and his distinction made in the *De Trinitate* between *allegoria quae factis fit* (allegory in historical events, deeds) and *allegoria quae verbis fit* (allegory in words, language).[32] What is unique in Bede is the attempt to yoke all of this under the rules of grammar. To a modern philosophic linguist, his attempt is not successful, since factual allegory depends on the objective (for Bede divinely set) realities of history (e.g., Abraham's having two sons prefigures God's having two peoples, Jewish and gentile), whereas verbal allegory, as Bede teaches elsewhere, is metaphorical and ambiguous (e.g., an eagle can symbolize Christ and much else; the moon can symbolize inconstancy or the Church).[33] However, Bede does formulate a synthesis of various symbolic modes, which established exegetical categories until Scholasticism. Furthermore, Bede might have argued from Pauline, Augustinian, and Gregorian perception that even given the polyvalence of verbal symbols, there exists a certain inherent propriety and rightness within the sign itself to make it essentially analogous to factual symbol. Factual and verbal allegory he applies to the traditional four modes of Scriptural interpretation, classically formulated by Cassian in Book XIV of his *Conferences* and by Gregory in the *Moralia*: literal (historical), typical, tropological (moral), and anagogic.[34] As he so often does in his commentaries and histories, Bede, in closing the section on allegory, calls upon Gregory as his exemplar: "My discussion of the Church according to the allegorical interpretation has followed the example of that most learned exegete Gregory, who in his *Moralia* was accustomed to call allegory specifically

---

[30] Keil, ed., *Grammatici latini,* IV: 401.

[31] Bede, *De schematibus et tropis,* ed. Kendall, CCSL 123A, pp. 164–66.

[32] See Antonio Isola, "Il *De schematibus et tropis* di Beda in rapporto al *De doctrina christiana* di Agostino," *Romanobarbarica* 1 (1976): 71–82.

[33] See Armand Strubel, "'Allegoria in factis' et 'Allegoria in verbis,'" *Poétique* 23 (1975): 351–53.

[34] Bede, *De schematibus et tropis,* ed. Kendall, CCSL 123A, pp. 166–69. The fourfold formula, for which Bede is responsible, is explained in the medieval distich:

Littera gesta docet, quid credas allegoria,
Moralis quid agas, quo tendas anagogia.

[The letter teaches event, allegory what you should believe,/ Morality teaches what you should do, anagogy what mark you should be aiming at.] Henri de Lubac, *Exégèse médiévale: le quatre sens de l'Écriture* (Lyons, 1960), I: 23; *Medieval Exegesis: The Four Senses of Scripture,* trans. Mark Sebanc (Grand Rapids, 1998), I: 1.

those sayings and deeds which he interpreted figuratively concerning Christ or the Church."[35]

On Orthography

Bede, *De orthographia*, ed. Ch. W. Jones, CCSL 123A, pp. 1–57.

Unlike Bede's two systematic grammatical texts just discussed, which are structured according to topics, the little book *De orthographia* is organized on a different principle altogether. He himself describes it as "a book about orthography, arranged according to the order of the alphabet" (*HE*, V. 24). Roughly alphabetized by first letter, after a quick run-through of single letter abbreviations (e.g., "L by itself stands for Lucius"), it consists entirely of short entries about the meaning and correct usage or spelling of words likely to cause difficulties for a medieval Latinist. Here is a sample entry: "*Caedo cecidi* per .ae. diphthongon: *Caeditur* et tilia ante iugo leuis (Virgilius); *cedo cessi* per .e. simplicem" ["The verb *caedo cecidi*, to cut, is spelled with an *ae* diphthong, as in this verse from Vergil's *Georgics*; but the verb *cedo cessi*, to withdraw, has a simple *e*"].[36]

Compiled from some seven grammatical works, the examples are drawn from both pagan and Christian texts; the entries often give Greek equivalents to the Latin words, as found in the source texts.[37] It was long assumed that Bede, who provides no preface or introduction, randomly and capriciously assembled the words, intending the collection to be used in the classroom. However, the classicist Anna Dionisotti has astutely and convincingly argued, from what Bede did with his sources and the nature of the resulting rearranged manual, that Bede has produced a lexical key to grammatical, orthographic, and semantic information, producing a medieval equivalent to Fowler's *Modern English Usage*. Bede's manual is designed for the library or scriptorium or the desk of the scholarly monk.[38] So, whereas the other grammatical works were clearly intended as textbooks, this piece more likely served the function of a reference book for the educated reader or writer.

The *De orthographia* was once considered "even less mature" than the *De arte metrica* until Anna Carlotta Dionisotti pointed out that a correction Bede made in the *Retractatio* to his *Expositio* on Acts (6: 8), concerning the meaning of the name Stephen, in *De orthographia* had been correctly interpreted as "crown" rather than "crowned."[39] That suggests that the *Expositio* (completed after 709), which had the etymology slightly incorrect,

---

35 Bede, *De schematibus et tropis*, ed. Kendall, CCSL 123A, p. 169.
36 Bede, *De orthographia*, ed. Charles W. Jones, CCSL 123A, pp. 7, 17.
37 Anna Carlotta Dionisotti, "On Bede, Grammars, and Greek," *RB* 92 (1982): 111–41 at 121. She corrects the exaggerated statement of Jones in the preface to CCSL 123A, p. x, that Bede "certainly used tracts of seventeen grammarians, and probably ten more" by showing the number to be "at most seven, probably in fewer volumes."
38 Dionisotti, "On Bede, Grammars, and Greek," *RB* 92 (1982): 111–41.
39 Bede, *De orthographia*, ed. Jones, CCSL 123A, p. 50, line 1082.

predated *De orthographia*, which had it correct, as does the later *Retractatio*. Again, the assumption that since the grammatical pieces are brief school works, they should antedate the more sophisticated scholarly works has been disproved, for on closer inspection they show themselves as both sophisticated and mature.

Tracts on nature and time

> Bede, *De natura rerum*, ed. Ch. W. Jones, CCSL 123A, pp. 173–234; *De temporibus*, CCSL 123C, pp. 579–611; *De temporum ratione*, ed. Ch. W. Jones and Th. Mommsen, CCSL 123B.

As part of the basic curriculum, Bede provided an enchiridion, *De natura rerum*, which he called "a separate book on the nature of things" (*HE*, V. 24). It serves as an introduction to cosmology, a companion to the hexaëmeron (exegesis on the first six days of creation in Genesis, chs. 1. 1 – 2. 3), and an adjunct to computus (measurement and time reckoning).[40] Reworking Isidore of Seville's *Liber rotarum* (also called *De natura rerum*) and pseudo-Isidore's *De ordine creaturarum*, Bede created a new text, which also incorporates much from the first half of the Roman encyclopedist Pliny's *Natural History*, carefully edited and re-ordered. As was his frequent custom (rare in the Middle Ages) in his biblical commentaries, Bede credited the sources from which he drew his material with a marginal citation. Although much of the book appears simple and even naive to readers in our scientific and technological age, his description of natural phenomena is as intelligent and rational as any to be found in the early Middle Ages, including Isidore's *Liber rotarum* (*De natura rerum*).

Bede opens the work with a prefatory poem of a couple of distichs:

> Naturas rerum uarias labentis et aeui
> Perstrinxi titulis, tempora lata citis,
> Beda Dei famulus. Tu fixa obsecro perennem
> Qui legis astra, super mente tuere diem.[41]

> [I, Bede, servant of God, have summarized in brief notices the various natures of things and the broad periods of the passing age. You who read the stars, I beseech you, look with fixed mind above to the everlasting day.]

---

40 On Bede's natural science, see Bede, *Opera de temporibus*, ed. Jones (Cambridge, MA, 1943), pp. 125–29; also Jones's entry on Bede in the *Dictionary of Scientific Biography* (New York, 1970), I: 564–66, and editorial preface to Bede, *Opera didascalia*, CCSL 123A, pp. xi–xii, 175, and 186. However, Peter Kitson, "Lapidary Traditions in Anglo-Saxon England, Part II: Bede's *Explanatio Apocalypsis* and Related Works," *ASE* 12 (1983): 73–123 at 88, demonstrates from Bede's use in that commentary of information in chapter 38 of Pliny's *Natural History* that, contrary to Jones's assertion, Bede also knew the second half of that work.

41 Bede, *De natura rerum*, ed. Jones, CCSL 123A, p. 189. Not everyone was impressed with Bede's poetic talents: a later glosser, while questioning whether the final couplet was Bede's, bestows faint praise: "Fuit enim Beda versificator tolerabilis" ["Bede was a tolerable versifier"], PL 90: 188B; critics with bad judgment exist in every age.

In fifty-one brief chapters Bede explains the earth, the heavens with the stars, the planets with their orbits, and then the atmospheric events, the oceans and some rivers, the earth as a globe, cause of earthquakes and the volcanic activity of Aetna, and ends with the geographical divisions of the earth.

In the preface of the *De temporum ratione*,[42] Bede alludes to the *De natura* and the *De temporibus* as earlier works, but how early is indeterminable. In chapter 38 of the *De natura* he accepts Pliny's eight-year tidal cycle, which he corrects in chapter 29 of the late work, *De temporum ratione,* to a nineteen-year cycle. The modern editor of *De natura* would place it even earlier than 703, the date of *De temporibus*.[43] It may indeed be that early, but that does not mean that Bede abandoned the subject; on his deathbed he was again correcting material in Isidore's *Liber rotarum (De natura rerum)* for his students.[44]

Near the beginning (703) and near the end (725) of his distinguished writing career, Bede composed works on time and its calculation: "A separate book on chronology; also, a longer book on chronology" (*HE*, V. 24). For the early Middle Ages the correct reckoning of time and dating of secular and sacred events was no easy matter, complicated by the liturgical necessity of coordinating the lunar (Jewish) calendar with solar (Roman) calendar.[45] It is a subject of which Bede became the master. In the later Middle Ages treatises on chronology bore the name *computus* and Bede's tracts are called that, though in Bede's day the word still meant the technique of reckoning especially as applied to creating and understanding ecclesiastical calendars. His first computistical manual, *De temporibus liber*, is a revision of books 5 and 6 of Isidore's *Etymologies* along with corrected supplements of Irish origin. The book has twenty-two chapters, each only a brief paragraph in length. Chapters 1 through 16 treat of time from the shortest measures to the longest: minutes, hours, days, months, years (including solstice and equinox, seasons, paschal dating), centuries, and finally the six ages of the world. Chapters 17–22 are a little chronicle giving the most important events in salvation history of each of the six ages. These latter chronicle chapters sometimes circulated as a separate work during the Middle Ages, as did the larger chronicle at the end of *De temporum ratione*.

As the frequency of the theme in his works confirms, Bede was extremely fond of the doctrine of the six ages of the world, which he inherited from Augustine and Isidore, and which clearly appealed to his orderly mind and strong sense of divine architectural planning. The six ages correspond to the six days of the creation in Genesis and the traditional six periods of man's

---

[42] Bede, *De temporum ratione*, ed. Jones, CCSL 123B, p. 263.

[43] Jones, ed., Beda, *De natura rerum liber*, CCSL 123A, p. 174; see also Max Laistner, *A Hand-List of Bede Manuscripts* (Ithaca, 1943), p. 139.

[44] Letter of Cuthbert in *HE*, p. 582.

[45] On computus as a problem-based pragmatic science, see Faith Wallis's lucid introduction to her translation of *Bede: The Reckoning of Time* (Liverpool, 1988, rpt. with corrections 2004), pp. xviii–xxxiv.

life from infancy to decrepitude.[46] Bede shared the common belief, therefore, that he was living in the last awful age before the final destruction. Where he differed was in the actual reckoning of the number of years in each age; instead of blindly accepting the figures which Isidore had unquestioningly taken from Jerome's translation of Eusebius's *Chronicle*, he himself calculated the time differences allotted in the Bible according to Jerome's translation from the Hebrew, with assistance from the historian Josephus where the Bible is unspecific. The result was that instead of the usual figure of more than 5000 years from the creation to the birth of Christ, Bede arrived at the sum of 3952 years. Such a disparity caused some eyebrow-raising in Northumbrian clerical circles, with the result that five years after releasing *De temporibus* (708), Bede was accused of heresy at a banquet in the monastery of Hexham at which his diocesan superior Bishop Wilfrid was present. He was charged with positing Christ's birth in the fifth age instead of at what was considered the correct time, the beginning of the sixth. Bede, who ardently shunned anything smacking of heresy and who also ardently considered time and God's work in time a serious matter, was appalled at this "repeated drunken attack by wanton rustics."[47] He responded to the report brought him by the Hexham monk and friend, Plegwin, with a ferocious letter, demanding that the detailed justification it contained be read in the presence of the bishop before whom no one had defended him.

The youthful piece, *De temporibus*, also caused another problem. Bede had to admit that it was too condensed for students to absorb. He remedied this by producing a new version, called *De temporibus liber maior* (*HE*, V. 24) but traditionally known as the *De temporum ratione*, from among the first words of the preface, in order to distinguish it from the earlier work.[48] This revision, the earliest comprehensive treatment of the subject, appeared some twenty-two years after the former work. However, Bede had not remained completely silent on computistical matters in the meantime: at some point he wrote a formal letter to Helmwald concerning solar increments that necessitate the intercalation of a leap-year day; this he later incorporated into the *De temporum ratione* as chapters 38 and 39. In the preface, paraphrasing Jerome and naming with him Augustine, Eusebius, and Josephus as his precedents, Bede carefully serves notice that his choosing to follow for his guide in this work the purity of the Hebraic Truth (that is, Jerome's Vulgate translation) is not intended as a slight to those chronographers who have followed the Septuagint (and its Old Latin) version of the Bible. He offers

---

[46] *De temporibus*, ch. 16; in *De temporum ratione*, 66, CCSL 123B, p. 463, he makes the comparison yet more explicit by calling man, following Greek philosophers, a microcosm (microcosmos) of the world with its ages.
[47] Bede, *Epistola ad Pleguinam*, in *Opera de temporibus*, pars 3, ed. Jones, CCSL 123C, pp. 617–26 at 617, lines 6–7: "quod me audires a lasciuientibus rusticis inter hereticos per pocula decantari."
[48] Bede's *De temporum ratione* is edited by Jones, CCSL 123B; Faith Wallis's *Bede: The Reckoning of Time* provides a superb translation with informative notes, and a critique and correction to Jones' commentary.

the work to his abbot Hwætberht for inspection and correction, and explains his bringing still another computus to the world by quoting Augustine: "It is necessary for many books to be made by many, in diverse manner but not in diverse faith, even about the same questions, so that the subject itself may get through to many, in one way to some, in another to others."[49] Then he ends, speaking for himself, saying that he has collected this material at the request of his brothers and if anyone takes offense or finds it superfluous, that person, maintaining fraternal charity, should go search the Fathers himself.

De temporum ratione is a commentary on the solar calendar and the paschal tables. After an initial elementary chapter on finger-calculation and a table of Greek and Roman letters signifying numbers, he has a chapter on the various aspects of time and traditional modes of its measurement (e.g., Olympiads [i.e., four-year intervals between the Greek Olympian games], indictions [Roman fiscal fifteen-year periods], lunar and solar years). In chapter 3 and onwards he proceeds, as he did in *De temporibus* but in much greater detail and with much added material, from the smallest to the largest units of time. He discusses the day, week, and month. After his description of the Roman months and dating (chs. 12–13) and the Greek months (ch. 14), he provides a chapter on English months, *De mensibus Anglorum*, with precious data for students of Germanic and Anglo-Saxon culture. He does this, "for it seems to me incongruous to speak of the annual reckoning of other peoples and to be silent about my own people's."[50] Since the English adopted the Roman calendar at an early date, Bede is really our only source for most of the information given here, scant though it is, about the months and the gods to whom they were dedicated.

> The first month, which the Latins call January, is Giuli; February is called Solmonath; March, Hrethmonath; April, Eostormonath; May, Thrimilchi; June, Litha; July, also Litha; August, Weodmonath; September, Halegmonath; October, Winterfilleth; November, Blodmonath; December, Giuli, the same name by which January is called. They began the year on the 8th calends of January [25 December], when we celebrate the birth of the Lord. That very night, which we hold so sacred, they used to call by the heathen word Modranecht, that is, "mother's night," because (we suspect) of the ceremonies they enacted all that night.[51]

Our only clue to the Anglo-Saxon deities Hretha and Eostre (Easter) is found in this chapter.[52] Bede concludes this section with chapter 16, on the twelve signs of the zodiac.

---

[49] Augustine, *De Trinitate*, I. 3, lines 25–28, ed. J. Mountain, CCSL 50, p. 33: "Ideoque utile est plures a pluribus fieri diuerso stilo, non diuersa fide, etiam de quaestionibus eisdem ut ad plurimos res ipsa perueniat, ad alios sic, ad alios autem sic."

[50] Bede's *De temporum ratione*, ed. Jones, CCSL 123B, p. 329: "neque enim mihi congruum uidetur aliarum gentium annalem obseruantiam dicere et meae reticere."

[51] Wallis, trans., *Bede: The Reckoning of Time*, ch. 15, p. 53.

[52] See Jones' commentary, *Bedae opera de temporibus*, pp. 350–51; Stenton, *Anglo-Saxon England*, pp. 97–98.

Next, he treats lunar movements. He continues on to the seasons and the solar variations. He analyzes the year and concludes with a section, most important for him and his students, on the right reckoning of the Easter dates. In chapter 65 Bede shows how the nineteen-year cycles of Dionysius can be joined to the larger unit, the Great Paschal Cycle of 532 years. The next-to-last chapter of this first part, chapter 66, beautifully presents the mystical or allegorical meaning of the Easter date, which he draws from Augustine's Letter 55, but couched in his own fine prose style. (Part of this chapter appears in the letter to King Nectan attributed to Abbot Ceolfrith in *HE*, V. 21, and makes us suspect that Bede at least composed the draft of the letter for Ceolfrith.) Bede climaxes the book with a consideration of the ages of the world. These chapters are termed the *Chronica maiora* and, like the earlier *Chronica minora* of his *De temporibus*, often circulated independently during the Middle Ages. This is especially true of chapter 66, on events of the sixth age. He greatly dilates the chronicle of the sixth age with more than seventy pages of European events (to the year of the world 4680, the year AD 729, during which "the Saracens, coming to Constantinople with an immense army, besieged it for three years ...");[53] he includes chapters on the remainder of the sixth age, Augustine's ideas on the time of Christ's Second Coming, and the times of the Antichrist. Bede concludes "with a rigorously Augustinian eschatological treatise"[54] rebutting "those who speculate that the existence of this world was determined from the beginning at 6,000 years," and who hold that the arrival of the day of Judgment "is generally to be expected around the end of the sixth millennium."[55] He then cautions against those who believe that the seventh age of 1000 years will be an earthly one. The final chapter, 71, adds two more ages to the six of *De temporibus*: the seventh age is the unfinished age of all the souls of the blessed from the death of Abel to the Last Judgment; the eighth age is the age of eternal joy or eternal woe after the end of this world. On this serene note he concludes: "And so our little book concerning the fleeting and wave-tossed course of time comes to a fitting end in eternal stability and stable eternity."[56]

A formal brief letter to an otherwise unknown monk named Wicthed constitutes a sort of appendix to the *De temporum ratione* and was often associated with that work in Bedan manuscript transmissions.[57] The letter wrestles with the Anatolian Canon concerning the dating of Easter (cited by

---

53 Wallis, trans., *Bede: The Reckoning of Time*, p. 236.
54 Richard Landes, "Lest the Millennium Be Fulfilled: Apocalyptic Expectations and the Pattern of Western Chronography 100–800 CE," in *The Use and Abuse of Eschatology in the Middle Ages*, ed. Werner Verbeke, Daniel Verhelst, and Andries Welkenhuysen (Leuven, 1988), pp. 137–211 at 176. In his survey of apocalyptic expectations Landes points out the major effect Bede's orthodox doctrine had on the Carolingians and later history in countering millenarianism.
55 Wallis, trans., *Bede: The Reckoning of Time*, pp. 239–40.
56 Wallis, trans., *Bede: The Reckoning of Time*, p. 249; *De temporum ratione*, ed. Jones, CCSL 1234B, p. 544: "Ergo noster libellus de uolubili ac fluctiuago temporum lapsu descriptus oportunum de aerterna stabilitate ac stabili aeternitate habeat finem."
57 Beda, *Opera didascalia*, 3, ed. Jones, CCSL 123C, pp. 635–42. Bede titles the work "De

Bede in chapter 30 of *De temporum ratione*), which was not recognized as a forgery until the Renaissance. Running counter to orthodox reckoning, it was used by the Irish as an authority against the Roman dating for Easter. Not skirting the issue, Bede judges that the text at some point must have been corrupted, perhaps deliberately.[58]

Bede considered all these didactic treatises, grammatical and scientific, as propaedeutics to the study of Scripture. He neither disdained nor neglected these basics. They extend from one end of his teaching career to the other, and from the simplicity of the early grammatical texts to the sophisticated, delicate complexity of the *De temporum ratione*, which was an immensely popular work throughout the Middle Ages. Moreover, he wrote these as tools for the schoolmaster, serving him in *viva voce* teaching. As he remarks while discussing the signs of the zodiac in *De temporum ratione*, "Much can be said about this, but it can be done to better effect by someone speaking than through the written word."[59]

sequinoctio iuxta Anatolium und" (*HE* V. 24, p. 568), but Jones in his editions calls it "Epistola ad Wicthedum," the addressee.

[58] Beda, *Opera didascalia*, 3, ed. Jones, CCSL 123C, sec. 11, p. 641.

[59] Bede, *The Reckoning of Time*, trans. Wallis, chapter 16, pp. 57–58; Beda, *Opera didascalia*, 3, ed. Jones, CCSL 123B, p. 336: "Multa hinc dici poterant, sed haec melius a colloquente quam a scribente fiunt."

3

The Biblical Commentaries

THE PRIMARY focus of Bede's life was the study of the Bible and the integration of its lessons to Christian life. All else was subservient to that. He states, "I have spent all my life in this monastery, applying myself entirely to the study of the Scriptures."[1] The "great mass of books" that Benedict Biscop and Ceolfrith had brought from the Continent for the monastery's fine library furnished the means to accomplish that task.[2] As a consciously orthodox scholar living in a strongly conservative monastery using a library chosen with great care by the founding abbots, Bede in his biblical commentaries follows the tradition and format inherited from the western Fathers, who in turn had practiced exegetical methods used by rabbinical and early Christian theologians like Origen, Tertullian, and Victorinus. While Bede had no wish to be singular, he made his own extensive contributions and played a major role in forming the canon of primary patristic authority. It was he who established the authoritative tetrarchy of Jerome, Augustine, Ambrose, and Gregory.[3] He asserts his intention "to follow the footsteps of the Fathers" in bringing the truth of the Scriptures to his age, while being fully conscious that he was interpreting the Bible authoritatively.[4] As he explains in the bio-bibliography at the end of the *Historia ecclesiastica*, he produced in brief format the comments of the Fathers "breuiter adnotare ... curaui" but also added his contribution to their formulations ("etiam ad formam sensus et interpretationis eorum superadicere curaui").[5] Always

---

[1] *HE*, V. 24, p. 567.

[2] *HAA*, I, c. 4, p. 367; c. 9, p. 373; *Lives of the Abbots*, trans. J. F. Webb in The Age of Bede, pp. 105–208 at 188, 194.

[3] See Bernice M. Kaczynski, "Bede's Commentaries on Luke and Mark and the Formation of the Patristic Canon," in *Anglo-Latin and its Heritage: Essays in Honour of A.G. Rigg*, ed. Siân Echard and Gernot Wieland (Turnhout, 2001), pp. 17–26; and her "The Authority of the Fathers: Patristic Texts in Early Medieval Libraries and Scriptoria," *Journal of Medieval Latin* 16 (2006): 1–27. For Bede's method of citing these four, and only these four, Fathers, see within p. 40, and n. 32.

[4] "Sequens vestigia patrum" is a leitmotif throughout Bede's exegetical works.

[5] As Bertrand de Margerie notes in "Bède le Vénérable, Commentateur original du Nouveau Testament," in *Introduction à l'Histoire de l'Exégèse*, IV: 187–228 at 188: "Bède décrit ainsi avec précision son double but par rapport aux commentaires antérieures des Pères: *adnotare*, *superadjicere* ... En d'autre termes, Bède nous communiquait, en cet aveu, un projet d'originalité dans la continuité." De Margerie then discusses a number of Bede's original interpretations of New Testament texts. Readers of Colgrave's translation of the Latin of *HE*, V. 24, p. 567, "haec in Scripturam sanctam ... ex opusculis uenerabilium partum breuier adnotare, siue etiam ad formam sensus et interpretationis eorum superadicere curaui," may be led astray by his wording: "to make brief extracts from the works of the venerable fathers on the holy Scriptures, or to add notes of my own to clarify their sense and interpretation."

scrupulous of the truth and vehemently opposed to heresy, Bede strives to convey the deepest meaning of the text by way of lucid interpretation within the orthodox tradition. Bede's exegesis is not aimed at an academic, philological, or abstract theological analysis of the text; rather, while manifesting great learning, his exegesis searches the core meanings of the Scriptures for the edification and development and maintaining of the spiritual life and, in its later stages especially, for the reformation of the individual and the Church.

The books of the Bible Bede chooses to interpret, often in response to a request, are of two types: those books that were already favorites of the Fathers, such as Genesis and Luke, and those that were largely ignored by earlier exegetes, such as Ezra and Nehemiah and New Testament Catholic Epistles. Both filled pedagogical needs; the former display Bede's talents as a monastic adapter and editor, and the latter testify to Bede's originality within the exegetical tradition. With the former he organizes and simplifies the best of the Fathers' comments for his English students, while interspersing his own commentary; with the latter, he provides his own exegesis as a supplement to the patristic legacy and emphasizes themes of personal concern, such as the reform of the Northumbrian Church. It is clear from the contents of the commentaries themselves that Bede in both types, the patristic anthology and his own exposition, closely follows the hermeneutic procedures of the Fathers, particularly Augustine and Gregory, while making his own contributions.[6] In the former he has decided which authority to follow, which opinion to incorporate and which to exclude, what comments to add, and what sort of synthesis to form, and in the latter, how best to present his insights and reformist policies within a patristic matrix. In all of his commentaries he provides both a literal and an allegorical interpretation of the text, but for the Old Testament his approach is more allegorical and for the New more literal. In his earlier commentaries he proceeds more segmentally, verse by verse, in the later commentaries more discursively and expansively.

In general, it is a fact that Bede's early exegetical treatises betray a much greater dependence on large patristic borrowings, whole sections being lifted from a source with some linking prose, syntactic adjustments, and abbreviations. His later treatises, though still heavily indebted to the Fathers, as Bede candidly admits, are more original, synthesizing traditional doctrine and personal observation, in which the sources are subsumed into the texture of the commentary while contemporary issues are emphasized.

Bede's method of commentary is the usual early medieval one of a phrase-by-phrase exegesis, explanation, and lucubration of a biblical book,

---

6 M. L. W. Laistner, *Thought and Letters in Western Europe, AD 500 to 900* (Ithaca, 1957), p. 163: "Yet, however great his debt to his predecessors may be, Bede does not copy uncritically. He is careful to select what will be useful and intelligible to his readers, he adds his own comments and observations, and he has knit the whole together in a way which raises his theological works well above the level of mere compilation or *catenae* and which bears clearly the impress of his own mind and personality."

from beginning to end. He summarizes his authorities and supplies his own reading of a text not treated to his satisfaction by an earlier author. Related to the practice of the monastic *lectio divina*, by which a text is affectively meditated upon and personally applied, this procedure extracts various potentialities in even apparently simple expressions.

Following his patristic predecessors, Bede provided both literal and allegorical interpretations of the biblical text.[7] The former explain the events in their historic complexity and resolve problems caused by scribal differences and differing versions of the Scriptures (the Old Latin and the Vulgate), or by fallible human expression of divine realities (such as attributing emotions to God). The latter explain the deeper meaning of the text, especially for the reader's own needs. The literal interpretation is identified with the Antiochene school of commentators, Theodore of Mopsuestia and John Chrysostom, and transmitted in the West by the *Instituta regularia divina* by Junilius. This method captivated the Irish exegetes, such as the authors of *De mirabilibus sacrae scripturae* (c. 655) and the *Liber de ordine creaturarum* (end of seventh century), who were keenly interested in historical, concrete, and often quaint detail;[8] it was also favored in the school of Canterbury under Eastern-trained Theodore (d. 690) and Hadrian (d. 710).[9] Although Bede was indebted to the Irish for much, especially in the area of computus, and although he likewise admired the teachers at the school of Canterbury, for his biblical exegesis he turned to the tradition of western patristic exegesis, which, while first establishing the literal meaning of the biblical text, embraced the allegorical for its efficacy in maintaining and fostering spiritual life.

The allegorical mode derived historically from Hellenistic praxis (especially in the interpretation of Homeric epic) and was applied to the Jewish bible by Philo of Alexandria, and thence to Christian patristic interpretation. The inspired word was understood to have a literal surface meaning but also deeper, hidden, spiritual meaning. The literal meaning serves as the husk, outer covering, and metaphorical sign of the profound truth it embodies. Philo combined the Platonic and Stoic allegorical method of construing literature with the rabbinical system of biblical commentary. The resultant procedure was used by the Christian patriarchs Clement and Origen, exploiting the Pauline teaching that the Old Testament prefigures

---

7   On Bede's practice in both arenas, see Calvin B. Kendall's excellent analysis in "The Responsibility of *auctoritas*: Method and Meaning in Bede's Commentary on Genesis," in *Innovation and Tradition in the Writings of the Venerable Bede*," ed. Scott DeGregorio (Morgantown, 2006), pp.101–19.

8   Pseudo-Augustine, *De mirabilibus Sacrae Scripturae* (PL 35: 2149–2200); *Liber de ordine creaturarum*, ed. and trans. M. C. Díaz y Díaz (Santiago de Compostela, 1972). See M. L. W. Laistner, *Thought and Letters in Western Europe*, (Ithaca, 1957), p. 146; Kathleen Hughes, "The Church in Irish Society, 400–800," in *A New History of Ireland, I: Prehistoric and Early Ireland*, ed. Dáibhi Ó Cróinín (Oxford, 2005), p. 328; Marina Smyth, *Understanding the Universe in Seventh Century Ireland* (Woodbridge, 1996), pp. 11–13.

9   *Biblical Commentaries from the Canterbury School of Theodore and Hadrian*, ed. Bernhard Bischoff and Michael Lapidge (Cambridge, 1994).

or foreshadows the New. Their methodology was carried on in the West by Ambrose, Augustine, and Gregory, but with Jerome they insist on the literal as well. Gregory and Bede point out that the Lord taught in parables and that he explained the parable of the sower in order to teach us also to look beneath the surface.[10] For the Christian as for the rabbinical Jew, the sacred Scriptures are full of meaning, and nothing in them can be devoid of significance. Thus, Bede writes: "The whole course of sacred Scripture is full of mystical figures, and not only in words and deeds, but also in those places and times in which it is enacted."[11] He repeats this assertion throughout his hermeneutics, sometimes citing Paul's "All things happened to them in figure, but they are written for our instruction" (I Cor. 10: 11).[12] The Bible contains truth in all its divine complexity and interrelated aspects; in it the Christian exegete sees a "marvelous sacramental concord" whereby nature and history serve as indicators of higher truths.[13] In the hands of a gifted literary exegete the allegorical method can elicit from the biblical text profound meaning and poetic richness. It can extricate the inner meanings of a pregnant phrase or complex allusion. On the other hand, it can also be a flight from the reality of the text to the abstract world of fancy. Bede sensibly warns that the basic meaning can be lost by such allegorizing: thus he writes, "But it must be carefully observed, as each one devotes his attention to the allegorical senses, how far he may have forsaken the manifest truth of history by allegorical interpretation."[14] So in such works as his commentary on the Acts of the Apostles with its *retractatio* he uses mostly an historic approach. In this Bede follows Augustine's mandates, set out in *On Christian Doctrine*, for adherence to historical truth and orthodoxy in which we are told to trust the text at the literal level first, provided it does not contradict the principle of charity.[15]

More than Gregory, Bede maintains that the literal, historical meaning of the text must not be abandoned or surrendered entirely to the allegorical interpretation. Bede's procedure is often allegorical and sometimes exuberantly so, and he defends the allegorical stretching and even wrenching of the text by an appeal to the metaphor of crushing aromatic herbs in order to release

---

[10] Gregory, *Homilia XL in Evangelia*, PL 76: 1131C; Bede, *In Lucae ev.* III, 8. 4–5, CCSL 120, p. 173, 309–12.

[11] Bede, *In Genesim* III, 14. 15, CCSL 118A, p. 188, lines 1610–14; trans. Calvin Kendall, *Bede: On Genesis* (Liverpool, 2008), p. 265.

[12] Bede, *De Tabernaculo*, I, 5–9, CCSL 119A, p. 5: " 'All things,' not only deeds or words which are contained in the sacred Scriptures but truly also the relationships of places, hours, and seasons, and also the circumstances in which they are done or spoken"; also *In I Samuhelem*, prologus, CCSL 119, p. 9, lines 4–6, Homilia *In Adventu*, I. 2, CCSL 122, p. 10, line 119.

[13] Bede, *In Lucae ev.* II, 6. 1, CCSL 120, p. 127, line 1088: "mira sacramenti concordia."

[14] Bede, *In Genesim*, I. 1, CCSL 118A, p. 3: "Sed diligenter intuendum ut ita quisque sensibus allegoricis studium impendat, quatenus apertam historiae fidem allegorizando derelinquat"; trans. Calvin Kendall, *Bede: On Genesis*, p. 69; cf. *In Lucae ev.* III, 10.29, CCSL 120, p. 222, lines 2206–09.

[15] Augustine, *De doctrina christiana*, Book 3, ch. 10. 14, ed. Joseph Martin, CCSL 32 (Turnhout, 1962), p. 86.

their fragrance.[16] However, the literal retains primacy. Although he shares the common rabbinical and Christian notion that the Song of Songs should not be understood in a carnal and literal sense,[17] in other commentaries he sometimes even excludes an allegorical interpretation in favor of a wholly literal one.[18] He works now in one system of interpretation, now in another, guided by the rule of faith, traditional orthodoxy, and Christian charity.

To describe the various allegorical functions a biblical text may have, Bede uses various terms indicating nuances in context even though his terminology varies: *sensus spiritalis* or *intelligentia spiritalis* to indicate the spiritual sense, spiritual intelligibility, of an event or statement; *figura* (figure), *typus* (type*)*, and *signum* (sign) to indicate a symbolic function in which one thing stands for another; *mysterium* (mystery, as allegorical meaning in the most extensive sense), *sacramentum* (sacrament, in its earlier pre-thirteenth century general meaning of "a sign of a sacred thing"), *allegoria* (allegory, a transferred sense), *arcanum* (secret truth) to express a hidden meaning.[19] Like Augustine, Bede is more concerned with elucidating the text in a literary critical way than in conforming to a rigid mode of doctrinaire theory; like Gregory, he is more eager to extract moral meaning than to pursue theological speculation.

Often Bede simply presents a single allegorical interpretation superimposed upon the literal meaning. At other times he presents a multiple allegorical meaning that can be fourfold: historical, typical, tropological, and anagogic.[20] These four senses Bede illustrates in his commentary on the Song of Songs, where, discussing the verse, "Your lips, my spouse, are dripping honeycomb" (Song 4: 11), he explains:

> A honeycomb is honey in the comb, and honey in the comb is the spiritual sense of the Divine Scriptures in the letter which is rightly called a dripping honeycomb; for a honeycomb drips when it has more honey than its wax chambers can hold, doubtless because the fecundity of the Holy Scriptures is such that a verse which was written in a short line fills many pages if one squeezes it by careful examination to see how much sweetness of spiritual understanding it contains inside. As only one example, the psalmist says: *Praise the Lord, O Jerusalem!* [Ps 147: 12] According to the letter, this surely exhorts

---

16 Bede, *Homelia* 8, CCSL 122, p. 233, lines 4–8.
17 Bede, *In Cantica canticorum* V, 8. 1, CCSL 119B, p. 337, lines 1–4: "Et in multis enim et in omnibus et in hoc maxime loco testatur hoc carmen quia nil carnale et iuxta litteram resonet sed totum se spiritaliter ac typice uelit intelligi." ["Frequently and everywhere, and especially in this passage, this Song testifies that it resounds with nothing carnal or according to the letter, but wishes that the whole of it be understood spiritually and typically," trans. Arthur G. Holder.]
18 Bede, *In I Samuhelem*, II, 15. 11, CCSL 119, p. 130, lines 2625–30; also 15. 35, p. 136, lines 2869–70.
19 For further discussion of these terms and functions, see Kendall, "Responsibility," pp. 112–14. In a survey of such terminology in Bede's Commentary on Genesis, Charles W. Jones in "Some Introductory Remarks on Bede's Commentary on Genesis," *Sacris Erudiri* 19 (1969–70): 115–98 at 151, concludes: "Terms normally considered technical have no definite or consistent meaning in Bede's exegesis."
20 For instance, Bede, *De Tabernaculo*, II, CCSL 119A, p. 91, lines 1957–60; *In I Samuhelem*, II, 10, CCSL 119, p. 87, lines 799–824.

the citizens of that city in which God's temple was found to sing praises to him; but according to allegory, Jerusalem is the Church of Christ spread throughout the whole world; again, according to tropology (that is, to the moral sense), every holy soul is rightly called "Jerusalem"; again, according to anagogy (that is, to the meaning that leads to higher things), Jerusalem is the dwelling-place of the heavenly homeland which comprises holy angels and human beings. Now it aptly agrees with all of these (although in several different ways) that this Jerusalem which is ordered to praise the Lord means "vision of peace"; for a single holy soul cannot sing as many praises to God as can the whole Church throughout the world, nor can the praises sung by the Universal Church while she is on pilgrimage on earth away from the Lord be as perfect as those she sings in the presence of her Lord when she is blessed to reign in heaven; neither can the peace which the saints have while [they live] in hope of seeing God and being delivered from evil be considered equal to the vision of that peace which they have in repose, when having been delivered from every evil they delight in God who is the highest good. Therefore the honeycomb is not only full of honey but it is also dripping from the lips of the Bride when the Church's teachers show that it contains the manifold abundance of inner sweetness, whether in the figures of the law, or in the prophetic sayings, or in the mystical words and deeds of the Lord himself, and then prepare from them the sumptuous dishes that are most pleasing to her faithful members (that is, to worthy listeners) and most salutary for their souls.[21]

Bede was the definitive authority in the Middle Ages for this fourfold formulation.[22] In *De Tabernaculo* the four feet on the tabernacle serve as an analogy for this way of interpreting Scripture.[23] Since each of the four levels of meaning can be either of deed (that is, of some action such as the crossing of the Red Sea) or of word (of some expression, such as "Your eyes are doves ") or both, the resulting combinations are so numerous that a single passage in Scripture would demand, Bede surmises, many pages for even a cursory exposition. Despite the brief stock examples he cites and the large potential for allegorical development he recognizes, in practice Bede's analysis, like Gregory's, is usually two- or at most threefold. Bede speaks of the "rules of allegory."[24] In common with many ancient writers, the Fathers, and medieval exegetes generally, Bede shares a fondness for numerical symbolism, in accord with the biblical text, a favorite of the great numerical expositor Augustine, "You have ordered all things in measure, and in number, and in weight" (Wisdom 11: 21).

There are traditionally accepted meanings of biblical items, such as a

---

21 Bede, *In Cantica canticorum*, CCSL 119B, III. 4. 10, p. 260; trans. Arthur G. Holder (not yet published).

22 Bede, *De schematibus et tropis*, CCSL 123A, II, 2, pp. 166–69; see Henri de Lubac, *Exégèse médiévale: Les quatre sens de l'Écriture* (Lyons, 1959), I. 664.

23 Bede, *De Tabernaculo*, CCSL 119A, p. 25.

24 Bede, *In Lucae ev*. III, 7. 37, CCSL 120, p. 167, line 42: "Quod et regulis allegoriae pulcherrime congrui ..." Plummer, ed., *Bedae Opera historica*, pp. lix–lx, n. 8, provides a list of these "leges allegoriae" in Bede's works.

dove for the Spirit: "Because the Holy Spirit descended upon the Lord [Luke 3: 22], the word 'dove' or 'doves' rightly signifies the spiritual sense and gifts."[25] However, the rules of allegory mean in a larger sense the propriety and fitness of an analogy or figure as it conforms to the rule of faith and charity. In *Quaestio VI* of *Octo quaestionum liber* Bede tackles the problem of seemingly subjective interpretation of biblical texts, so that sometimes bad men and bad actions are held up as good models and exemplary types. Citing examples from Gregory the Great's commentary on Job, Bede says, "Nor should it seem absurd to you that the bad actions of the reprobate should signify something good, or on the other hand that the good works of the righteous should bear a contrary signification."[26] Bede points out that such contrary attribution is very common in Scripture itself.[27] Even though the good are truly just models, particular qualities or circumstances of the bad might allow a meaning from which good can be elicited, and vice versa. Hence, appealing to biblical and patristic precedents, Bede defends subjective, impressionistic, and even apparently contradictory allegorical types and analogies as appropriate *ad hoc* exegesis.

By way of Augustine, Bede learned a specific set of exegetical techniques, the "Rules of Tyconius."[28] Augustine had given the Donatist heretic Tyconius his due by extolling his seven rules as key to expounding obscurities and subtextual assumptions in Scripture. These rules are really literary critical in that they involve exploitation of figures of speech. The Rules list the various ambiguous or confusing predications that are made as the result of synecdoche or a similar submerged figure. In the letter to Eusebius (the monastic pseudonym of Hwætberht, who became abbot in 716) prefacing the *Expositio Apocalypseos*, Bede first states that the Apocalypse is structured in seven parts; he then keeps the symmetry of the heptad by outlining the seven Tyconian rules.[29] The first, with a christological, ecclesial, and eschatological focus, concerns references to the Lord and his body: the mystical body (the

---

25 Bede, *In Cantica canticorum*, I, 1. 14, CCSL 119B, p. 208, 686–89.
26 Arthur G. Holder, trans., *On Eight Questions*, in W. Trent Foley and Arthur G. Holder, trans., *Bede: A Biblical Miscellany* (Liverpool, 1999), Question 6, p. 167.
27 See Bede's comment, *In Genesim* IV, CCSL 118A, p. 236, lines 1515–20: "Solitum namque est in scripturis, et per bonos mala, et per malos aliquoties bona designari. Nam et beatus papa Gregorius reges impiissimos Saulem et Iechomiam in figura Domini saluatoris ponere non dubitauit, et e contrario per factum Vriae fidelissimum perfidiam Iudeorum dicit esse designatam." ["For it is customary in the Scriptures not only for evil things to be signified by good men, but also at times for good things to be signified by wicked men. For the Blessed Pope Gregory did not hesitate to offer the really wicked kings Saul and Jeconiah as figures for our Lord the Savior, and on the other hand he says that the faithlessness of the Jews was signified by the very faithful deed of Uriah," translated by Calvin Kendall.] See also Bede, *In Tobiam* 2: 10 – 11: 3–5, CCSL 119, p. 5, and *In I Samuhelem*, II, 10, 25, CCSL 119, p. 92, lines 995–98, where Bede uses much the same words along with the example of the use of black, gold, and red in manuscript copies of the scripture.
28 Tyconius, *The Book of Rules*, trans. William S. Babcock (Ithaca, 1989). On the subject, see Pamela Bright, *The Book of Rules of Tyconius: its Purpose and Inner Logic* (Notre Dame, 1988).
29 Bede, *Expositio Apocalypseos*, ed. Roger Gryson, CCSL 121A (Turnhout, 2001), pp. 221–33; Bede, *Explanation of the Apocalypse*, trans. Edward Marshall (Oxford and London, 1878), translated from the poor Latin edition of PL 93: 129–206.

Church) is distinct from the head but identified with it. The second is the twofold nature of the Church, made up of saints and sinners in the communion of faith and therefore both sinful and saintly, so that, for instance, she can be referred to as dark but lovely (Song of Songs 1: 4). The third concerns the Pauline distinctions of promises and the law; the spirit and the letter; of faith and works; of free will and predestination; as well as the Matthean and Johannine contrast of good and evil within the Church. The fourth Tyconian rule is about genus and species (generic prophecies vs. prophecies particular to individuals, cities, states). The fifth is about times (the meaning of "day") and numbers and the various symbolic uses of them. The sixth is recapitulation, which Bede, following Augustine, understands to be an anachronistic or dislocated temporal reference, in which an event is mentioned before its true chronological place. (For Tyconius, by contrast, recapitulation meant the simultaneous speaking of the type and antitype, the promise and the fulfillment.) The seventh, about the devil and his body, is the completion and obverse of the first rule: as the Church is the body of Christ, so the wicked, particularly heretics, are the body of the devil. Although Tyconius intended his methodology to apply to "the immense forest of prophecy" of Scripture, Bede found the rules most useful in explicating the complex imagistic text of Revelation, and to some extent his other commentaries, such as on Genesis, on the Tabernacle, and on the first book of Samuel. For instance, when discussing David as a figure of Christ in Book IV of *In Samuhelem*, he implicitly invokes rule one by pointing out that in certain actions, such as warfare against the Philistines, David represents individual Christians.[30]

Bede was far more scrupulous than the majority of medieval commentators in acknowledging his principal authorities. In his prefaces Bede regularly informs his readers of his principal sources and, unusually for the medieval period, in the case of his commentaries on Mark and Luke by a designation in the margin of the author of the excerpt (A–V = Augustine, A–M = Ambrose, H–R = Hieronymus, i.e. Jerome, G–R = Gregory). In the preface to his commentary on Luke he specifically requests that those who copy his writings should on no account omit the marginal references to his sources that he has entered in his own copy.[31] It is noteworthy that Bede, while citing the four doctors he was responsible for establishing as the canonical "Big Four," does not give explicit citations to any other of the Fathers, such as Cassian or Hilary.[32]

30 Bede, *In I Samuhelem*, CCSL 119, pp. 213–14, lines 64–103.
31 M. L. W. Laistner, *Thought and Letters in Western Europe* (Ithaca, 1957), p. 163. Laistner's assumption, however, that Bede followed the same practice in all his commentaries is unwarranted.
32 Information from correspondence with Paul Meyvaert. Whether Bede in all his works noted only the four Fathers in his marginal notation is not certain. However, the marginal ascriptions to Eucherius, Arculfus, Hieronymus (Jerome) in three manuscripts of *De locis sanctis*, CCSL 175, pp. 152, 254, 257, and 261, are not abbreviated as Bede was accustomed to do, as in the ascriptions to the four Fathers; and Bede's principal source for *De locis sanctis*, Adamnus, cited by Bede in the introduction, does not appear in the margins. These two bits of evidence suggest that a scribe and not Bede originally inserted those references. On Bede as the first to establish

Bede shows a concern for the accuracy of the text and sometimes questions whether scribes have copied a text faithfully. Aware of the problems inherent in translations from Hebrew or Greek into various Latin versions, he exploits the ambiguities by suggesting different interpretations. Laistner notes, "His interest in the text criticism of the Bible was unique in his age,"[33] and Meyvaert provides a number of interesting examples of Bede's "shrewd sense of textual problems."[34] Carmela Vircillo Franklin has shown how Bede effectively mines both the Vulgate and Vetus Latina (Old Latin, prior to Jerome's Vulgate) versions of the Bible and various patristic sources to give a complex reading of verses in Genesis.[35]

Bede began his exegetical exercises on books of the New Testament; thereafter he concentrated on books of the Old Testament. Many of the books he tackled later had not been commented on directly by earlier Fathers and theologians. His purposes were therefore first to furnish from established sources traditional commentary in a simplified form for his English students and then, usually on request, to fill for them the gaps in which no treatise yet existed by supplying both traditional and contemporary commentary. Although he learned some Greek early in his career, he took great pains to gain a better mastery of it for his later work; as a result he published a revised version of his commentary on the Acts of the Apostles based on his careful readings of the Greek text. Because the Hebrew Bible was not to be found in England or northern Europe in Bede's day, and no one like Jerome's teacher in Palestine was available to instruct him in the language, he could cite only a few Hebrew words and their etyma from Jerome.[36]

Bede composed ten Old Testament commentaries, an interesting mix: *On Genesis, On Samuel, Thirty Questions on Kings, On the Tabernacle, On the Temple, On Ezra and Nehemiah, On Proverbs, On the Song of Songs, On Habakkuk, On Tobit.* To the list should be added the three brief questions from *Eight Questions* that pertain to the Old Testament (two from II Samuel and one on the word "ignitum" in Psalm 118 and Proverbs 30);[37] the letter-tract

---

the Fathers' quadrumvirate, "calqued on the list of the four Evangelists," see Bernice Kaczynski, "The Authority of the Fathers: Patristic Texts in Early Medieval Libraries and Scriptoria," *Journal of Medieval Latin* 16 (2006): 1–27 at 2–3.

33 Laistner, *Thought and Letters*, p. 161.

34 Paul Meyvaert, "Bede the Scholar," in *Famulus Christi*, ed. Gerald Bonner (London, 1976), pp. 48–51 at 51.

35 Carmela Vircillo Franklin, "Bilingual Philology in Bede's Exegesis," in *Medieval Cultures in Contact*, ed. Richard F. Gyug (New York, 2003), pp. 3–17.

36 Colette Sirat, *Hebrew Manuscripts of the Middle Ages* (Cambridge, 2002), p. 36, states concerning Hebrew codices: "In Christian Europe the oldest surviving books date from not earlier than 1050, a century or a century and a half later [than in Muslim lands]." David Howlett, "Israelite Learning in Insular Latin," *Peritia* 11 (1997): 117–152, contends that from transcribed words and bits of Hebrew phrases that appear in Insular writers from the seventh century they knew the Hebrew language; but his evidence shows only that the Insular authors had garnered a few isolated words, not that they had command of the language.

37 Text edited by Michael Gorman, "Bede's *VIII Quaestiones* and Carolingian Biblical Scholarship," *RB* 109 (1999): 32–74, in the Appendix, 62–74. Gorman mistakenly asserts, p. 33, that "six are

41

on the resting places of Israel in its desert wanderings; another letter-tract on a phrase in Isaiah, 24: 22; and the abbreviated Psalter as a devotional manual. He also composed a set of descriptive titles for sections of the Old Testament, which he called *capitula lectionum* in his bio-bibliography at the end of the *Historia ecclesiastica*; they have been deduced recently in large part by Paul Meyvaert.[38] Bede's New Testament commentaries are six: *On Luke* and *On Mark*, *On the Acts of the Apostles*, *Collectaneum on the Pauline Epistles*, *On the Seven Catholic Epistles*, and *On the Apocalypse*. In addition, there are Bede's *Capitula Lectionum* for the New Testament.[39]

Bede lists his commentaries in his bio-bibliography in the *Ecclesiastical History* according to the traditional biblical canon. However, organization based on the dates of composition reveals a process of maturation and thematic development from the earlier to the later commentaries. The dating is for the most part hypothetical and tentative because Bede furnishes little specific information about when he wrote his individual commentaries; moreover, some of his works he composed or revised over a period of time. A relative scale, though, can be surmised from the few internal signs for dating and from his development of a more discursive style, with personal additions, and his involvement with contemporary issues.[40]

COMMENTARIES ON THE OLD TESTAMENT

On Genesis

In principium Genesis, usque ad natiuitatem Isaac et eiectionem Ismahelis, libros IIII [The Beginning of Genesis up to the Birth of Isaac and the Casting Out of Ishmael: four books], ed. C. W. Jones, CCSL 118A. *Bede: On Genesis*, translated by Calvin B. Kendall, with an extensive introduction and notes (Liverpool, 2008).

Although Jones' 1967 edition is generally reliable, Kendall has re-evaluated the dating of the versions, augmented Jones' list of manuscripts, added a

from the New Testament and two from the Old," instead of five from the New and three from the Old.
[38] See Paul Meyvaert's admirable investigation, "Bede's *Capitula Lectionum* for the Old and New Testaments," *RB* 105 (1995): 348–80.
[39] See Meyvaert, "Bede's *Capitula Lectionum*," esp. pp. 360–61.
[40] For arguments for the dating of Bede's exegetical works, see M. L. W. Laistner, *A Hand-List of Bede Manuscripts* (Ithaca, 1943); Paul Meyvaert, "'In the Footsteps of the Fathers': The Date of Bede's *Thirty Questions on the Book of Kings to Nothelm*," in *The Limits of Ancient Christianity*, ed. William E. Klingshirn and Mark Vessey (Ann Arbor, 1999), pp. 267–86; Scott DeGregorio, "Bede's *In Ezram et Neemiam* and the Reform of the Northumbrian Church," *Speculum* 79 (2004): 1–25; Arthur Holder, "The Feminine Christ in Bede's Biblical Commentaries," in *Bède le Vénérable entre tradition et postérité*, ed. Stéphane Lebecq, Michel Perrin, Olivier Szerwiniack (Lille, 2005), pp. 109–118; and his "The Anti-Pelagian Character of Bede's *Commentary on the Song of Songs*," forthcoming in the Proceedings of the 2001 Gargano Conference on the Study of the Bible in the Early Middle Ages, ed. Michael Gorman; and Alan Thacker, "Bede and the Ordering of Understanding," in *Innovation and Tradition in the Writings of the Venerable Bede*, ed. Scott DeGregorio (Morgantown, 2006), pp. 52–60.

detailed description of previous editions, and made textual corrections and emendations.[41]

For Bede, as for Augustine, Genesis is of the greatest importance because it is the Old Testament's account of creation, the structure of the world, the temptation and the fall of Adam, with all the consequences of sin for the human race. It serves as the negative pole for the positive new creation of the New Testament with redemption by the new Adam, Christ.[42] However Bede, while Augustinian, is not so concerned with sin and grace in this commentary as with "*natura externa*, God's gracious creation."[43] Bede concentrates on the original beauties of nature and the character of mankind, with its unique gift of language. Thematically the work is structured on the themes of exile, "the fundamental metaphor for the condition of human life on earth" (and the leitmotif of Old English elegy), and of privileging of the younger over the older.[44] It must be admitted that Bede, who most likely never met a Jew or Muslim in his northern monastic life, thematizes as evil, dark, and diabolical the Judaism that rejected Christ and the Islam reported to attack contemporary Mediterranean Christians.[45]

It is conjectured that Bede composed Book I (parts a and b) c. 717–18, adding Book II in 720, and completing the commentary with Books III and IV in 722–25.[46] Bede's Preface to Bishop Acca, to whom he dedicated five of his commentaries,[47] was composed for the two books of the shorter version and not revised for the longer version. In it he acknowledges the lengthy patristic commentaries on Genesis by Basil the Great, Ambrose, and Augustine, and explains that his commentary is an abbreviated chrestomathy of their works adjusted to the needs of the simple reader. These parts exhibit Bede's early qualities as an editor and commentator. As a condensed form of patristic hexaemeral exegesis, demonstrating how "the world proceeded in perfectly proper order from unformed matter to harmonious form,"[48] the first book posits a traditional geocentric universe but makes a number of acute

---

[41] Kendall, trans., *Bede: On Genesis*, pp. 46–53, 57–59, 59–61, 327–33.

[42] For instance, *Libri Quatuor in Principium Genesis*, I. 2. 9, ed. Jones, CCSL 118A, pp. 46–47, lines 1453–1480. See Jean Daniélou, *From Shadows to Reality: Studies in the Biblical Typology of the Fathers* (London, 1960), pp. 16, 28. See also Thomas O'Loughlin, *Teachers and Code-Breakers: The Latin Genesis Tradition, 430–800* (Turnhout, 1999), pp. 235–37, 312, and 323–24.

[43] Jones, "Bede's Commentary," p. 117, citing Bede's remarks on Genesis 1: 11–13. See, for instance, Bede, *In Genesim*, I. 1. 26, pp. 25–26, lines 759–77; I. 2. 20–22, p. 56; I. 3. 8, p. 63, lines 2002–20.

[44] Kendall, *Bede: On Genesis*, Introduction, pp. 14, 19.

[45] Discussed by Kendall, Introduction, pp. 21–27. See also Andrew P. Schiel, *The Footsteps of Israel: Understanding Jews in Anglo-Saxon England* (Ann Arbor, 2004), Introduction and chapters 1 and 2; Alan Thacker, "Bede and the Ordering of Understanding," *Innovation and Tradition in the Writings of the Venerable Bede* (Morgantown, 2006), pp. 55–57.

[46] This conjectural arrangement suits the evidence better than Jones' dating and supposition that Bede did Ia and Ib separately, rather than that abbreviators excised Ia for separate use. See Kendall, *Bede: On Genesis*, Introduction, pp. 40–45.

[47] See Lapidge, "Acca of Hexham," *Analecta Bollandiana* 123, p. 66.

[48] Bede, *In Genesim*, I. 14, p. 15, lines 399–400; trans. Kendall, *Bede: On Genesis*, p. 80.

astronomical observations.[49] After commenting on chapter 2, verse 3, Bede inserts a favorite topic (elaborated further in *De temporum ratione*, c. 66), the six ages of the world, in which each of the seven days of Genesis is paralleled with an age of the world.[50] Much of the latter part of the first book, "a coherent analysis of the nature and psychology of the Fall,"[51] contains large chunks from *De Genesi ad litteram*, where Augustine authoritatively deals with the question. However, as Carmela Vircillo Franklin has demonstrated, Bede combines verses in the Vulgate and Vetus Latina versions of the Bible with comments from the Fathers to give a richer interpretation to individual verses.[52] And, when coming to Genesis 4: 3, Bede shows that even though he generally follows in the footsteps of the Fathers, he is also his own man. Since the Bible does not give a reason why God rejects Cain's offering, Ambrose ascribes the cause (as do modern commentators) to Cain's profession as a farmer instead of a grazer, but Bede objects that since husbandmen such as Noah were righteous, the reason must be that Cain did not act with proper piety and service.[53] Much of Book II (6. 5 – 9. 19) deals in extensive and apt detail with Noah's ark, which allegorically represents Christ and his Church. Book III, dealing with chapters 10–14 of Genesis, has a fine if traditional spiritual interpretation of the city of Babylon, whose builders use brick and bitumen (the dirty, earthly deeds of the devil).[54] Like Gregory, Bede opposes the linguistic confusion at the Tower of Babel with the linguistic unity at the miracle of Pentecost.[55] Book III concludes with the history of the yet childless Abraham in Genesis 14. In Book IV there are beautiful moments of allegorical exegesis, as for instance Sarah's three measures of flour signifying three levels of meaning (historical, typological, anagogical), and the spiritual meaning of the three loaves of bread that Sarah bakes in ashes, so that the ashes represent the literal covering and the sweet loaves the spiritual sense, the butter she serves is the perfection of teaching and the milk the simplicity of the literal sense (Genesis 18: 6);[56] however at the literal level Bede does not shirk discussing the moral issues involved in Abraham's sleeping with his daughters or Lot's offering his daughter to the Sodomites to spare the angel-guests. A contemplative reading of Bede's four books of commentary

---

[49] Bede, *In Genesim*, I. 17a–18b, pp. 17–19.
[50] For complete reference to the Bedan theme of the six ages, see Kendall's note 149 on pp. 100–101 of *Bede: On Genesis*.
[51] Kendall, *Bede: On Genesis*, Introduction, p. 42.
[52] Franklin, "Bilingual Philology," pp. 8–16, gives examples from Bede's commentary on Genesis 3: 14, 4: 25–26, and 8: 7.
[53] Bede, *In Genesim*, II. 4. 3–4, CCSL 118A, p. 74, lines 42–46. Jones the editor notes "*Beda hic Ambrosius, De Cain et Abel*, I, x, 42 (cf. iii, 11 et vii, 25) *contradicit.*" See Kendall's note, p. 141, n. 6, in *Bede: On Genesis*.
[54] Bede, *In Genesim*, III. 11. 9–10, CCSL 118A, p. 157, line 542, to p. 162, line 708.
[55] Kees Dekker, "Pentecost and Linguistic Self-Consciousness in Anglo-Saxon England: Bede and Ælfric," *JEGP* 104 (2005): 345–72 at 352–54, emphasizes Bede's interest in language and sanction of a role for the vernaculars, to bring about the ability to praise God and teach the mysteries in the remote corners of the world, such as England (p. 372).
[56] Bede, *In Genesim*, IV. 18. 6–7, CCSL 118A, pp. 212–15; Kendall, *Bede: On Genesis*, p. 292.

on Genesis 1–21 provides an excellent example of Bede's skills at extended exegesis, but, even more rewarding, a long spiritual interpretation of the biblical text.

In his commentary on Genesis Bede showed that he could successfully incorporate and emulate patristic exegesis. "Moreover, in Bede's writings we have a systematic exploitation of Genesis that is as competent as any work on the topic could be until the rise of modern scholarship."[57]

In the three following commentaries, *De Tabernaculo*, *De Templo*, and *In Ezram et Neemiam*, Bede demonstrated that, on his own, he could analyze Old Testament biblical works that had not been treated as a whole by any of the Fathers. The three works form something of a trilogy, though the first two are more obviously thematically kin, whereas the third, while sharing the topic of the Temple and its worship, also treats of the restoration not only of the Temple but of the Jewish state and culture. Furthermore, all three biblical texts provide subjects that Bede could easily and profitably allegorize.

On the Resting Places of the Children of Israel

De mansionibus filiorum Israel, PL 94: 699–702. *On the Resting Places of the Children of Israel*, translated with notes and brief introduction by Arthur Holder in *Bede: A Biblical Miscellany* (1999), pp. 29–34.

In response to Bishop Acca's query, the *De mansionibus* enumerates and describes the Israelites' stopping-places during their desert wandering, described in Numbers, chapter 33. Following Jerome's interpretations, Bede adds the allegorical and moral meanings of those resting areas for the Christian journeying through this desert of life on the way to the Promised Land of heaven, a favorite theme in Bede.[58]

On the Tabernacle

De Tabernaculo et vasis eius ac vestibus sacerdotum libri III [*Three Books on the Tabernacle, its Vessels, and the Priestly Vestments*], ed. D. Hurst, CCSL 119A, pp. 1–139. *Bede: On the Tabernacle*, translated with notes and introduction by Arthur G. Holder (1994).

---

57 Thomas O'Loughlin, *Teachers and Code-Breakers: The Latin Genesis Tradition, 430–800* (Turnhout, 1999), p. 312, who adds, n. 58: "This is evidenced not only in the use made of his works by Aquinas and later writers such as Cornelius à Lapide, but in the number of other exegetical works on Genesis, and scientific works based on Genesis, that are attributed to him." Throughout *Teachers and Code-Breakers* O'Loughlin shows how important Bede was to the tradition and what he contributed to it.

58 On the interpretations of Origen, Jerome, and Bede about the *mansiones* see Jennifer O'Reilly, "Bede on Seeing the God of Gods in Zion," in *Text, Image, Interpretation*, ed. A. Minnis and J. Roberts, pp. 3–29 at 7–10. She incorporates that exegesis into Bede's larger understanding of the pilgrimage journey of this life to God's promised land of heaven.

Bede's *On the Tabernacle* is the first Christian extended commentary on the portable shrine of the divine presence fashioned by Moses; it spawned a number of twelfth-century commentaries on the topic.[59] With its companion piece, *On the Temple*, it demonstrates "Bede's rather exceptionally architectural approach to Revelation."[60] He sees the tabernacle as representing the Church militant, on its earthly pilgrimage; he will then address the temple as the Church triumphant: "Here the Church is built amidst the labour and toil of this transient life, thirsting and hungering for the everlasting kingdom, but there it is completed in the vision and possession of true peace."[61] The principal sources Bede uses for describing and expounding the tent shrine are, besides Exodus 34: 12 – 30: 21, Josephus's *Jewish Antiquities*, Jerome's Letter 64 to Fabiola about the priestly vestments, and Pope Gregory's *Pastoral Care*. He also refers to a double-page drawing of the tabernacle in Cassiodorus's *Codex Grandior*, and draws to some extent on Pliny's *Natural History*, Jerome's *On Hebrew Names*, and Isidore's *Etymologies*.[62] Although the tabernacle was destroyed in 587 BCE, what it represents in every detail for the Christian Church symbolically perdures. As Bede says in his introduction to Book I:

> Since with the Lord's help we are going to speak about the figure of the tabernacle and its vessels and utensils, first we ought to examine and attentively consider the topography of the place and the circumstances that obtained when these things were commanded to be made. For "all these things," as the Apostle says, "happened to them in figure but were written down for us" (I Cor. 10: 11). "All these things" [includes] not only the deeds or words that are contained in the Sacred Writings, but also the description of the locations and hours and times and the things themselves, as well as the circumstances under which they were said.[63]

In *On the Tabernacle* Bede is most concerned with the spiritual sense. It is in this treatise that he becomes the first writer to give a full account of the fourfold sense of Scripture, with reference to the four feet of the table in Exodus 25: 26, as historical, allegorical, tropological, and anagogical. Elsewhere in this and other treatises, such as *On Genesis*, he posits a threefold sense; but for the most part he distinguishes just two senses, one literal (historical), and the other spiritual, also called "typic," "sacramental,"

---

59 Henri de Lubac, *Exégèse médiévale*, 2 vols. in 4 parts (Paris, 1959–64), 2. 1: 406; *Bede: On the Tabernacle*, trans. Arthur G. Holder (Liverpool, 1994), p. xv.

60 Charles W. Jones, "Remarks on Bede's *Commentary on Genesis*," p. 169; cited by Holder, *Bede: On the Tabernacle*, p. xv, with further references in n. 2 to Bede's exegesis on various sacred structures in the Bible.

61 *Bede: On the Tabernacle*, 2. 1, trans. Holder, p. 45. The meaning of Jerusalem as "the vision of peace" (Jerome, *De nominibus Hebraicis*, CCSL 72, ed. P. de Lagarde, 121: 9–10), is often so explained in Bede.

62 *Bede: On the Tabernacle*, trans. Holder, p. xvi.

63 *Bede: On the Tabernacle*, trans. Holder, p. 1.

"mystical," or "allegorical."[64] Bede does not lose sight of the literal meaning and the larger context of the biblical narrative, but he does emphasize and concentrate on the symbolic meanings that the various sacred elements and particular objects suggest. Such a reading produces a poetic effect, in that objects are metaphors for deeper signification. If the reader allows the process, extraordinary beauty and meaning emerge. A brief example will have to suffice. When discussing the ten colored curtains of the tabernacle, Bede says:

> The tabernacle of the Lord is made from curtains variegated with diverse sorts of colours because the Holy Church universal is built from many elect persons, from many churches throughout the world, and from the flowers of diverse virtues. All its perfection is contained in the number ten because in whatever direction the Church has been spread throughout the world, among diverse nations and tribes and peoples and tongues, it stands completely firm in the single love of God and neighbour which was contained in the Decalogue of the law.[65]

Reading the whole commentary of such extended meaning may seem excessive to some but most will find it pleasing, even captivating.

On Samuel

In primam partem Samuhelis libri IIII [Four Books on the First Part of Samuel], ed. D. Hurst, CCSL 119.[66]

This work, written about 716, Bede labeled an important enterprise that involved a "great deal of sweat,"[67] but for some reason it never entered the main exegetical stream as his other commentaries did.[68] It nonetheless represents his mature work and, as Alan Thacker notes, "one of the most elaborately allegorical."[69] As in other commentaries Bede divides the work into thematic sections. Book I, in seven chapters, deals with Samuel's career from childhood to judge and leader. Book II, in eight chapters, tells of the

---

64 Bede, *De Tabernaculo*, 1, CCSL 119A, p. 24, line 776 to p. 25, line 81; Henri de Lubac, *Exégèse médiévale*, 2, 2: 422; *Bede: On the Tabernacle*, trans. Holder, p. xviii.

65 *Bede: On the Tabernacle*, trans. Holder, Book II, 2, p. 48, commentary on ch. 26: 1.

66 There is no translation as yet of this, Bede's longest Old Testament commentary. I am in the process of doing one. For a translation of some sections see the Appendix to my "Bede's Style in his Commentary on I Samuel," in *Text, Image, Interpretation: Studies in Anglo-Saxon Literature and its Insular Context in Honour of Éamonn Ó Carragáin*, ed. Alistair Minnis and Jane Roberts (Turnhout, 2007), pp. 233–51 at 247–51.

67 Bede, *In I Samuhelem*, ed. David Hurst, CCSL 119 (Turnhout, 1972), I prol., line 55; III prol., line 1.

68 See my "Bede's Neglected Commentary on Samuel," in *Innovation and Tradition in the Writings of the Venerable Bede*, ed. Scott DeGregorio (Morgantown, 2006), pp. 121–42.

69 Alan Thacker, "Bede and the Ordering of Understanding," pp. 37–63 at 54. In his n. 58 on p. 54 Thacker calls attention to Bede's own reference (at *In I Sam.* 4., prol., p. 212, line 23) to his commentary as "allegoricae expositionis libellum."

Israelites' demand for a king, to which God reluctantly accedes, after which Samuel anoints Saul. Book III, in seven chapters, recounts the actions of the deeply troubled Saul as leader and king threatened by the young hero David. Book IV, in nine chapters, extols the ascendant David, while the dishonored Saul falls in battle and dies. Each book is preceded by a distinctive prologue. The first justifies his allegorical approach by referring to three crucial texts in Scripture, two Pauline and one Petrine: "For what things soever were written, were written for our learning" (Romans 15: 4, Douai translation); "Now all these things happened to them in figure: and they were written for our correction, on whom the ends of the world have come" (I Cor. 10: 11); "And all the prophets, from Samuel and afterwards, who have spoken, have told of these days" (Acts 3: 24). With that key reference to Samuel, Bede says he will carve out ("exsculpere") the allegorical heart of the text, so that to the historical literal reading favored by the Jewish tradition he will with Christ's help add the spiritual symbolic meaning for the contemporary Christian. After all, Bede, says, the fact that Elcana had two wives can only have meaning for the celibate monk if those persons represent spiritual qualities or states.[70] Bede, seeking the meaning of I Samuel for Christian times, neatly encloses the prologue in a rhetorical envelope when he invokes the aid of St. Peter, whom he quoted at the beginning. The second prologue attempts to sort out the complicated chronology of the reigns of Saul, David, and Solomon, which even modern exegetes have not been able to resolve. The third prologue summarizes what has been done in the first two books and prepares for the discussion in the third, in which Saul symbolizes the Jewish rule giving way to that of David, who represents Christ leading his Church. The fourth prologue records Bede's devastation at the resignation of his beloved abbot Ceolfrith, which caused him to delay before taking up the final book, in part a mystical interpretation of David's defeat of the Philistines at Keilah (I Sam. 23: 1). Throughout the commentary Bede assiduously explores personages, names, events, and numbers for valuable symbolic meaning for the Christian recognizing providential exemplary acts in this divinely guided history.[71]

On the Temple

> *De Templo libri II*, ed. D. Hurst, CCSL 119A, pp. 141–234. *Bede: On the Temple*, trans. Seán Connolly with comprehensive introduction by Jennifer O'Reilly (1995).

In creating this detailed companion commentary to *On the Tabernacle* Bede builds and expounds on the New Testament texts 1 Peter 2: 4–10, I Corinthians 3: 11, and especially Ephesians 2: 20–22:

---

[70] Bede, *In I Samuhelem*, I prol., lines 23–34.
[71] For specific examples see my "Bede's Neglected Commentary on Samuel," pp. 130–36.

You are built upon the foundations of the apostles and prophets, with Christ Jesus himself as the cornerstone. In him the whole structure is joined together and grows into a holy temple in the Lord, in whom you also are built together spiritually into a dwelling place of God.

As Jennifer O'Reilly explains, the fathers from Origen through Ambrose and Augustine to Gregory the Great had developed the temple theme,[72] but Bede's is the first commentary that develops the theme in a sustained allegorical analysis in the context of Solomon's temple. However, Bede in this and in his other writings shows intense interest in and knowledge about building crafts and explains every element of the Temple, its construction, and adornment, expounding at both the literal and allegorical levels.[73]

After a tripartite prologue Bede opens Book I with a succinct summary of the meaning of the Temple "as a figure of the holy universal Church, which, from the first of the elect to the last to be born at the end of the world, is daily being built through the grace of the king of peace, namely, its redeemer." Although Bede had already explored the meaning of the Temple to some extent in three homilies, here he systematically proceeds verse-by-verse through the description of Solomon's temple in III Kings 5: 6 –7: 51. In chapter 2 he explains that just as Solomon was assisted in the building of the Temple by the pagan King Hiram of Tyre, meaning that masters of worldly affairs can assist the Church in its development, and, more importantly, that just as Solomon sought help from Hiram and his workmen, so in the building of the Church the Lord picked ministers of the word from both Jews and gentiles, brought philosophers converted to true wisdom, and teachers chosen from among the gentiles. Bede stresses that the living members of the Temple are all God's people,[74] and in chapter 17. 4 of Book II he says:

After all, it was not just bishops and priests alone but to all God's Church that the Apostle Peter was speaking when he said, "but you are a chosen generation, a kingly priesthood, a holy nation, a people for his possession" [I Peter 2: 9]. And the ancient people of God were also singled out by the honour of this dignity as he himself said to Moses, "Thus shall you say to the house of Jacob, and tell the children of Israel"; and a little further on, "And you shall be to me a kingdom of priests and a holy nation" [Exodus 19: 3 and 19: 6].[75]

The twelve bronze oxen supporting the laver, which stands for Baptism, represent not only the twelve apostles carrying the Gospel to north, south, east, and west, but also all the ministers of the word.[76] The building of Solomon's temple in seven years and its dedication in the eighth of course

---

72 In the introduction, *On the Temple*, pp. xxiii–xxviii.
73 Concerning Bede's pragmatic knowledge of construction, particularly carpentry and masonry, see Paul Meyvaert, "Bede and the Church Paintings at Wearmouth-Jarrow," *ASE* 8 (1979): 63–77.
74 See also Bede, *De Templo*, 19.1, p. 84.
75 Bede, *On the Temple*, trans. Connolly, II. 17. 4, p. 68.
76 Bede, *On the Temple*, trans. Connolly, II. 19. 1 and 19. 5, pp. 84–85 and 87–88.

gives Bede the opportunity to apply it in the final chapter of Book II, 25. 2, to the development of the historical Church and its completion and dedication in the eighth age of the world.

Thirty Questions on the Book of Kings

> *In Regum librum xxx Quaestiones*, ed. D. Hurst, CCSL 119, pp. 289–322. *Thirty Questions on the Book of Kings*, trans. W. Trent Foley, in *Bede: A Biblical Miscellany*, trans. W. Trent Foley and Arthur G. Holder (1999), pp. 81–87.

The four parts of the Book of Kings (now usually designated as I and II Samuel and I and II Kings)[77] contained some problematic passages that Nothelm, assistant to Archbishop Albinus and himself later Archbishop of Canterbury, queried Bede about. *Thirty Questions on the Book of Kings*, which scholars date to about 715,[78] deals largely with the literal and historical sense of the passages, though a few (questions 1, 2, 14, 16, 30) give allegorical interpretations. Bede's question 4 (on the length of time the Ark of the Covenant remained in Kiriath-jearim) and questions 11–13 (on the dimensions of Solomon's temple) are examples of how "problems of chronology and measurement clearly delight him."[79] There is fascinating lore and orderly explanation in Bede's responses dealing with a number of biblically related questions, such as the making of salt and the apparent retrograde movement of the sun.[80]

Items 8, 9, and 10 are undated but seem to be from Bede's mature period.

Eight Questions

> *De octo quaestionibus*, PL 93: 455–62; new edition by Michael Gorman, in the Appendix to his "Bede's *VIII quaestiones* and Carolingian Biblical Scholarship," *RB* 109:1–2 (1999): 62–74. Translated by Arthur Holder in *Bede: A Biblical Miscellany*, pp. 145–65.

These discussions of problematic passages in the Old and New Testaments are now considered for good reason to be genuinely Bede's, while the rest, questions 9–15 (PL 93: 462–78), are not. Gorman has produced a new and reliable edition. There are nine extant manuscripts containing this treatise, dating from the twelfth to the fourteenth century, and many Carolingian scholars studied and used the text.[81]

---

[77] On Bede's title, *On the Book of Kings*, see Foley, trans., *Thirty Questions*, pp. 81–82.
[78] On the dating see Foley, *Thirty Questions*, pp. 86–87.
[79] Paul Meyvaert, "Bede the Scholar," p. 47, quoted by Foley, *Thirty Questions*, p. 83.
[80] Bede, *In Regum librum*, Questions 21 and 25; *Thirty Questions*, trans. Foley, pp. 124–25, 129–30, with Foley's excellent notes.
[81] See Michael Gorman, "Bede's *VIII Quaestiones* and Carolingian Biblical Scholarship," *RB* 109:1–2 (1999), 32–74; rpt. in *The Study of the Bible in the Early Middle Ages* (Florence, 2007), pp. 299–345.

On the Song of Songs

> *In Cantica Canticorum libri VI*, ed. D. Hurst, CCSL 119B, pp. 165–375. *Bede: On the Song of Songs*, trans. Arthur Holder (in press).

The reader might expect the prologue to provide an introduction to the commentary but instead Bede gives a 500-line, highly rhetorical rebuttal of Julian in the prologue and subsequent commentary. A number of misconceptions about the work have accumulated. Arthur Holder has addressed these:

> Among the misconceptions that appear in scholarly treatments of this text are the following: 1) that the work was composed in several stages, with the commentary proper having been written prior to the opening polemical prologue against the fifth-century Pelagian author Julian of Eclanum, 2) that Bede's quotations from Julian indicate that the earlier author had interpreted the Song in a literal Antiochene fashion, as referring to human sexual love, 3) that Bede explicitly rejected a Mariological interpretation of the Song, and 4) that there are no grounds for dating this commentary any more precisely than to say it must have been written prior to 731, since Bede listed it among his works at the end of the *Historia ecclesiastica*. A careful reading of the entire commentary, tracing connections between the polemical prologue and the rest of the work, will serve to clear up each of these four scholarly misconceptions.[82]

Holder resolves the first misconception by observing that Bede begins the prologue with the future participle, *scripturus* ("I am going to write") and ends with "Now let us turn our pen to the exposition of the Song of Songs."[83] Bede's usual practice is to compose the prefaces before the commentaries. Bede's commentary is full of rebuttals against Pelagian doctrine, so it was not as if he wrote the commentary before realizing Julian's heretical stance. Holder addresses the second misconception by noting that Julian in fact did interpret the Song allegorically. Thirdly, Holder says, Bede did not reject a mariological interpretation, because he simply did not consider the bride in the Song to be identified with Mary. That interpretation arose only with Paschasius Radbertus in the ninth century. Finally, Holder presents a case for Bede's anti-Pelagian commentary on the Song as coming from the same period as his commentary on the Seven Catholic Epistles, written between 709 and 716, at the time "when Bede and his fellow Northumbrians were actively engaged in promoting the Roman [paschal dating] observance among their friends and neighbours."[84] Although Bede follows Augustine in his criticism

---

[82] Arthur Holder, "The Anti-Pelagian Character of Bede's Commentary on the Song of Songs," in *Biblical Studies in the Early Middle Ages*, ed. Claudio Leonardi and Giovanni Orlandi (Florence, 2005), pp. 91–103 at 92.

[83] Bede, *In Cantica canticorum*, prol., CCSL 119B, p. 167, lines 1–4; p. 180, lines 501–2.

[84] Holder, "The Anti-Pelagian Character of Bede's Commentary on the Song of Songs," p. 101.

of Julian, the text of Julian's works on the Song that Bede quotes, although judged authentic, is found nowhere else except in Bede.[85]

A mere dozen lines at the end of the prologue serve as an introduction to Bede's commentary proper:

> We have reckoned it appropriate to sample these things from Julian's work as a warning to those who read it. Now let us turn our pen to the exposition of the Song of Songs and, earnestly following the footsteps of the Fathers and with the help of the grace of God which we are defending, let us devote as much salutary study as we can to that book which is very difficult to understand. I urge the reader not to think it irrelevant if in this work I propose to explain more fully about the nature of the many trees or aromatic herbs that are contained in this text, in accordance with what I have learned in the books of the ancients. For I have done this not out of a desire to seem presumptuous, but mindful of the ignorance that befalls me and my people as a result of having been born and bred far outside the world, that is on an island in the ocean, so that we cannot know about things that go on in the first parts of the world (I mean places like Arabia and India, Judea and Egypt), except through the writings of those who have lived there.[86]

The five-book commentary that follows provides a prime example of Bede's allegorical exegesis.[87] This approach to the amatory Song was sanctioned both by Jewish rabbinical teachers and by Christian exegetes from Hippolytus and, notably, Origen onwards.[88] It is historically ironic that the Bible's most erotic poem became the most frequently expounded upon of all the Old Testament books by medieval clerics and monks, and Bede with the later Bernard of Clairvaux and the Cistercians is among the foremost monastic commentators. As a poem celebrating the union between the Church and Christ rather than a paean to sexual congress, Bede classifies the poem, as did Origen, as a spiritual epithalamium with dramatic dialogue.[89] As Bede explains in *De arte metrica*, "In a dramatic or enacted poem, speaking characters are introduced

---

[85] See Albert Bruckner, *Die vier Bücher Julians von Aeclanum an Turbantius: Ein Beitrag zur Characteristik Julians und Augustins* (Berlin, 1910; rpt. Aalen, 1973), pp. 113–16.

[86] Bede, *On the Song of Songs*, Preface, trans. Holder, p. [8].

[87] Bede says in his bibliography in *HE*, V. 24 that the commentary is in seven books ("In cantica canticorum libros VII"), but Book I is the preface containing the apology against Julian and Book VII is a collection of extracts from various works by Gregory the Great that treat verses from the Song. Hurst's CCSL 119B edition gives the text as an introduction followed by six books.

[88] For a history of the allegorical interpretation of the Song, see Roland E. Murphy, *The Song of Songs: A Commentary on the Book of Canticles or The Song of Songs*, ed. S. Dean McBride, Jr. (Minneapolis, 1990), pp. 11–41. Unfortunately, Murphy shares Beryl Smalley's underestimation, in *The Study of the Bible in the Middle Ages* (Oxford, 1962), pp. 35–36, of Bede's exegetical contribution. For a more positive assessment but also recognizing it as a "strange work," see E. Ann Matter, *The Voice of my Beloved: The Song of Songs in Western Medieval Christianity* (Philadelphia, 1990), pp. 97–101 at 97.

[89] Contrary to the opinions of Matter, *The Voice of my Beloved*, p. 100, and Benedicta Ward, *The Venerable Bede* (Harrisburg, 1990), p. 75, I agree with Arthur Holder, "The Patristic Sources of Bede's Commentary on the Song of Songs," *Studia Patristica* 34 (2001): 370–75 at 371, that Bede did not have direct access to Origen's commentary; the influence of Origen is by way of Apponius.

without any commentary by the poet … Among our works, the Song of Songs belongs to this genre."[90] After the prologue and chapter listings ("capitula") the verses of the Canticle are headed by the supposed speakers, "vox sinagogae," "vox ecclesiae," and "vox Christi." Although Bede, like Origen and Gregory the Great, occasionally applies the text to the voice of the contemplative soul, from this list and from the commentary itself it is clear that the principal actors are Christ and the Church. Later writers identify more exclusively the *sponsa* with the individual soul (e.g., the Victorines) or with Mary (e.g., Rupert of Deutz, d. 1129). Bede's allegory is restrained by comparison with Bernard's; he presents a coherent portrait of the nuptial relationship between Christ and the Church, and sets the pattern for later medieval commentaries celebrating the spouse as the unblemished Church, without stain, in contrast to the sinners who composed its temporal membership.[91]

Following his stated intention in the prologue, Bede provides a number of literal details about the plants and herbs, details which he takes mostly from Pliny, before giving those same plants an allegorical interpretation. As an example of how fruit in the Garden may be understood, notice what Bede, commenting on Song 4: 2, "Your cheeks are as a piece of pomegranate, besides that which is hidden within," does with the pomegranate:

By cheeks, as we remarked above, is designated shame, because to be sure a sudden redness is accustomed to suffuse them in blushing. Moreover, the pomegranate is, like scarlet dye, suitably applicable to the mystery of the Lord's passion because of its rosy hue. For it was fitting that the mode of our redemption be intimated by the frequent use of figures in sacred song and the other writings of the prophets. Because the Church does not blush at the cross of Christ but even rejoices in insults and sufferings on behalf of Christ and is accustomed to bear the standard of the cross itself (*vexillum crucis*), it is suitably said to have cheeks like the pomegranate. And it is not without meaning that the pomegranate is here described not as a whole but a piece, because in the broken-open pomegranate a part is red (*ruboris*) and a part that is hidden inside is shiny white (*candoris*). Therefore the spouse has the redness of the pomegranate in her cheeks when she confesses the mystery (*sacramentum*) of the Lord's cross in words. She also shows the whiteness (*alborem*) of the same broken pomegranate when, struck by affliction, she also exhibits the chastity of a pure heart in deeds, since the very cross of her redeemer opens what is contained within, salvific grace. Likewise she shows pomegranate color in her cheeks when her first and more eminent members, that is, the martyrs, pour forth their blood for Christ, and adds white color when the same ones shine forth during their passion or, after their completed suffering, with their miracles. Nor should we pass over that the pomegranate encloses a mass of

[90] Bede, *De arte metrica*, I. xxv, in *Opera didascalia*, CCSL 123A, ed. C. B. Kendall (Turnhout, 1975), pp. 139–41; translation by Ann W. Astell, *The Song of Songs in the Middle Ages* (Ithaca, 1990), p. 164.
[91] See Helmut Riedlinger, *Die Makellosigkeit der Kirche in den lateinischen Hoheliedkommentaren des Mittelalters* (Münster, 1958), pp. 400–403; cited in Murphy, ed., *Song*, p. 24.

grains within an outside rind; hence it is called a pomegranate in the singular (*malum granatum*), in that the grains are unable to be seen when the fruit is whole, but when broken they increase innumerably. For thus the holy church in so far as it is broken by adversity so much the more brilliantly lays open so many grains of virtues it contains within the covering of one faith. And rightly is added, "besides that which is hidden within," because all are able to hear the profession in the church of the vivifying cross, all can see the afflictions of that church, and the infidels are able along with the faithful to admire the brilliance of its gifts (*carismatum*) by which it cures the sick, raises up the dead, cleanses the lepers, ejects demons, and so forth. She alone knows, however, with how great a love of invisible life she is held, with how great a vision of her founder, with how great a love she is inflamed by the progress of her members.[92]

It is difficult for the modern reader to accept the shifting, seemingly arbitrary interpretation of the text. At one moment the teeth of the beloved represent the Christian teachers chewing hard doctrines for the digestion of the Church members or chewing up heretical doctrines, at another, the breasts of the beloved are the same teachers, giving milk instead of solid food to the weaker, immature members of the Church.

An example of how the symbolic association varies between Bede and contemporary analysis is his exegesis on "Each of them with his sword upon his thigh because of nighttime terrors" (Song 3: 8). While Bede is aware that in the Bible "the organ of procreation is customarily represented by the word for thigh,"[93] and a post-Freudian interpreter would recognize the sword as emblematic of the penis, for Bede "soldiers of Christ have swords upon their thighs when they restrain the impulse of carnal desires with the rigor of the spiritual word,"[94] so that "they not defile the true Solomon's bed, which they are supposed to be guarding."[95] But once one enters into Bede's allusive play, the interpretation becomes both instructive and charming.

Bede supplements his own commentary with a final book (equivalent to a modern chapter) that is a collection of Gregory the Great's various comments on the Song. Bede prefaces the little anthology with the gracious remark, "If there is some reader especially enamoured of our own efforts, let it be as though our humble building were to receive a golden roof at the hand of a great master-builder."[96]

---

[92] Bede, *In Cantica canticorum*, II. 4. 3, p. 248, lines 170–205, my translation. For further discussion of this passage, see my "Bede and the Cross," in *Sancta Crux/ Halige Rod: Cross and Culture in Anglo-Saxon England*, ed. Karen Jolly, Catherine Karkov, and Sarah Keefer (Morgantown, 2008), pp. 21–38, at 33–34.

[93] Bede, *In Cantica canticorum*, CCSL 119B, p. 239, line 328: "Per femur carnalis solet propago designari."

[94] Bede, *In Cantica canticorum*, CCSL 119B, p. 239, lines 333–34.

[95] Bede, *In Cantica canticorum*, CCSL 119B, p. 239, lines 328–34; *On the Song of Songs*, trans. Holder.

[96] Bede, *In Cantica canticorum*, Book 6, CCSL 119B, p. 359, cited by William McCready, *Miracles and the Venerable Bede* (Toronto, 1994), p. 6.

On Isaiah 24: 22

In response to another query from Bishop Acca, Bede's letter (still available only in Migne's text, PL 94: 202–10) deals with a phrase, Isaiah 24: 22, which seems to prophesy a punishment in hell that will end after many days. The Vulgate text reads, *Et claudentur ibi in carcere et post dies multos visitabuntur* ["They shall be shut up there in prison; and after many days they shall be visited"].[97] Bede wrestles with this "questione periculosissima" ["very dangerous question," PL 94:709C], admitting it is hard to determine exactly what the Prophet Isaiah had in mind with these words, and calling on Jerome's commentary and other biblical texts for clarification and confirmation.[98] With Jerome he insists that the text cannot be forced to mean that those condemned to hell will eventually be freed, and then he explains it in terms of what Catholic theologians have since formulated as the individual judgment at death and the final judgment at the end of the world. This long letter not only reveals Bede in a somewhat tentative hermeneutic mode but also exemplifies in his expatiation his abiding apocalyptic concerns, the final great testing, the visitation of the Antichrist, and the Day of Judgment.

On the Canticle of Habakkuk

In Canticum Habacuc Prophetae, ed. J. E. Hudson, in CCSL 119B, pp. 377–409. *Canticle of Bede the Priest on the Canticle of Habakkuk*, trans. Seán Connolly (1997), pp. 65–95.

As Bede explains in his preface to a nun ("dilectissima in Christo soror" – the only female dedicatee in his works),[99] the Canticle of Habakkuk has multiple importance, because of its liturgical use in the Office of Fridays at Lauds as "a proclamation of the Lord's passion"[100] and because "it also gives a mystical account of [Christ's] incarnation, resurrection and ascension, as well as of the faith of the Gentiles and the unbelief of the Jews."[101] The biblical

---

97 The Vulgate and the Septuagint represent fairly close renderings of the Hebrew, but the phrase is variously translated, nuanced, and interpreted by modern exegetes.

98 *Commentaires de Jérôme sur le prophète Isaïe*, ed. Roger Gryson and V. Somers, Books 8–11 (Freiburg, 1996), p. 948. Modern exegetes consider verses 21–23 of Isaiah 24 to be an "editorial addendum." See Joseph Blenkinsopp, ed. and trans., *Isaiah 1–39*, The Anchor Bible vol. 19 (New York, 2000), p. 356.

99 See also Bede, *In Canticum Habacuc*, p. 409, the conclusion of 3. 19, lines 770–71; Connolly, trans., *Canticle*, p. 95, "Dearly beloved sister and virgin of Christ." On Bede's attitude to the educated woman, see Benedicta Ward's " 'To my dearest Sister': Bede and the Educated Woman,' in *Women, the Book, and the Godly: Selected Proceedings of the St. Hilda's Conference, 1993*, ed. Lesley Smith and Jane H. M. Taylor (Woodbridge, 1995), pp. 105–11.

100 *In Canticum Habacuc*, 3. 219, is the third Scriptural reading of the Hour of Lauds in the Divine Office.

101 *Canticle*, trans. Connolly, ch. 1, p. 65. On the unbelief (*perfidia*) of the Jews, see Plummer, ed., *Bedae opera historica*, II: 18–19; further on *perfidi/perfidia* see de Lubac, *Exégèse médiévale*, II. 1: 153–81. On Bede's attitude towards Jews see Andrew Scheil, *The Footsteps of Israel*, pp. 30–110.

lemmata that Bede quotes indicate that he is generally glossing an Old Latin (*Vetus Latina*) text rather than the Vulgate, though he sometimes includes the variant readings (e.g., at 3. 3, 3. 10, 3. 13, 3. 14).[102] He favors the Old Latin version, which is closely related to the Septuagint Greek,[103] because of its use in the Divine Office.[104] If some of Bede's glosses are predictable, many are quite beautiful and charming in their invention and application.

On Ezra and Nehemiah

> Beda, *In Ezram et Neemiam libri III*, ed. D. Hurst, CCSL 119A, pp. 235–392. Bede, *On Ezra and Nehemiah*, trans. Scott DeGregorio, with excellent introduction, notes, and corrections to readings in Hurst's edition (2006).

After a short prologue Bede proceeds to comment in two books on Ezra and on Nehemiah in a third. The subject of the commentary is not only the building of the second Temple after the first was destroyed by the Babylonians but also, importantly, the reconstitution of the Jewish nation and people. As DeGregorio notes in his introduction, key passages in Books 2 and 3 emphasize the topic concerning the need for contemporary spiritual rebuilding of the individual and of society by repentance and reform. Alan Thacker noted the central theme of reform in Bede's later writings, such as the *Life of St. Cuthbert*, the *Ecclesiastical History*, the Letter to (Arch) bishop Cuthbert, and it is quite strong in this commentary.[105] Indeed, by the repetition and intensity of the theme of reform in this work Bede may seem rather querulous. Since Ezra "leads his people from sin in Babylon to salvation in Jerusalem, he is for Bede a figure of Christ the heavenly Priest and Scribe who, journeying into the sin of this world by becoming incarnate, leads humankind from earthly tribulation to the peace of the celestial Jerusalem."[106]

For those who suspect Bede to be a monastic antifeminist, his positive remarks about the female singers among the males in the Israelite assembly should give pause:

---

102 Bede's Old Latin version of the Canticle differs rather extensively in phrasing from the "versio antiqua" printed by P. Sabatier in *Bibliorum sacrorum latinae versiones antiquae seu Vetus Italica* (Reims, 1743), II: 966–970; we will have to await the publication by Bonifatius Fischer et al., eds., of the Canticle in the full edition of *Vetus Latina* (Freiburg, 1949–).

103 See the text in Lancelot C. L. Brenton, trans., *The Septuagint with Apocrypha: Greek and English* (London, 1851; rpt. Peabody, MA, 1986), p. 1108.

104 The Old Testament canticles used in the Office kept their earlier Old Latin guise. See Richard Marsden, *The Text of the Old Testament in Anglo-Saxon England* (Cambridge, 1995), pp. 5–53, 214–15; Heinrich Schneider, *Die altlateinischen biblischen Cantica* (Buron, 1938), pp. 46–50; F. Cabrol, "Cantiques," in *DACL*, 1975–1994.

105 Alan Thacker, "Bede's Ideal of Reform," in *Ideal and Reality in Frankish and Anglo-Saxon Society*, ed. Patrick Wormald et al. (Oxford, 1983), pp. 130–53; Scott DeGregorio, "Bede's *In Ezram et Neemiam* and the Reform of the Northumbrian Church," *Speculum* 79 (2004): 1–25.

106 *Bede: On Ezra and Nehemiah*, trans. DeGregorio, Introduction, p. xxxiii.

It is proper also that, along with the male singers, female singers should be included on account of their female sex, in which there are many people found who not only by the way they live but also by preaching enkindle the hearts of their neighbours to the praise of their Creator, as though with the sweetness of a holy voice, assist the labour of these who build the Lord's temple.[107]

In Book 2 Bede considers the Temple as a figure of manifold meaning: it represents the individual soul, the whole Church, and the body of Christ. As to the last, the Temple had a side entrance; the opening into Christ's side on the cross, made by the centurion's spear, is the door to salvation, out of which flows the water of Baptism and blood of the Eucharist.[108]

In Book 3 Bede, while dwelling verse by verse on the allegorical meaning of text, at the passage about the Jewish merchants extorting pay during the famine and even marketing children and fields, interjects:

In this passage, it behooves us not to scrutinize the allegorical meaning but to observe the literal meaning of the text itself by performing it as diligently as we can, namely so that quite apart from the daily fruits of almsgiving, we should take care whenever a general time of famine and want has afflicted the people not only to give poor people what we can but also to forgive that tribute by right, in order that the Father might forgive us our debts too.[109]

It is disappointing that in the lengthy passage at Nehemiah 12: 27–35, on the Jews' celebration "with song, on cymbals, harps, and lyres," Bede makes no application or reference to monastic chant and music.

Bede ends with a fervent prayer to God:

You who have given me, the humblest of your servants, both the love and the aid to consider the wonders of your law, and have manifested to me, unworthy though I am, the grace not only to grasp the ancient offerings in the treasury of the prophetic book but also to discover new ones beneath the veil of the old and to bring them for the use of my fellow servants.[110]

In this late commentary Bede's own voice seems, not only here at the end but throughout, more clearly and intensely present than in his earlier exegetical works. Both in content and style the commentary manifests Bede's monastic outlook, attitude, and concerns.[111] The commentary reflects the monastic

---

107 *Bede: On Ezra and Nehemiah*, 2. 65, trans. DeGregorio, p. 32.
108 DeGregorio, p. 98, n. 1, notes Bede uses the text of I Kings 6: 8 in five works: *In Ezram et Neemiam, In Genesim* 2 (CCSL 118A, p. 109, lines 1275–99), *Hom.* 2. 1 (CCSL 122, p. 190, line 239 – p. 191, line 266), *In Regum librum* 12 (CCSL 119, p. 305, line 1 – p. 306, line 42), *De Templo* 1 (CCSL 119A, p.165, line 758 – p. 166, line 784). On Bede's theme of the opening in Christ's side see my "Bede and the Cross," in *Sancta Crux/ Halig Rod*, ed. Catherine Karkov, Karen Jolly, Sarah Keefer (Morgantown, 2007), pp. 23–38.
109 *Bede: On Ezra and Nehemiah*, trans. DeGregorio, Book 3, p. 185; see also p. 195 at line 1174.
110 *Bede: On Ezra and Nehemiah*, trans. DeGregorio, p. 226.
111 Scott DeGregorio, "Bede, the Monk, as Exegete: Evidence from the Commentary on Ezra-Nehemiah," *RB* 115 (2005): 343–69.

asceticism advocated by the Benedictine Rule (although Bede followed the eclectic rule devised by Benedict Biscop)[112] and the ruminative processes distinctive of monasticism; it also demonstrates Bede's apostolic and pastoral concerns. All of Bede's commentaries are put to the service of edification and Christian behavior; exegesis is a tool for moral and social reform as well as for biblical and ascetic instruction. Although all his exegetical works display pastoral concerns and moral exhortation, his calling attention to the need for reform of the clergy and for instruction of the laity in the English church becomes increasingly urgent in his mature, later exegesis. As Scott DeGregorio has emphasized, the same call for reform appears in Bede's exegetical as in his historical works: "In contrast to his early commentaries, Bede's mature exegesis is decisively infused by the aims and concerns of his later non-exegetical works such as the *Ecclesiastical History* and the *Letter to Egberht*."[113]

The Abbreviated Psalter

> *Collectio psalterii Bedae Venerabili adscripta*, ed. Gerald M. Browne (2001). *The The Abbreviated Psalter of the Venerable Bede*, trans. Gerald M. Browne (2002).

Although Bede does not include this little devotional work in his bibliography, its style and content identify it as surely his. Extant are only three manuscripts of the work, but they are all early: the ninth century. From each of the Psalms Bede chose one or more verses that capture the spirit and theme of each prayer. The verses are so aptly chosen they form a fine testimonial to Bede's editorial acumen and Scriptural sensitivity.[114] In one instance when the literal text causes a hindrance for Christian sentiment he substitutes a transferred reading: for Ps. 136: 9, "Blessed is he who takes your children and dashes them against the stones," he substitutes "Blessed is the man who fears the Lord."[115]

On Tobit

> *In librum beati patris Tobiae*, ed. D. Hurst, CCSL 119B. *Bede: On Tobit and on the Canticle of Habbakkuk*, trans. Seán Connolly, pp. 39–63.

Bede in his bibliography at the end of the *Historia* lists the work as "In librum beati patris Tobiae explanationis allegoricae de Christo et ecclesia librum

---

112 On the relationship between the Benedictine Rule and that of the eclectic one at Wearmouth-Jarrow, see above, Ch. 1, pp. 4–5.

113 Scott DeGregorio, "'Nostrorum socordiam temporum': The Reforming Impulse of Bede's Later Exegesis," *Early Medieval Europe* 11. 2 (2002): 107–122.

114 See Benedicta Ward, *Bede and the Psalter*, Jarrow Lecture (Jarrow, 1991), p.10, cited in Bede, *Abbreviated Psalter*, trans. Browne, p. 10.

115 See Bede, *Abbreviated Psalter*, trans. Browne, pp. 12–13.

I,"[116] indicating its nature as one of his allegorical biblical treatments, as he does also in the introduction:

> ... its inner meaning excels the mere letter as much as the fruit excels the leaves. For if it is understood in the spiritual sense it is found to contain within it the greatest mysteries of Christ and the Church; inasmuch as Tobit himself denotes the people of Israel which alone served God with true faith and acts of virtue when all the Gentiles were given over to idolatry.[117]

Bede's presentation of Tobit as the ideal pious Jew is augmented by his allegorical interpretation of the text as a moral for Christian living. In doing so Bede strangely omits large sections of the story, such as chapter 4, that are plaudits for Tobit's moral behavior. Bede also passes over in silence Tobit and Sarah's wedding night and prayer (8: 4). He does deal with Tobit's famous dog (6: 1 and 11: 9): "One must not dismiss with scorn the figure of his dog which is a traveler and the companion of an angel."[118] Allegorical numerology comes into play in Bede's chapter 23 exploiting Tobit 8: 22, on Raguel's slaughtering for the banquet two fat cattle (representing prosperity and adversity) and four rams (representing the four Gospels, four cardinal virtues, and the four quarters of the world).[119]

COMMENTARIES ON THE NEW TESTAMENT

On Luke

In Lucae evangelium expositio, ed. D. Hurst, CCSL 120, pp. 5–425.[120]

Like the commentary on the Acts of the Apostles, Bede's commentaries on the Lucan and Marcan Gospels are major in subject and length: the Commentary on Luke consists of 425 pages with 15,841 lines in its modern edition; Mark is a little more than half that size. Both commentaries have an extensive manuscript and textual history and have had great influence over the centuries.

The six-page, 220-line prologue to the Lucan commentary begins with Bishop Acca's letter urging Bede to undertake the arduous task of a commentary on this gospel even though it has been commented on by Ambrose and others, whose commentaries were too erudite for Bede's English students. Bede responds by agreeing to the big task, in which he is involved "as

---

[116] *HE*, V. 24, p. 568.
[117] *Bede: On Tobit*, trans. Connolly, ch. 1, p. 39.
[118] *Bede: On Tobit*, trans. Connolly, ch. 30, p. 37.
[119] *Bede: On Tobit*, trans. Connolly, ch. 23, pp. 3–54.
[120] Although most of Bede's Old Testament and a number of New Testament commentaries have now been translated, neither of his great commentaries on the gospels of Luke and Mark have been, and to date apparently no one has proposed translating them.

author, secretary, and publisher" ("ut mihi dictator simul notarius et librarius existerem"). In assembling the commentary he notes he will carefully cite his patristic sources by a system of marginal references (A–M = Ambrosius, A–V = Augustinus, G–R = Gregorius, H–R = Hieronymus).[121] He adds that "some things which the Lord of light has revealed I have added as marks of my own sweat, when it seemed opportune." However, he hastens to point out that those who have accused him of idiosyncratic originality in his assigning the symbol of the lion to Matthew and of the man to Mark (instead of the reverse) in his earlier commentary on the Apocalypse, ought to realize that it was not his notion but Augustine's. He then quotes Augustine at length from the *De consensu evangelistarum* to prove it.[122]

Bede breaks up the commentary into six nearly equal books, with an introductory paragraph for each. For the fourth book, which begins with Christ's ejection of the mute demon (Luke 11: 14), he includes a personal invocation. Citing I Peter 5: 5, "God opposes the proud but gives grace to the humble," he says:

> Wherefore, beginning the fourth book of commentary on the Gospel with the reading in which the spirit of pride is driven out by the finger of God, I suppliantly implore your clemency, Christ, that your good Spirit may guide me in the right way and keep him who is from the North far from me, so that with the evil ones driven from me I may investigate the commands of God and with the opened eyes of my mind I may proceed as a devout reader to consider the marvels of your Law.[123]

The vast commentary draws heavily upon the writings of Ambrose, Jerome, Augustine, and Gregory the Great. Bede is the first to canonize the now-traditional quartet as the main Latin Fathers of the Church, in numerical alignment with the four Evangelists.[124] The commentary explores the literal and moral meanings of the text and to a lesser degree the allegorical. Throughout, but especially in discussing the infancy narratives Bede attacks christological heretics and their subordinationist doctrines. An indication of how strong the impulse was for Bede to combat heresy is his treatment of the initial words of Luke's Gospel, 1: 1–4. Most understand simply Luke's introductory clause "Since many have undertaken to set down an orderly account of the events that have been fulfilled among us ..." to be a recognition of various accounts. However, Bede interprets the words "to mean the cause for [Luke's] writing the Gospel was especially to prevent giving an opportunity to pseudo-evangelists of preaching falsehood, who, as

---

121 *In Lucae ev.*, CCSL 120, ed. D. Hurst, p. 7, lines 109–10; see also the editor's *Praefatio*, p. v.
122 *In Lucae ev.*, *Prologus*, CCSL 120, ed. Hurst, pp. 7–10, lines 123–27.
123 *In Lucae ev.* IV, CCSL 120, ed. Hurst, p. 230, lines 23–30, and note 32 above.
124 *In Lucae ev.*, *Prologus*, CCSL 120, ed. D. Hurst, p. 7; see Bernice M. Kaczynski, "Bede's Commentary on Luke and Mark and the Formation of a Patristic Canon," in *Anglo-Latin Literature and its Heritage: Essays in Honour of A. G. Rigg*, ed. Siân Echard and Gernot Wieland (Turnhout, 2001), pp. 17–26 at 24.

their documents testify even today, attempted to introduce the perfidy of their sects under the name of the apostles," such as Thomas, Bartholomew, and Matthew.[125] In the many passages in which he mentions heresies Bede shows he is well informed about heresiarchs, whom he names, and their various doctrines, which he rebuts.[126]

Bede's commentary contains many hortatory components but a particularly striking section is at the conclusion to the work, where he encourages us to be like the Apostles preparing for the coming of the Holy Spirit so that with quiet mind and without discord we may "follow in the footsteps of him" who was obedient even to death.[127]

On Mark

"On the Gospel of Mark: Four Books," *HE* V. 24; *In Marci evangelium expositio*, ed. D. Hurst, CCSL 120, pp. 427–648.

This was composed some years after his commentary on Luke, as Bede says in the Prologue.[128] When the two synoptics have concurrent texts Bede's commentary on Mark usually inserts large blocks from his Lucan commentary. Nonetheless, the original parts of this commentary represent some of Bede's most mature exegesis. Although he often and with due credit interweaves appropriate sections from the four Fathers, his own contribution is intelligent and fairly extensive.[129] Of the forty passages unique to Mark's gospel, Trent Foley has observed, Bede does not comment on twelve of them, including two from the Passion narrative (Mark 15: 6–10, and

---

125   *In Lucae ev.*, CCSL 120, p. 19: "Quoniam quidem multi contati sunt ordinare narrationem" … "Quo manifestissime praoemio significant eam sibi maxime causam euangelii fuisse scribendi ne pseudoeuangelistis facultas esset falsa praedicandi qui ut eorum hodieque monumenta testantur sub nominee apostolorum perfidiae conati sunt inducere sectas …"

126   Bede's assaults against heretics and heresies occur frequently in the commentary on Luke, where he attacks, besides the pseudoevangelists, the Gnostics Basilides and Apelles (1: 1–4, p. 19, lines 18–20); the Arians, Photians, Manichaeans (1: 16–17, p. 26, lines 273–77); the Nestorians (1: 32, p. 32, lines 510–17, and p. 34, lines 593–98); Arians (2: 50–51, p. 73, lines 2146–49); the Manichaeans and Apollinarists (2: 52, p.74, lines 2159–68); the Pelagians (8: 46, p. 191, lines 973–80); the Arians again and other subordinationists (11: 17, p. 232, lines 70–74); heresy, superstition, Jewish perfidy, and fraternal schism (17: 14, pp. 312–13, lines 682–85); Simon Magus and pseudochrists (17: 23, p. 316, lines 817–22); Marcion, Mani, Tatian, Encratites (17: 27, p. 317, lines 867–73); Marcionites (18: 31–33, p. 330, lines 1382–86); Simon Magus and antichrists (21: 8, p. 365, lines 77–82); Manichaeans (24: 37, p. 418, 2180–99); Eutyches (24. 39, p. 418, 2216–20).

127   *In Lucae ev.*, VI, pp. 424–25, lines 2427–60.

128   Bede, *In Marci ev.*, ed. D. Hurst, CCSL 120, p. 432, lines 48–50. As in his commentary on Mark, Bede mentions his *De tabernaculo* written about 721, the dates of composition for *In Marci ev.* are somewhere between 721 and 731.

129   For a not altogether laudatory but perceptive and detailed analysis of Bede's exegetical contribution on Mark, see W. Trent Foley, "Bede's Exegesis of Passages Unique to the Gospel of Mark," in *Biblical Studies in the Early Middle Ages*, ed. Claudio Leonardi and Giovanni Orlandi (Florence, 2005), pp. 105–24.

Mark 15: 44–45).[130] Of those forty passages, Bede apparently provides an original commentary on twenty-two. On most of these Bede gives a figurative or moral sense of the text but for some, the literal sense as well.[131] In the first section, for instance, he discusses on his own the interesting fact that the gospels all have different time-frames, with what historical event each begins and ends, and the appropriateness of those differences.[132] He does not hesitate to indicate a tropological meaning when suitable. Thus, commenting on Mark 11: 11, "And he entered Jerusalem, and went into the temple," he edifyingly remarks:

> The fact that having entered the city he first visited the temple presages for us a form of piety which we follow. When we enter a village or town or some other locale in which there is a house of prayer consecrated to God, we should first turn aside to that, and after we have commended ourselves to the Lord through the pursuit of prayer, we can then leave to do those temporal affairs for which we have come.[133]

He also calls attention to important spiritual meanings on the allegorical level that the text suggests to him. For instance, in the subsequent passage which describes Christ's driving the money changers from the temple, he first notes how the Church can also be polluted by gossip and chatter "or some other vice." In commenting on the next verse he moves to the *sensus moralis*, pointing out that the individual soul is the temple which the Lord cleanses and purifies.[134]

In Bede's own moral and figurative interpretations of passages particular to Mark's gospel, as Foley notes, "three themes stand out above the rest: Christology, the soul's salvation and sanctification, and the mission of the church on earth."[135] As examples of the first, Bede calls attention to the fact that Matthew titles Christ "Son of Man" whereas Mark calls him "Son of God." In Mark 4: 35–36, Mark distinguishes Christ's human nature when he slept in the boat during the storm but his divine nature when he awoke to still the sea's fury. As for the second theme, Mark provides a number of examples cited by Foley, such as the detail that the young man, having thrown off his cloak, fled naked, "for it is better to serve the lord naked than by cleaving to the things of the world, to court the danger of being tested and being removed from God to one's enemies," just as Joseph fled from Potiphar's wife (Genesis 39: 12).[136] Passages in Mark describing Jesus's arduous missionary activity provide Bede with models for pastoral activity, in contrast to feasting clerics

---

130 Foley, "Bede's Exegesis," p. 110.
131 Foley, "Bede's Exegesis," pp. 112–22.
132 Bede, *In Marci ev.*, I, pp. 437–38.
133 Bede, *In Marci ev.*, III, p. 575, lines 1296–1303.
134 Bede, *In Marci ev.*, III, pp. 578–79, lines 1416–51, 1463–75.
135 Foley, "Bede's Exegesis," p. 115. On the following pages, 116–22, Foley gives examples of Bede's three thematic interests, along with commentary.
136 *In Marci ev.*, IV, CCSL 120, p. 620, lines 983–9, quoted by Foley, p. 120.

and certain bishops who feed their bodies but not the souls of the faithful. And as Christ fled from honors and adulation, all believers but especially the church's preachers and teachers must fight the temptation to vainglory.[137]

On the Acts of the Apostles

Expositio Actuum Apostolorum et retractatio and *Nomina regionum atque locorum de Actibus Apostolorum*, ed. M. L. W. Laistner, CCSL 121.[138] *Commentary on the Acts of the Apostles*, trans. Lawrence T. Martin (1989).[139]

The commentary is early, dated between 709 and 716.[140] To establish and compare the lemmata of the text Bede used three Vulgate manuscripts, including the famous Codex Amiatinus (or one of its sister volumes) and three Old Latin (Vetus Latina) versions. One of the latter was joined to the Greek text of Acts, the version found in Bodleian Library MS Laudianus Graecus 35, which Bede cites often for textual comparison. Because Bede refers to "Graeca exemplaria" in the plural, he apparently consulted at least one other Greek manuscript of Acts.[141] Since the Acts of the Apostles deals with the historical development of the early Church and also with its significance for Christians of later generations and peoples, Bede furnishes this text with both literal and allegorical commentary. Attention in Acts to the complex evolution of the early Church is interesting to Bede not only because of the information about the early historical life of the institution responsible for spreading the Gospel to all peoples but also, more particularly, the relevance of the information to the continuous evangelization of the West, including of course the Christianization of Britain.[142]

Bede's commentary on Acts became one of his more popular and influential; there are more than eighty manuscript copies still extant (and twenty-four of the *Retractatio*). A major reason for its popularity is no doubt that no Father in the West before Bede had done a complete prose commentary

---

[137] Examples cited by Foley, pp. 120–22.

[138] The CCSL edition is a reprint, minus the excellent introduction, of Laistner's edition published by the Medieval Academy in 1939.

[139] Unfortunately Martin translates only the *Commentary*, providing translations of parts of the *Retractatio* in his notes. For his reasons for not translating the complete *Retractatio* see his explanation on pp. xxiii–xxiv, in which he admits that comparing the two works "can therefore give us an interesting picture of Bede's development as an exegete," and the *Retractatio* "adds much new material based on his continued meditation on the Acts text and his reading of other sources" (p. xxiii), but it was not translated because "the major part of of the *Retractatio* is devoted to comments of a textual nature … of limited relevance today" (p. xxiv).

[140] The commentary is dedicated to Acca, who became Bishop of Hexham in 708/709; see Laistner, ed., *Expositio*, pp. xv–xvi; Martin, trans., *Commentary*, p. xviii.

[141] M. L. W. Laistner, "The Latin Versions of Acts Known to the Venerable Bede," *Harvard Theological Review* 30 (1937): 37–50, summary at 48–49; Martin, *Commentary*, p. xix.

[142] In his commentary on Acts 28: 31b Bede quotes Jerome that Paul "was released so that Christ's gospel might also be preached in the regions of the West." See also Bede's *Prologus* to *In epistulas VII catholicas*, ed. D. Hurst, CCSL 121, p. 181, lines 5–7; *Commentary on the Seven Catholic Epistles*, trans. D. Hurst, preface, p. 3, lines 6–8.

on the text. Arator had composed a poetic version in hexameters with an elaboration of the symbolic meaning in the biblical narrative; in his preface Bede acknowledges his use of Arator's poem and in the commentary he uses the poem as a source nineteen times.[143] For other information Bede relies on Jerome, Augustine, Rufinus, Gregory the Great, and, to a lesser extent, on Ambrose, Isidore and others; from classical sources he uses Josephus and Pliny.[144] The whole work, however, is very much Bede's own; it is quite readable, and he uses a number of figures of speech and structural wordplay to great effect.[145] As in all his exegetical works, the commentary centers on Christ, the Church, and the sacraments.[146]

Although Bede composed the commentary early in his exegetical career, late in life he composed the *Retractatio*, in the spirit of Augustine's *Retractions*; that is, a commentary written in late life with reflections, revisions, corrections, and additions to the earlier work.[147] Although it is chronologically among the last of his works, it will be discussed here because it is closely keyed to the *Commentary*. The *Retractatio*, about a third of the size of the original commentary, corrects a few errors in the earlier work, defends Bede's position on some points against critics, and, more independent than the *Commentary*, adds information gained from further study. Among the many important comments in this late work is his judicious condemnation of the apocryphal text on the death of Mary, *Transitus Mariae*, as fictional and suspect.[148]

The glossary of geographical names in Acts that Bede appended to this commentary, but which is often found separately in manuscripts, is discussed below in the section on gazetteers, pp. 71–72.

On the Seven Catholic Epistles

In epistulas VII catholicas, ed. M. L. W. Laistner and D. Hurst, CCSL 121, pp. 179–342. *Commentary on the Seven Catholic Epistles*, trans. D. Hurst (1985).[149]

---

143 Martin, *Commentary*, Index, p. 207.
144 Laistner, *Expositio*, pp. xxxviii–xxxix; Martin, *Commentary*, p. xxxi.
145 Martin, *Commentary*, p. xxvi.
146 Paul Meyvaert, "Bede the Scholar," in *Famulus Christi*, p. 47; John William Houghton, "Bede's Exegetical Theology: Ideas of the Church in the Acts' Commentaries of St. Bede the Venerable," (Ph.D. diss., Notre Dame University, 1994).
147 It was assumed that the *Retractatio* was written after 731 because Bede does not mention it in his bibliography at the end of the *Historia ecclesiastica*, 5. 24, but Laistner points out that Bede's entry is actually "In actus apostolorum libros II," and the *Retractatio* therefore is likely considered the second book (see *Expositio*, II. Date of Composition, pp. xiii–xvii). Nonetheless, the *Retractatio* is patently a late work, somewhere between 725 and 731.
148 Laistner, ed., *Retractatio*, CCSL 121: 134, 1–135, 35; 138, 45–139, 74; 144, 14–145, 19; Martin, *Commentary*, p. 122.
149 Annoying for the reader of Hurst's Latin edition is the fact that the individual commentaries are not labeled and the beginning and the ending of the epistles are not clearly marked. The reader relying on Hurst's translation should be aware of a few unfortunate locutions: for instance, on p. 11, last line, "the righteous flourish for a short while" should of course be "the *un*righteous flourish for a short while"); p. 15, line 16, Hurst translates "dominae," referring to Potiphar's

When Bede sent to Acca his Commentary on Acts he included his commentary on the Letter of John. When the commentaries on the other six epistles were readied is unknown, but, as Laistner says, "their general character aligns them with the treatises on Acts and on the Apocalypse."[150] The number of extant manuscripts indicates that these were the most popular of all Bede's exegetical expositions: to the 112 manuscripts recorded by Laistner can now be added another five.[151]

In the preface Bede attempts to explain that the order of the Seven Letters represents both the sequence of conversion to the Faith (first Jerusalem, then the Jews in diaspora, and finally the gentiles) and of their dates of composition.[152] Bede is aware that the attributed authorship of the various letters has been questioned, but he insists on their authenticity.[153] All the letters are moral exhortations in epistolary guise for the practice of Christian wisdom and virtues, so Bede's commentaries are largely of that genre, while adducing other biblical passages and comments by the Fathers.

In the Commentary on James, Bede, in keeping with the tenor of the letter, emphasizes its moral message for the Christian disciple, only once or twice giving an allegorical interpretation of a verse. Bede's exegesis is at once sensitive and sensible. For instance, on the verse "The rich man will languish in his ways" (1: 11), Bede remarks: "He is not talking about every rich man but one who trusts in the uncertainty of riches. For in contrasting a rich man with a humble brother, he has shown that he was speaking about that sort of rich man who is not humble." He then goes on to point out that Abraham was rich but received a poor man after his death into his bosom, leaving a rich man in torments, because he had scorned being humble and merciful in life.[154] In the famous section on faith and works, 2: 14–26, Bede compares Paul's emphasis on faith and James' emphasis on works, by pointing out that the two are reconcilable, that Paul himself speaks of "faith working through love" (Gal. 5: 6). For "only he truly believes who carries out in deed what he believes."[155] Whereas in Galatians 2: 1–14 "Paul was instructing those who were boasting of their works without the grace of faith," James is insisting that those who have received the sacraments of faith must follow up with

wife as Joseph's "mistress"; p. 199, line 18, "graves" for "grapes"; p. 231, line 2, "persons thinks" for "persons think."
150 Laistner, *Hand-List*, p. 31.
151 Laistner, *Hand-List*, pp. 30–37. An updated handlist of Bedan manuscripts, including *In epistulas catholicas*, is being prepared by Joshua Westgard and myself.
152 According to modern biblical scholarship, "The present order of the General Letters and of each series of the Pauline Letters is in terms of their length, going from the longer to the shorter letters," *The New Oxford Annotated Bible*, ed. E. M. Metzger and Roland E. Murphy (New York, 1994), p. 204 NT.
153 *In 2 Petrum*, I. 18, CCSL 121, p. 266, lines 205–20; *In 2 Johannem*, 1, p. 329, lines 1–12.
154 *In Jacobum*, I. 11, CCSL 121, pp. 186–87; *Commentary on the Seven Catholic Epistles, Commentary on James*, trans. D. Hurst, pp. 12–13.
155 *In Jacobum* II. 15–17, line 156, Bede cites Gal. 5: 6, "fides quae per dilectionem operatur"; Bede's impressive commentary on James 2: 14–26, beginning with a quotation from Augustine, extends from p. 197 to p. 202.

good works, for "a person is made righteous from works and not from faith only" (2: 24). One wonders whether Martin Luther had read and considered Bede's extensive and sensitive commentary on what for him were such troublesome verses.

The hortatory First Letter of Peter introduces the striking metaphor of Christians as living stones and of Christ as the cornerstone (I Peter 2: 4–8), which Bede, like the poet of the Old English Advent poem,[156] exploits much further. For instance, he describes the faithful as

> fitted like living stones into the spiritual building when at the discrimination of a learned teacher they have their undesirable actions and thoughts cut off and are squared off by the blow of a hammer, as it were. And just as some rows of stones in a wall are held up by others, so all the faithful in the Church are held up by the righteous who preceded them, they themselves by their teaching and support hold up those who come after even to the last righteous person.[157]

In his *Commentary on the Apocalypse*, 2: 28, "And I will give him the morning star," Bede, accepting the identification made by Tyconius, wrote that "Christ is the morning star who, when the night of this world is ended, promises and discloses to the saints the eternal light of life."[158] In the Commentary on II Peter, though, commenting on the verse, "And the morning star arises in your hearts" (1: 19), Bede asks:

> What is the morning star? If you say the Lord, that is too little. The morning star is our own excellent understanding. For if this arises in our hearts, it will be enlightened, it will be made clear. It will become love, such as we now wish and long for yet do not possess, and we shall see of what sort it will be in each other, just as now we see each other's faces.[159]

The length of Bede's commentaries on the three letters of John is proportionate to the length of the letters themselves. I John is five chapters

---

156 See Robert B. Burlin, ed., *The Old English Advent: A Typological Commentary* (New Haven, 1968), pp. 56–66.

157 Trans. Hurst, p. 82; *In epistulas VII catholicas*, II. 5, p. 234: "Sed tamquam lapides uiui at spiritale aedificium aptantur qui per discretionem eruditi doctoris amputatis actibus et cogitationibus superfluis uelut ictu quadrantur securis. Et sicut ordines lapidum in pariete portantur alii ab aliis, ita portantur fideles quique a praecedentibus in ecclesia iustis, portant ipsi sequentes per doctrinam et tolerantiam usque ad ultimum iustum ..." Note Bede's use of his favorite motif word, "discretionem" ("discrimination," "right judgment").

158 *Expositio Apocalypseos*, CCSL 121A, ed. Gryson, p. 265, lines 160–62; translated and commented on by Gerald Bonner in his *Saint Bede in the Tradition of Western Apocalyptic Commentary*, Jarrow Lecture 1966, p. 9. Bonner is responsible for placing this verse on the wall behind Bede's tomb in the Durham Cathedral Galilee chapel.

159 Commentary on II Peter 1: 19, trans. D. Hurst, *Commentary on the Seven Catholic Epistles*, p. 132; *In 2 Petrum*, CCSL 121, p. 267, lines 231–36: "Quis est Lucifer iste? Si dominum dicas, parum est. Lucifer ipse praeclarus intellectus noster est. Ipse enim oritur in cordibus nostris, ipse illustrabitur, ipse manifestabitur. Dilectio enim qualem nunc optamus et quoniam non est suspiramus et quailis erit singuli in singulis uidebimus quo modo nunc facies nostras alterutrum uidemus." In the Commentary on Jude, verse 13, the morning star is also identified *in bono* with John the Baptist and *in malo* with Satan.

long (and all but the first chapter have more than twenty verses); the whole of II and III John are only a few verses long. However, Bede's commentary on I John is long – forty-five pages in Latin and sixty-nine in translation – reflecting Bede's deep interest in the Johannine themes of faith and charity. The first and last parts of the commentary, like the letter itself, deal with doctrinal issues concerning Christ's divine and human nature and sinful mankind's need for salvation, but Bede lists the heresies contrary to this orthodoxy, those of Apelles (1: 2), Manichee (1: 5), Pelagius (1: 8, 1: 10, 3: 1, 3: 3, 5: 19), and Arius (3: 1).[160] The refutation may be expressed in lively metaphor: using the question in Matthew 7: 16, "Do people gather grapes from thorns or figs from thistles?" at 4: 1 he writes:

> Therefore, these are fruits by which the evil spirits who speak in false prophets can be discerned, namely, the thorns of schism and the dreadful thistles of heresies by which, by wounding their faith, they defile those who approach them heedlessly, just as on the contrary the fruits of good [works], namely, charity, joy, peace in the Holy Spirit, are appropriately signified by the pleasant odor of grapes and the sweetness of figs.[161]

The core of the commentary turns to the workings of charity and the life of grace. Throughout Bede interweaves passages from Augustine's Epistle on the First Letter of John.[162] As in his *Retractationes* to his Commentary on the Acts of the Apostles, Bede shows his knowledge of Greek in his commentary on I John 3: 4 (p. 303, line 96) by explaining that the Latin word "lex" is "νόμος" in Greek. The conclusion of I John (5: 21) is "Little children, keep yourselves from idols." Bede uses the verse to provide a concluding summary to the letter by interpreting "idols" as "the teaching of heretics which lead to everlasting death, because like those who fabricate idols in place of God, they by their wicked teachings change the glory of the imperishable God into the likeness of perishable things. Keep yourselves also from 'covetousness, which is the service of idols' [Col. 3: 5], be on guard lest you prefer the allurements of the world to the love of the Creator."[163] The brief commentaries on II and III John reinforce this theme.

The last of the Catholic Epistles, by Jude, is also a moral exhortation, but its condemnation of false teachers and heretics, with references to the faithless Israelites in the desert, the rebellious angels, and Satan (verses 5–16), provides Bede with an opportunity to address his favorite topic, the

---

160 On the various forms of subordinationism by which the Son is regarded as subordinate to the Father or the Holy Spirit as subordinate to both, consult any good theological dictionary, such as *The Oxford Dictionary of the Christian Church*.

161 Commentary on I John 4: 1, p. 310: "'Numquid colligunt de spinis uuas aut de tribulis ficus?' Hi sunt ergo fructus a quibus eos qui sibi incaute appropriant fidem lacerando contaminant, sicut e contra fructus bonorum, caritas scilicet, gaudium, pax in spiritus sancto, per flagrantiam uuarum ficorumque dulcedinem apte figurantur."

162 Augustine, *In Ioannis epistulam ad Parthos tractatus x*, PL 25: 1977–2062.

163 *Commentary on Seven Catholic Epistles*, trans. D. Hurst, p. 228.

dangers of heresy. Bede is troubled by the letter's citing the Book of Enoch (verses 14–15) because "this is classed by the Church among the apocryphal scriptures," but even though he is wary of apocryphal works, he makes the best of it here, as he does in the *Retractatio in Actus Apostolorum* when referring to the apocryphal "passiones apostolorum."[164] The beautiful doxology, verses 24–25, at the end of the Letter also provides a text for Bede to confute Arian subordinationism.

Excerpts from Augustine on the Pauline Epistles

> *In Apostolum quaecumque in opusculis sancti Augustini exposita inueni, cuncta per ordinem transcribere curaui* [unedited]. *Excerpts from the works of Saint Augustine on the Letters of the Blessed Apostle Paul*, trans. David Hurst (1999).

Surprisingly there is no printed edition yet of Bede's Latin text.[165] Before his death David Hurst was preparing a critical edition "from five early manuscripts" that was not published; in fact, among the seven extant manuscripts there is only one complete manuscript of the work.[166] The edition has been entrusted to the scholars I. Fransen and R. Demeulenaere.[167]

Incorporating much of the *collectaneum* of Augustine's works by the abbot Eugippius (fl. c. 509) but arranging the collections according to the Pauline canon instead of Augustinian theme, Bede's Pauline collection had considerable influence on Carolingian exegetes such as Hrabanus Maurus and Florus of Lyon, who created a similar collection of Augustine's citations of Paul.[168] Since Bede was heavily influenced by Pauline doctrine as mediated and expanded by Augustine, it is not surprising that he would form a chrestomathy of Augustinian commentaries on Paul's letters. Of the 457 passages from Augustine some are only a few lines while others are two or three pages long. The selections reveal not only Pauline theology but also Augustine's rhetorical verve. Thus, commenting on "You were called to freedom, brothers and sisters" (Galatians 5: 13), Augustine comments:

> No Christian should say, "I'm free, I've been called to freedom. I was a slave but I've been redeemed, and by my redemption I've been set free. I shall do what I want; if I'm free, no one can keep me from doing what I want." However, if you commit sin because of what you want, you are the slave of sin. Then do not use your freedom to sin freely, but use it not to sin. Only if your will is

---

164 *Commentary on Seven Catholic Epistles*, trans. D. Hurst, pp. 249–50; *In epistulas VII catholicas*, ed. Hurst, CCSL 121, p. 340, lines 207–33.

165 The 1499 chrestomathy edited by Petrus Securibilis and attributed to Bede is in fact by Florus of Lyons. See André Wilmart, "La collection de Bède le Vénérable sur l'Apôtre," *RB* 38 (1926): 16–52, at 21–22. Wilmart uncharacteristically errs by naming the editor Geoffrey Boussard, who wrote only the prefatory letter to the editor Securibilis, as Mabillon correctly remarked in his "Bedae elogium historicum," PL 90: 11B.

166 D. Hurst, trans., *Excerpts*, p. 10; Laistner, *Hand-List*, p. 38.

167 See *Clavis patrum latinorum*, CCSL, no. 1360, p. 448.

168 D. Hurst, trans., *Excerpts*, p. 9.

holy will you be free. You will be free if you are a servant – free from sin, a servant to righteousness.[169]

The collection is replete with such aphoristic nuggets.

Commentary on the Apocalypse

Bedae presbyteri Expositio Apocalypseos, ed. Roger Gryson, CCSL 121A (2001).[170] *Explanation of the Apocalypse by Venerable Beda*, trans. Edward Marshall (Oxford and London, 1878).[171] It is notable that the newest (and best) edition of any of Bede's exegetical works is this by Gryson, and the oldest English translation of one of Bede's commentaries is this by Marshall.

As an exegete and ecclesiastical historian Bede was interested in first and last things as well as in the evolution of human history. It is not surprising then that his early biblical commentaries are on Genesis and Revelation along with the Acts of the Apostles. His commentary on the Apocalypse, apparently his earliest commentary (written between 703 and 709), is deliberately short, ostensibly because of the indolence of his English race.[172] It proved quite popular on the Continent, as the 113 extant manuscripts attest. The commentary is preceded by Bede's 22-line poem about the author John and his apocalyptic subject.[173] There follows the preface addressed to Eusebius (the monk Hwætberht). In that preface Bede explains that the Apocalypse, addressed to the seven churches in Asia (Rev. 1: 1), contains seven parts, "periochae," within thirty-eight chapters; and just as seven seals enclose the Book, the seven Tyconian rules unseal the meaning. The commentary is strongly allegorical, an approach which the symbolism and mystery of the text itself mandates. It displays a great dependence on the comments of the Fathers and earlier exegetes, particularly Tyconius, Augustine, and Primasius. Its entries are succinctly brief, in accord with the exegetical genre, which Bede, following Jerome, styles *commaticum genus interpretandi*.[174] For example,

"And I have the keys of death and hell" [Rev. 1: 18]. Not only, he says, have I conquered death by resurrection but I also have dominion over death itself. And

---

169 Selection 295, trans. D. Hurst, p. 220, from Augustine's Homily 38 on the Gospel of John.
170 In the introduction Gryson provides a magisterial manuscript history of Bede's work and on opposite pages of Bede's text supplies a rich array of "fontes et loci paralleli" (sources and parallel texts).
171 Although Marshall's translation is out of print, it is available on line at www.apocalyptic-theories.com/theories/tmainframe.htm. Faith Wallis is preparing a new translation.
172 "Nostrae siquidem, id est Anglorum gentis inertiae consulendum ratus ... et idem quantum ad lectionem tepide satis excoluit," Bede, *Expositio Apocalypseos*, ed. Gryson, CCSL 121A, *Praefatio*, 141–45, p. 233.
173 Bede, *Expositio Apocalypseos*, ed. Gryson, *Versus Bedae presbyteri*, pp. 218–19.
174 Bede, *Expositio Apocalypseos*, ed. Gryson, ch. 37, p. 559, line 370, p. 559.

this he also bestowed upon the Church saying, "Whose sins you forgive, they are forgiven, and those you retain, they are retained" [John 20: 23].

Or:

"And I saw in the right hand of him who was seated on the throne a book written inside and outside" [Rev. 5: 1]. This vision demonstrates the mysteries of sacred Scripture laid open by the incarnation of the Lord. Its concordant unity contains the Old Testament as outside and the New as inside.[175]

However, when Bede comes to explain the significance of the twelve precious stones that form the foundations of the heavenly Jerusalem (Rev. 21: 19–20), he abandons the *commaticum genus interpretandi* and expounds on the properties of the precious stones forming the foundation of the city, drawing extensively upon numerous sources of lapidary lore (Pliny, Solinus, Epiphanius, Jerome, Ambrose, Gregory, Isidore, Anglo-Latin glosses and the Hiberno-Latin tract *De duodecim lapidibus*, and possibly the Latin Damigeron) to present an original systematic exposition of the text.[176]

At the end of that passage in chapter 37 he explains:

I may perhaps seem to have set forth these remarks concerning the precious stones at greater length than belonged to the *commaticum* mode of interpretation. For it was necessary diligently to expound their natures and provenance, then very carefully to investigate their sacred meaning, not omitting to pay attention to their order and numbers. As touching, indeed, the real profundity of the matter, it seems to myself that I have said very little, and that briefly and superficially.[177]

After this lapidary lore, Bede returns at Rev. 21: 21 to the short commentary mode, carried on until the end. He finishes with a request for prayers from "any that have thought this little work worth reading or transcribing."[178]

BIBLICAL AIDS

In addition to his biblical commentaries Bede provided some ancillary texts to assist the student in his understanding of sacred history and geography.

---

[175] Bede, *Expositio Apocalypseos*, ed. Gryson, III, lines 90–94, p. 249; VI, lines 1–5, p. 287.

[176] On the extent and importance of Bede's contribution to the lapidary tradition and for a discussion of his sources of information, see Peter Kitson, "Lapidary Traditions in Anglo-Saxon England, Part II: Bede's *Explanatio Apocalypsis* and Related Works," *Anglo-Saxon England* 12 (1983): 73–123. However, one should note Gryson's critique of Kitson, with corrections and additions, in the Introduction to his edition, 4.7 "Les douze gemmes," pp. 173–77.

[177] Bede, *Expositio Apocalypseos*, ed. Gryson, ch. 37, p. 59, lines 370–79. Trans. Kitson, "Lapidary Traditions, Part II," p. 75, n. 9.

[178] Bede, *Expositio Apocalypseos*, ed. Gryson, ch. 38, p. 577, lines 101–107; *Explanation*, trans. Marshall, pp. 171–72.

On the Holy Places

De locis sanctis, in *Itineraria et alia geographica*, ed. I. Fraipont, CCSL 175, pp. 245–80. *On the Holy Places*, translated with notes by W. Trent Foley in *Bede: A Biblical Miscellany*, pp. 1–26.

In Book 5, ch. 15, of the *Ecclesiastical History* Bede speaks of the *De locis sanctis* by the Irish abbot of Iona, Adomnán (whom Bede calls Adamnan), based on information given the abbot by a putative Bishop Arculf, supposedly a studious pilgrim in the Holy Land.[179] In chapters 16 and 17 Bede presents extracts from it. Actually, Bede quotes from his own abridgement of Adomnán's work, into which he incorporated some descriptions from Eucherius's account of Jerusalem and Judaea as well as bits from Hegesippus's adaptation of Josephus's *History of the Jews*. He speaks of his epitome at the end of chapter 17: "If anyone wishes to know more of [Adomnán's] book, he may find it in the volume itself or in the abridgement of it which I have lately made."[180] He again acknowledges his indebtedness to Adomnán in the epilogue to his version of *De locis sanctis*, CCSL 175, pp. 279–80. However, he does not include the work in the list of his other works at the end of the book; perhaps the little work as an edited abridgement was in his judgment not enough his own work. In fact, he has improved on Adomnán's peculiar prose.

On the Holy Places is an early work, written between 702 and 703, which, as Bede tells us in the ten-line verse introduction to the treatise, describes the territory and sites that Holy Scripture makes memorable. The quaint manual demonstrates, as do the rest of the texts in this collection of Holy Land guides, that artefacts such as the Lord's headcloth, the shroud woven by the blessed Virgin, the twelve stones that Joshua ordered taken from the Jordan, and the stones on which Christ's clothes were laid at his baptism, were not merely invented for later gullible Crusaders.

Gazetteers

Two geographic dictionaries for locating and explaining places mentioned in the Bible have been attributed to Bede, although he does not include them in his own list of works. The first, *Nomina Locorum ex beati Hieronimi presbiteri et Flavi Iosephi Collecta Opusculis*, printed as a sequel to *In primam partem Samuhelis,* is now considered inauthentic even though it appears as a supplement in the two early manuscripts of Bede's *In I Samuhelem*.[181] The second, quite likely genuine,[182] is a geographical dictionary briefly explaining

179 Thomas O'Loughlin, *Adomnán and the Holy Places* (London and New York, 2007), has shown that Adomnán's work is a fabrication of theological literature about an "imagined Palestine" by a putative Bishop Arculf (pp. 210–11).
180 Bede, *HE*, V. 17, pp. 512–13.
181 Bede, *In I Samuhelem*, ed. D. Hurst, CCSL 119, pp. 273–87.
182 Its authenticity Laistner convincingly defends in the introduction to his edition of Bede's *Expositio Actuum Apostolorum et retractatio* (Cambridge, 1939), pp. xxxvii–xxxviii.

the names and places that appear in the Acts of the Apostles: *Nomina regionum atque locorum de Actibus Apostolorum.*[183] It is found attached to Bede's commentaries on Acts. This gazetteer draws upon a number of authorities such as Pliny, Jerome, Isidore, and Adomnán, as well as Bede's own *De locis sanctis* to explain geographical names and locations referred to in Acts and in his commentary. The alphabetical list ranges from Acheldemac ("a field of blood which is shown today in Aelia on the west side of Mount Zion ...") to Thessalonica ("a city in Macedonia") and Theatrum. A modern reader may well expect to learn about esoteric locations such as Mysia and Seleucia but may be amused at that final entry: "Theater (Acts 19: 29): a place borrowing a word from viewing, because in it the people standing and looking down from above viewed dramatic scenes."[184] The necessity for such a gloss indicates how far removed the English monastic medieval world was from late antique secular Roman culture. It also indicates Bede's knowledge of Greek etymology.

---

[183] *Nomina regionum atque locorum de Actibus Apostolorum*, ed. M. L. W. Laistner, CCSL 121, pp. 165–78.

[184] *Nomina regionum atque locorum*, CCSL 121, p. 178, referring to Acts 19: 29, "Theatrum: locus ab spectaculo uocabulum mutuans, quod in eo populus stans desuper atque spectans ludo scenicos contemplaretur."

4

Homilies, Hagiography, Martyrology, Poems, Letters

THESE popular medieval genres, once of little modern interest except to specialists, have elicited a good deal of study in recent years, and Bede's extensive contributions to the genres, like his other works, have also generated considerable attention.

Homilies

"Homilies on the Gospel: two books" (*HE*, V. 24); Beda, *Opera homiletica*, CCSL 122, pp. 1–378; Bede, *Homilies on the Gospels*, trans. Lawrence T. Martin and David Hurst (1991).

For Bede, preaching that teaches the meaning of Scripture, correct theological understanding, and moral rectitude has a special, even sacramental, significance. Preachers are the successors of the prophets and apostles. In his view, preaching is the function not only of the priest but of all those rightly instructed in the faith. Thus, in a Christmas homily, explaining that the shepherds did not keep silent about the nativity mysteries revealed to them but proclaimed them, Bede says about Christian shepherds:

It is not only bishops, presbyters, deacons, and even those who govern monasteries, who are to be understood as pastors, but also all the faithful, who keep watch over the little ones of their house, are properly called "pastors," insofar as they preside with solicitous watchfulness over their own house. And the office of pastor should [be acknowledged] in anyone of you who presides over even just one or two brothers by daily guidance, since he is ordered to feed them with a banquet of the word insofar as he is able. Moreover, every single one of you, brothers, who is believed to live as a private person holds the office of pastor, and feeds a spiritual flock, and keeps watch by night over it, if, gathering a multitude of good acts and pure thoughts to himself, he tries to govern them with just control, to nourish them with the heavenly pastures of the scriptures, and by vigilant shrewdness to keep [them safe] against the snares of evil spirits.[1]

---

[1] Bede, Homily I. 7 on the Gospels, *Homilies on the Gospels*, trans. Lawrence T. Martin and David Hurst (Kalamazoo, 1991), I: 69; *Homilia* I. 7, CCSL 122, p. 49, lines 100–117: "Non solum pastores episcopi presbyteri diaconi uel etiam rectores monasteriorum sunt intelligendi sed et omnes fideles qui uel paruulae suae domus custodiam gerunt pastores recte uocantur in quantum eidem suae domui sollicita uigilantia praesunt. Et quicumque uestrum saltim uni aut duobus

As Alan Thacker notes, "Bede was thus concerned with a group whose qualifications were not primarily institutional, and indeed he deliberately refrained from identifying his *doctores* and *praedicatores* with the ordained hierarchy of bishops, priests, and deacons ... He even envisaged women as preachers."[2]

Bede took the function of preaching seriously indeed, as his collection of sermons on the gospels, renowned and used widely throughout the Middle Ages, demonstrates. Bede composed fifty homilies, in two books of twenty-five each, ordered in the sequence of major feasts and Sundays of the liturgical year according to the Romano-Neapolitan use. Those fifty homilies were widely copied. Eventually a number of his homilies were transferred to different days to accommodate them to the later liturgy. While numerous sermons were attributed to him over the course of the Middle Ages, many indeed were his but concocted by others by excerpting sections from his commentaries, especially on Mark and Luke, and assigning them to the Sundays when the gospel texts occur in the liturgy.[3] Since they are designed for general use,[4] they provide few personal or local details about Bede and his immediate world, but they are clear indicators of Bede's religious attitudes and mature artistry. Although individual pieces may have come from an earlier period, most likely he assembled the collection between 730 and 735. Bede's method of preaching is not greatly different from his exegetical procedure; that is, he takes the assigned gospel text for the day's feast and probingly comments on its verses, extracting its meanings, for the edification of the attentive Christian. It is a meditative process of rumination, savoring the spiritual content.[5] Since his sermons are essentially reflective, with the purpose of meditation on the divine mysteries, interior compunction, and interior attainment of virtue, they differ from the public sermons of the Fathers. He does borrow pertinent parts from their works, but he transforms

---

fratribus cotidiano regimine praeest pastoris eisdem debet officium quia in quantum sufficit pascere hos uerbi dapibus fratribus iubetur. Immo unusquisque uestrum, fratres, qui etiam priuatus uiuere creditur pastoris officium tenet et spiritalem pascit gregem uigiliasque noctis custodit supra illum, si bonorum actuum cogitationumque mundarum sibi adgregans multitudinem haec iusto moderamine gubernare caelestibus scripturarum pascuis nutrier et peruigili solertia contra immundorum spirituum insidias seruare contendit."

2   Alan Thacker, "Bede's Ideal of Reform," *Ideal and Reality in Frankish and Anglo-Saxon Society*, ed. Patrick Wormald et al. (Oxford, 1983), pp. 130–53 at 131. He cites Bede's *De Templo*, p. 194, and *In Ezram*, p. 257.

3   See Laistner, *Hand-List*, pp. 114–16, for the summary results of Dom Germain Morin's researches into the original Bedan homiletic collection as well as for Laistner's own findings. The editions of Giles and Migne reflect the medieval accretions to Bede's collection and its later confused order; indeed, one homily is printed twice, as I. 17 and II. 24 in PL 94, cols. 89–96 and 262–67. Only the modern edition of Dom David Hurst, CCSL 122, is reliable for genuinity and order. For a list of the factitious homilies extracted from Bede's commentaries on Mark and Luke, see Hurst's appendix, pp. 381–84. For the dating of the collection, see his preface, p. vii.

4   Except for one that commemorates Benedict Biscop, *Homelia* I. 13, CCSL 122, pp. 88–94.

5   On Bede's elaborate use of the metaphor of rumination, see Gernot Wieland, "Caedmon, the Clean Animal," *American Benedictine Review*, 35 (1984): 194–203, and the bibliography cited.

them all into his monastic modality.[6] His homilies do not display the rhetoric and oratorical flights of Ambrose's sermons to his Milanese church. They do not exhibit the pyrotechnics and rhetorical verve of Augustine's *Enarrationes in Psalmos*, preached to a noisy African congregation. They do not even directly resemble the papal sermons of Gregory the Great, though Gregory's attitudes and spirituality Bede greatly admired and imitated. They possess their own qualities of clarity, sincerity, and sobriety. They remind one of the complex simplicity of Gregorian chant, in contrast to the bravura of a polyphonic orchestrated chorale.

Bede's homilies resemble his own commentaries in general tone and technique. Even in their sobriety they demonstrate a considerable range of stylistic diversity.[7] Sermons for the great high feast days of joy – Christmas, Easter, Pentecost – display more overall shape, structural symmetry, figures of speech, cadenced endings, liturgical formulae, and higher style. Homilies for vigils, Advent, and Lent display a simpler mode, and a more verse-by-verse approach. However, even for the more austere occasions there is no lack of artistry. Take, for a random example, Homily II. 14 for Rogation Days (or The Greater Litanies).[8] The gospel for the day is Luke 11: 9–13. After introducing the general intention of the text, Bede explains that "asking" refers to our praying, "seeking" the search to live rightly, and "knocking" our persevering constancy. He develops the semantic fields of asking, seeking, and knocking for thirty lines. Then with a series of *ipse/nos* [he/we] phrases, Bede contrasts the healing power of the Lord with our diseased condition (lines 46–64). Next he turns to the reliability of God's response to those "calling upon him in truth" (Ps. 144: 18): "Inuocant quippe dominum in ueritate qui in hoc quod orando dicunt uiuendo non contradicunt" ["They call upon the Lord in truth who say in their praying what they do not contradict in their living"]. He moves from the concept of those seeking the Lord in truth to their opposites, those who seek badly, citing James 4: 3. He succinctly describes the four types of those seeking badly with a phrase *male petunt* followed by pleasingly varied clauses introduced by *qui*, 89, *qui*, 97, *quia*, 104, *et illi*

---

6   For a conspectus of his use of Scripture and the Fathers in his homilies, see CCSL 120, *Index scriptorum*, pp. 387–99 and 401–3.

7   See the two valuable if partly debatable articles on Bede's homiletic art by Philip J. West, "Liturgical Style and Structure in Bede's Homily for the Easter Vigil" and "Liturgical Style and Structure in Bede's Christmas Homilies," *American Benedictine Review* 23 (1972): 1–8, 424–38. In making his point in the second article about the artistry of the sermon for midnight on Christmas (I. 6), West belittles the form and treatment of the vigil homily that precedes it (I. 5), calling it "almost impoverished" (p. 425). Actually, Bede is using two different methods, both artistic, for the two different occasions: the one a simple reflection on the verses of the gospel, echoing the simplicity of the text and spirit of the vigil Mass, the other, an elaborately structured and linguistically brilliant exposition for the resplendent night. West blames Bede for subjecting the homily for the vigil Mass to an "allegorical interpretation of the Gospel's six main verbs: *transeamus, uideamus, uenerunt festinantes, uidentes, cognouerunt,* and *reuersi.*" West then praises Bede for holding allegory "to a minimum" in his sermon for Christmas Day (I. 8). In view of Bede's (and the Fathers') allegorical art, West's criticism is misinformed.

8   Bede, *In litaniis maioribus*, in *Opera homiletica*, ed. Hurst, CCSL 122, pp. 272–79.

qui, 107, all neatly turned to exhortation and leading to the section closure: "It is true that all these kinds of seekers in so far as they seek badly (*male petunt*) will not merit to receive; let us strive, beloved, to seek well and to be worthy of obtaining what we seek" (lines 123–25). He proceeds to the next biblical verses, Luke 11: 11–12, "And what father among you, if his son asks for bread, will give him a stone? Or if for a fish, will he give him a serpent for the fish? Or if he shall ask for an egg, will he hand him a scorpion?" He first stresses at the literal level the comparison between an earthly father and the heavenly Father, emphasizing the sublimer qualities of the latter. Then he takes up the figural meanings *iuxta typicam intelligentiam* (line 149) of bread (signifying charity, the principal food of the spirit), of fish in the water (faith in the element of God and surrounded by the pressures of adverse surroundings), and of the egg (hope for the future). These are the goods we are to ask of the Father (line 186). God will not give us hardness of heart (stone), allow the poison of infidelity (serpent), or encourage backsliding (the sting in the scorpion's rear). Bede concludes the homily by identifying the "good spirit" given by God in Luke 11: 13 with the Holy Spirit who comes with the seven gifts prophesied by Isaiah (11: 2–3). The sermon ends on a confident note of encouragement and promise (lines 258–69). The homily is not elaborately rhetorical, but it does use a number of tropes and figures in a quietly effective way. It is not structured like a classical oration, but it moves forward effectively and cumulatively to a strong conclusion. It does not move the emotions wildly, but it exhorts warmly.

Although Bede's homilies are primarily moral exhortations through the use of allegory and symbol, like his commentaries they also contain instructions about the history and meaning of biblical events and objects. For instance, in Homily II. 24 on the Dedication of a Church, for which the gospel text is John 10: 22–30, after the 173-line moral exhortation in which he speaks of the individual as well as the Church as the temple, he adds a long coda about the history of the Jewish Temple. He explains that John's text refers to the Temple rededicated in 164 BC after its desecration by Antiochus Epiphanes. He explains its construction, size in width and height, and its parts, all the while extracting moral significance from the details. So Bede's listeners receive both moral and historical instruction.

Saints' Lives

"Also the histories of the saints: a book on the life and passion of St. Felix the Confessor, which I put into prose from the metrical version of Paulinus; a book on the life and passion of St. Anastasius which was badly translated from the Greek by some ignorant person, which I have corrected as best I could, to clarify the meaning. I have also described the life of the holy father Cuthbert, monk and bishop, first in heroic verse and then in prose" (*HE* V. 24).

Bede composed these pieces with the conviction that God has conferred virtues and superior gifts on certain men and women who have responded courageously to his special call. With Augustine, Bede believed that their lives demonstrated the actualization of the potential humans have for spiritual perfection through grace; their lives represented models for us to emulate and their careers embodied ecclesiastical and even political ideals. The miracles they performed in life and after death were revelations of God's power and his intervention in history. In them God's justice is made manifest in a fallen world in which injustice and corruption are mankind's usual experience. Bede accepted and exploited the literary conventions that had been established traditionally for the description of those saints' lives.[9] In this genre, the saint's career had to conform to accepted essential patterns and be characterized by a set of standard deeds that served as credentials and proof of divinely inspired life. Moral qualities, not individual characteristics, were paramount.

The life could be expressed in prose or poetry, or transferred from prose into poetry or vice versa. Bede exercised his talents in both forms. While listing Aldhelm's works he calls the dual format *opus geminatum*.[10] It represents a development of the classical training program of *conversio*, an exercise of turning prose into poetry and vice versa.[11] Prudentius, Juvencus, Caelius Sedulius, Arator, and Venantius Fortunatus developed the practice in Christian Latin literature. Although Aldhelm's prose version of *De virginitate* is actually more difficult than his poetic rendition, for their hagiography Bede and Alcuin used prose to provide accessibility and clarity, poetry to provide artifice and grandeur. A straightforward prose account could be read aloud to the community and be more or less understood at a first reading. It served to edify the simple as well as the learned. A simple style, with the use of direct quotation and unobtrusive rhetoric, was the norm. However, a higher style, in poetic form, was used as panegyric for the saint. For the *Vita Felicis* Bede paraphrased in chaste prose the ornate poetic version of the life and miracles

---

9   For a comprehensive survey of hagiography see René Aigrain, *L'hagiographie: ses sources, ses méthodes, son histoire* (Paris, 1953). For an understanding of the literary conventions used by hagiographers, see the studies by Hippolyte Delehaye, such as *Les passions des martyrs et les genres littéraires*, 2nd ed. (Brussels, 1966), and *The Legends of the Saints*, trans. Donald Attwater (New York, 1962). For a stimulating essay on hagiography, see ch. 4 of Charles W. Jones's *Saints' Lives and Chronicles in Early England* (Ithaca, 1947), pp. 51–79. For a summary of the influential Augustinian view of the miraculous, see Benedicta Ward, *Miracles and the Medieval Mind* (Philadelphia, 1982), introduction and ch. 1, pp. 1–4.

10   *HE*, V.18. On the development of the *opus geminatum* see, with the attendant bibliography, Peter Godman, "The Anglo-Latin *opus geminatum*: from Aldhelm to Alcuin," *Medium Aevum* 50.2 (1981): 215–29, and his edition of Alcuin, *The Bishops, Kings, and Saints of York* (Oxford, 1982), pp. lxxviii–lxxxviii; also Gernot Wieland, "*Geminus Stilus*: Studies in Anglo-Latin Hagiography," *Insular Latin Studies*, ed. Michael Herren (Toronto, 1981), pp.113–33. Wieland's study is particularly informative about the purposes and uses of the geminated format (p. 125): "The conclusion to be drawn from this is not that the *gemina opera* were written to exemplify 'the interchangeability of metrical and non-metrical discourse,' but that the prose was written to complement the verse and the verse was written to complement the prose."

11   Quintilian, *Institutiones oratoriae*, ed. M. Winterbottom, Oxford Classical Texts (Oxford, 1970), Book 10, 5.4, describes *conversio* as the change or transfer from one type of composition to another, poetry to prose and vice versa.

of the third-century saint, Felix of Nola.[12] Writing quite early in his career, probably before 709, Bede explains what he has done to his source, the series of panegyrics by Paulinus of Nola (353–431) celebrating the *Natalicia* (that is, the birthday into heaven, January 14) of Felix:

> The bishop Paulinus of Nola has described most beautifully and fully in hexameter verses the most felicitous triumph of blessed Felix, which he merited with God's help in the same Campanian city of Nola. Because they are fitting for those versed in metrics rather than for simple readers, for the benefit of the many it has pleased me to elucidate the account with plainer words and to imitate the industry of the author who translated the text of the martyrdom of blessed Cassian from the metrical work of Prudentius into common and suitable speech.[13]

Comparing Bede's clean, short, easily readable prose version with the elaborately florid poetic panegyrics of Paulinus is instructive.[14] Although Bede picks up some of Paulinus's wordplay, especially at the beginning and end on the name Felix (meaning "happy," "blessed"), the relatively simple structure, short sentences, uncomplicated syntax, and prosaic vocabulary of his text make it suitable for reading aloud to the monks in chapter or refectory.[15] Why did Bede take the trouble to rewrite a life of this particular southern Italian saint? First, the cult of St. Felix is part of the southern Italian influence on the Anglo-Saxon liturgy, much of it under the aegis of Hadrian when he became prior of St. Peter's (later, St. Augustine's) at Canterbury.[16] Other evidence of this influence on Wearmouth-Jarrow includes 1. Bede's ordering his homilies according to the Roman-Neapolitan tradition, 2. the southern Italian features of books produced in the Wearmouth-Jarrow scriptorium, particularly its Bibles (the pandects, such as the Codex Amiatinus), 3. the Bedan testimonies to the cultural influences of Theodore and Hadrian in the *Ecclesiastical History*. Moreover, as with his educational tracts and his

---

12 Thomas W. Mackay has an analysis of the work in his "Critical Edition of Bede's *Vita Felicis*", Ph.D. diss., Stanford University, 1971 (Ann Arbor: University Microfilms International, 1972), and in his article, "Bede's Hagiographical Method: His Knowledge and Use of Paulinus of Nola," in *Famulus Christi*, pp. 77–92. Since Mackay's edition of Bede's *Vita Felicis* is still not available in print, references will be to the text in Migne's PL 94: 789–98.

13 Migne, PL 94: 789B.

14 The best edition of the poems of Paulinus is CSEL 30 (1894), edited by Wilhelm de Hartel. The *Natalicia* celebrating Felix are Poems 12 to 29; the biography used by Bede is found in Poems 15 and 16, the *Nachleben* especially in 18, and the buildings of Nola in 28. For a description and translation of the poems, see P. G. Walsh, ed., *The Poems of St. Paulinus of Nola* (New York, 1975).

15 In the preface to the prose life of St. Willibrord, Alcuin describes the purpose of the *opus geminatum* thus: "At your behest I have put together two small books, one moving along in prose, which could be read publicly to the brothers in church, if it seems worthy to your wisdom; the other, running along with Pierian feet, which ought only to be ruminated by your students in the private room," *Vita Willibrordi archiepiscopi Traiectensis*, ed. W. Levinson, MGH Scriptores rerum Merovingicarum, VII (1920): 113.

16 See Mackay, Introduction to his critical edition, pp. xxv–lxi, esp. liii–liv, and "Bede's Hagiographical Method," p. 78; Peter Hunter Blair, *World of Bede*, pp. 119–20.

exegetical commentaries, Bede is filling a gap in the Northumbrian Christian cultural void. Finally, this successful exercise in the transfer from poetry to prose is a charming and entertaining narrative, with its tale of Felix's using physical and verbal stratagems to elude the pursuing Romans, of stolen cattle finding their way home to a grieving old man by the intervention of Felix, of uncooperative tenants refusing to move their shabby dwellings and belongings from the immediate vicinity of Paulinus's elegant chapel.

Another surprising hagiographic undertaking is Bede's reworking of the badly written life and passion of St. Anastasius, the Persian monk martyred in 628 by Chosroes II, whom Bede also commemorates in his *Greater Chronicle* and his *Martyrology*.[17] Anastasius's relics were honored in Rome, and his cult was probably brought to England by Theodore and Hadrian (again that southern Italian connection). Until 1982 Bede's version of the *Life of St. Anastasius* was considered lost, but Carmela Franklin and Paul Meyvaert by painstaking analysis have made a strong case that the version "badly translated from the Greek by some ignorant person," as well as Bede's reworking of it, are extant.[18] The careful revision of the *Life*, respectful of the integrity of the text, aims to make sense of everything, and the clean and orderly prose bespeaks Bede's art. The fact that this rendering is only a correction and not a total recasting of the life and passion of St. Anastasius may be the reason why in the later Middle Ages Bede was not credited as author of this version.[19]

Bede's most important hagiographic writing is an *opus geminatum* on the life of Northumbria's great ascetic, St. Cuthbert (c. 634–687), successively monk, recluse, and bishop of Lindisfarne. That Cuthbert became northern England's most renowned saint can be attributed to the widespread popularity of Bede's prose *Life* not only in England but also on the Continent. Both Bede's versions (but especially the later prose one) represent a thorough reworking of an earlier (between 699 and 705) anonymous prose life by a brother or "brothers of the church of Lindisfarne."[20] The anonymous life is not without its virtues; as a matter of fact, some eminent Bedan admirers – Plummer, Colgrave, Levison, Jones – have preferred it to his two versions, but Lenore Abraham and especially Walter Berschin have countered with an extended defense of the superiority of Bede's version.[21] Despite its large borrowings

---

17 Dubois and Renaud, eds., *Édition practique des martyrologes de Bède, de l'Anonyme lyonnais et de Florus* (Paris, 1976), p. 20; Carmela Vircillo Franklin, *The Latin Dossier of Anastasius the Persian* (Toronto, 2004), p. 186.

18 Franklin's *Latin Dossier*, especially ch. 6, "The Passio S. Anastasii in Anglo-Saxon England," supersedes her and Paul Meyvaert's article, "Has Bede's Version of the *Passio s. Anastasii* come down to us in *BHL* 408?" *Analecta Bollandiana* 100 (1982): 373–400.

19 Franklin and Meyvaert, "Bede's Version," pp. 394–95.

20 *HE*, Prologue, pp. 6–7.

21 The strongest censure was leveled by Bede's most admiring critic, Charles Plummer, who in his Introduction to Bede's *HE*, I: xlvi, wrote: "In the case of Cuthbert's Life it cannot, I think, be said that Bede has bettered his original. He has improved the Latinity no doubt, and made the whole thing run more smoothly. In fact he seems to take delight in altering the language

from such sources as the *Epistola Victorii Aquitani ad Hilarium*, Athanasius's *Vita Antonii*, Sulpicius Severus's *Vita sancti Martini*, and the *Actus Silvestri* in the first sections, and despite its obvious use of traditional motifs from hagiographic lore, particularly Irish, the four books of the anonymous *Vita* present a fairly detailed but quick-moving narrative of Cuthbert's life.[22] It possesses simplicity and spriteliness; its strained attempts to relate the saint's actions to those of prominent types in the Bible are winsome. Indeed, its unsophisticated freshness and spareness contrasts both with Bede's learned poetic panegyric and with his carefully structured, stylistically superior, and generically more suitable prose account. The criticism directed against Bede's versions seems to stem from a misunderstanding of medieval literary genre and Bede's objective for these works. Bede reorders the events of Cuthbert's life, bringing symmetry into the account and stressing the increasing spiritual power that Cuthbert develops successively as hermit, bishop, and monk, culminating in his death and the miracles that followed.

The metrical version represents the kind of literary exercise that Juvencus and Sedulius performed on the gospels by transforming the humble prose account into highly stylized hexameter verse, the same kind of artistic heightening that hymnists did for the liturgy, and that Christian men of letters such as Augustine sanctioned as a means of glorifying God.[23] The prose version, on the other hand, serves another purpose. Bede's words in the preface to Bishop Eadfrith and the congregation of monks at Lindisfarne clearly intimate that he has been commissioned by them to write an official life of the recent saint whose fame and cult are no longer local but widespread. The life would also serve to support the importance of Lindisfarne as an episcopal seat. D. P. Kirby surmises,

> The probability is that Acca and the surviving Wilfridians were threatening Lindisfarne's episcopal status from 715 to 723–24 and that the traditions about Cuthbert were reinterpreted in the face of this threat and his cult more intensely proclaimed, the whole process culminating in the writing of Bede's *Life*, in response to such pressures.[24]

---

for the mere sake of alteration, while keeping closely to the sense. But he has obliterated many interesting details of time and place, he shows a marked tendency to exaggerate the ascetic and miraculous element, he amplifies the narrative with rhetorical matter which can only be called padding, inserts as facts explanations of his own, and has greatly spoiled one beautiful anecdote. On the other hand, his account of Cuthbert's death, derived from an eye-witness, is of real and independent value." For other critical assessments, see the remarks and documentation of Lenore Abraham, "Bede's *Life of Cuthbert*: A Reassessment," *Proceedings of the Patristic, Medieval, and Renaissance Conference* 1 (1976): 23–24, and Carole E. Newlands, "Bede and Images of Saint Cuthbert," *Traditio* 52 (1997): 73–109 at 78, nn. 25 and 26.

22 On the narrative qualities of the anonymous *Vita Cuthberti* see Theodor Wolpers, *Die englische Heiligenlegende des Mittelalters*, Buchreihe der Anglia 10 (Tübingen, 1964), pp. 74–75.

23 Augustine, *De doctrina christiana*, ed. J. Martin, CCSL 32 (Turnhout, 1962), Book 4. c. 19. 38, p. 144; Augustine, *De doctrina christiana*, ed. and trans. R. P. H. Green (Oxford, 1995), pp. 244–45; cf. Wieland, "*Geminus Stilus*," in *Insular Latin Studies*, ed. Michael Herren, pp. 124–26.

24 D. P. Kirby, "The Genesis of a Cult: Cuthbert of Farne and Ecclesiastical Politics in Northumbria

Although it is hard to believe that Bede would be a part of opposition to Bishop Acca, his diocesan superior and admired friend to whom he dedicated a number of his works, the cult of Cuthbert and Bede's *Life* certainly added luster to the see they wished to demote. As the best writer around, Bede accepted the task of writing the life and miracles of the saint in a form acceptable for *lectio divina*, for perusing not only in private devotion but also for annual public reading on the feast of the saint. He therefore took the anonymous Lindisfarne life as the most reliable textual history of Cuthbert's life and added to that his findings derived from witnesses, particularly Abbot Herefrith. In order to improve the style of his source, he completely rewrote the life in his own lucid fashion, rearranging the sequence of events, smoothing transitions, adding quotations and augmenting plot to form a continuous narrative. By drawing out the spiritual and moral lessons to be derived from hagiographic reading, he observed the requirements of the genre. As J. F. Webb points out, "His main aim was not historical accuracy but imaginative truth within the framework of a conventional literary form, the saint's life."[25] Bede wrote the metrical version, composed of 979 expert hexameter lines, between 705 and 716, according to the reference to Osred's reign in verses 552–55.[26] In the dedicatory preface Bede tells the priest John that he was unable to include all of Cuthbert's wondrous deeds because new ones were daily being done through his relics and old ones were newly being brought to light. He then adds the striking comment: "One of those wondrous deeds I myself experienced *per linguae curationem* [by a guidance *or* by a curing] of the tongue, as I have already told you, while I was singing his miracles."[27] Whether this means that Bede received direction and guidance through Cuthbert's inspiration as a saintly muse or whether he was cured of some lingual affliction is unclear because the Latin *curatio* bears both meanings, "administration, attention, treatment, guidance," or "cure, healing"; modern critics favor the former.[28] As the *apparatus criticus* of Jaager's edition makes

---

in the Late Seventh and Early Eighth Centuries," *Journal of Ecclesiastical History* 46.3 (1995): 383–97, at 397.

[25] J. F. Webb, trans., *Lives of the Saints* (Harmondsworth, 1965), p. 23. Webb's introduction to Bede's prose life is a cogent rebuttal to Plummer's opinion quoted on pp. 79–80, note 21 above.

[26] On the dating from this reference, see Manitius, *Geschichte der lateinischen Literatur des Mittelalters* (Munich, 1911–31), I: 84; Werner Jaager, ed., *Bedas metrische Vita Cuthberti* (Leipzig, 1935), p. 4.

[27] Bede, *Vita Cuthberti*, ed. Jaager, p. 57, lines 17–19. For a critique of Jaager's edition see Michael Lapidge, "Prolegomena to an Edition of Bede's Metrical 'Vita Sancti Cuthberti,'" *Filologia mediolatina* 2 (1995): 127–63 at 163: by clarifying "the various phases of redaction, it is possible to make a more accurate judgement of the variant readings which they convey. Jaager's text of the poem, though excellent in many ways, is defective in its failure to uncover anything of this transmissional history, with the unfortunate result that (for example) the [early] readings of the Besançon manuscript are jumbled together in the apparatus criticus with those of the 'vulgate' version, and readings offered by the various stages of redaction are treated eclectically, without any attempt to determine when and how they arose." See also Helmut Gneuss and Michael Lapidge, "The Earliest Manuscript of Bede's Metrical Vita S. Cudbercti," *Anglo-Saxon England* 32 (2003): 43–54.

[28] On the word *curatio* see *Thesaurus Linguae Latinae*, IV, 1476–77. For a discussion of the various

clear, Bede's metrical version owes very little to the wording of the anonymous life, but it does remain closer to the order and arrangement of that source than does his prose version. Bede includes all miracles of the anonymous life except those only summarily mentioned without detail. And Bede adds a dozen chapters' worth of material.[29] However, his poetic version provides less historical detail than the anonymous and certainly less than his prose version; in the poetic version he placed greater emphasis on Cuthbert's wonders.

Stylistically the poem, while following the late antique classical tradition of Juvencus, Sedulius, and Arator, from whom Bede takes phrases and vocabulary, is, as Michael Lapidge has demonstrated, in style and prosody remarkably Vergilian.[30] However, there are borrowings, in descending order of frequency, from Cyprianus Gallus, Venantius Fortunatus, Paulinus of Nola, Dracontius, Prudentius, Aldhelm, Paulinus of Périgueux, Alcimus Avitus, Damasus, Serenus Sammonicus, Ovid, Horace, Prosper, Orientius, Augustine, and Persius.[31] His metrics and prosody are enviably correct; he uses rhyme and alliteration sparingly (indicating how little Bede carries over the Anglo-Saxon poetic verse tradition into his Latin). The proem is nicely constructed, moving from the general view of the Lord's numerous and various saints as lights of the Church to examples of individuals, each shining particularly for his own locale – e.g., Peter and Paul for Rome, Cyprian for Africa, John Chrysostom for Constantinople, and finally Cuthbert for the English. Bede at the outset thus places Cuthbert in a cosmic setting as the patron of the English who is honored universally. In this spirit and with the world as audience, Bede presents in studied and solemn verse the glorified Cuthbert. In contrast to the solemnity of the proem and the gravity of the prophetic warning of the destruction of the monastery (ch. 37), some of the account is charming, mock-pastoral and mock-heroic. The amusing mixture of Vergilian bucolic and epic verse in the following passage reveals not only Bede's command of classical verse but also his sense of humor.[32]

---

understandings of Bede's gift in both the medieval and modern periods, see Dorothy Whitelock, "Bede and his Teachers and Friends," in *Famulus Christi*, ed. Bonner, p. 21 and nn. 15–21, to which Whitelock concludes: "If it is permissible to take *curatio* in this more original sense, Bede is claiming that he received miraculous inspiration from St Cuthbert while he was composing his verse *Life*. I prefer to believe this interpretation."

29 See Jaager's introduction and statistics, pp. 2–3, and Colgrave's concordance of the three lives, in *Two Lives of St. Cuthbert*, p. 375.

30 Michael Lapidge, "Bede and the Poetic Diction of Vergil," in *Poesía Latina Medieval (Siglos V–XV)*, ed. Manuel C. Díaz y Díaz and José M. Díaz de Bustamente (Florence, 2005), pp. 739–48. Lapidge counters with detailed analysis the earlier view (represented by Sharon Turner, Thomas Wright, Whitney Bolton) that Bede was "a competent but uninspired versifier" by showing that "he was an exceptionally good poet" and arguing convincingly that "Bede's debt to Vergil goes far beyond the level of verbal reminiscence: that his whole conception of poetic language and metrical technique was informed by his attentive – inspired even – study of Vergil's diction" (p. 740).

31 Jaager, *Bedas metrische Vita Cuthberti*, "Stylistisches," p. 15.

32 Jaager's three brief references to Vergil's *Georgics* in this passage, I. 244 [which should read I. 224] and II. 14 for lines 415 and 416, and I. 509 for line 423 do not at all convey the amount of Vergilian imitation in the passage. Cf., for example, *Georgics*, I. 50, 111, 219–24; II. 237;

Quique suis cupiens victum conquiere palmis
Incultum pertemptat humum proscindere ferro
Et sator edomitis anni spem credere glebis.
Dumque seges modico de semine surgeret ampla,
Tempus adest messis; rapidae sed forte volucres
Flaventes praedare senis nituntur aristas.
Talia qui placidus saevis praedonibus infit:
"Quid precor inlicito messem contingitis ausu,
Quae vestro sulcis non est inserta labore?
Pauperies an vestra meam transcendit, ut istud
Incurvam merito falcem mittatis in aequor?
Quod si forte deus iubet his instare rapinis,
Non veto; sin alias, vos finibus indite vestris."
Dixerat; et cessit mox plumea turba nec ultra
Militis audebat domini iam laedere iura.
Quin potius dulci pacis quasi foedere nexum
Unanimemque sui generis redamabat amicum,
Nam teneras ceu pastor oves hanc ipse regebat.

(Stanza XVII, lines 413–430)

[Desiring to get food by means of his own hands, he works to cut through the uncultivated soil with iron tool; and as a sower he entrusts the hope of the year in the tamed glebe. After an ample crop results from the bit of seed, it is time for the reaping. However, by chance quick birds strive to plunder the old man's golden ears of grain. Placid, he begins to speak to the savage thieves: "Why, I beg you, do you reach with illicit daring for the harvest, which was not planted in the rows by your labor? Or does your poverty exceed mine, that you should send your curved scythe justly into that plain? If perhaps God orders you to press on with this rapine, I do not forbid. If otherwise, put yourselves in your own territories." He had spoken, and immediately the plumed mob ceased and dared not further violate now the laws of the soldier lord. Rather, it formed a bond with him as by a sweet pact of peace, and loved him as a united friend of its race, for he ruled this group as a pastor his tender sheep.]

This passage, so Vergilian in diction, is not anomalous. Throughout the *Vita metrica*, as Lapidge notes,

The entire diction of that poem is saturated with the language of Vergil, not only the speech-formulas (*Haec ubi dicta, haec memorans, dixerat et, uix ea fatus erat*, etc.) and transition-formulas which propel the narrative (*hinc atque hinc, tempore non alio*, etc.), but also the cadences which conclude many of Vergil's hexameters (*ab ictu, ad limina tendit, pectore fatur, ad sidera palmas,*

IV. 158; *Aeneid*, VII. 721; XI. 301. As for the mock-epic quality, note that *Dixerat*, line 426, is used by Vergil for epic discourse twenty-five times in the *Aeneid*, but never in the *Eclogues* or *Georgics*. For Bede's use of Vergil in the metrical *Life*, see further Neil Wright, "Bede and Vergil," *Romanobarbarica* 6 (1981): 363, 367–71, and Lapidge, "Bede and the Poetic Diction of Vergil," cited above, n. 30.

etc.). Furthermore, Bede borrows entire Vergilian phrases at important narrative junctures.[33]

Bede's prosody is nearly always correct and his use of *caesurae* remarkably Vergilian in its sophistication; likewise, his structure of the hexameter, the figure of "accusativus graecus," poetic euphony and cacophony, and etymological wordplay are also notably Vergilian.[34]

Bede's prose life of Cuthbert owes very little to his metrical version but much to the anonymous prose life, although he restructured it stylistically and thematically. Forty miracles are related in Bede's; only eight of them are not in the anonymous.[35] Bede points out in the preface that he showed his notes to the monks of Lindisfarne for their criticism. Additional fine material, such as chapter 33, and his beautiful account of Cuthbert's death, related in chapters 37–39, he says he owes to Abbot Herefrith. In Bede's hands the *Vita* displays a skillful blend of the Roman and Irish ideals of monastic life. This is fitting not only because the writer himself owes so much to both traditions but also because the hero Cuthbert was an interlocking cornerstone for the two modes of life. In many respects Cuthbert resembles the enterprising Irish ascetics and pilgrim monks in his heroic penitential practices, his search for solitude, and his missionary activity. The arrangements of his Lindisfarne discipline and the relationship of bishop, abbot, and community reveal elements of both Irish and Continental monasticism, which Bede feels obliged to explain ("ne aliquis miretur") ["lest anyone should marvel"].[36] Bede does not include this detail from the anonymous life: that as prior Cuthbert instituted a rule "which we observe even to this day along with the rule of St. Benedict."[37]

The modern reader of Bede's *Vita Cuthberti* might consider it a skillful piece of hagiography without realizing that it is highly charged propaganda not only for the establishment of an English Cuthbert over the Irish holy and admirable but doctrinally suspect Aidan but also for an active monastic ideal apostolate that combines asceticism with pastoral care.[38] Bede in working from the earlier account by the anonymous author "refashions it to show Cuthbert's development from layman to monk, to hermit and bishop, and to stress his dual roles as a model of the active and contemplative life."[39]

---

33 Lapidge, "Bede and the Poetic Diction of Vergil," p. 740.
34 Lapidge, "Bede and the Poetic Diction of Vergil," pp. 741–48.
35 Colgrave, *Two Lives*, p. 14.
36 Colgrave, *Two Lives*, ch. 16, p. 206, and note, p. 347. For a discussion of the peculiarities of this monachism see A. Hamilton Thompson, "Northumbrian Monasticism," in *Bede: His Life, Times, and Writings*, pp. 60–101, esp. 72.
37 Colgrave, ed., *Anonymous Life*, III, 1, pp. 94–97: "et nobis regularem uitam primum componentibus constituit, quam usque hodie cum regula Benedicti obseruamus."
38 See Clare Stancliffe, "Cuthbert and the Polarity between Pastor and Solitary," in *St Cuthbert, his Cult and his Community to AD 1200*, ed. Gerald Bonner, David Rollason, and Clare Stancliffe (Woodbridge, 1989), pp. 21–44.
39 Catherine Cubitt, "Memory and Narrative in the Cult of Early Anglo-Saxon Saints," in *The Uses of the Past in the Early Middle Ages*, ed. Yitzhak Hen and Matthew Innes (Cambridge, 2000), pp. 29–66 at 42.

Moreover, as Alan Thacker has pointed out, Bede represents Cuthbert as an ideal of reform:

> Cuthbert is presented as an exemplary monk, ascetic, and bishop, fulfilling in these roles all the requirements of a Bedan *rector*, *doctor*, and *praedicator.* He is seen as the Northumbrian equivalent of the great holy men of the Christian past, and as the ideal Gregorian, who acts in the spirit of the Benedictine Rule and closely resembles Benedict himself and (to a lesser extent) other heroes of the *Dialogues*.[40]

As Carole Newlands also notes, Bede's prose life emphasizes, in contrast to earlier hagiographic tradition, the development, in carefully marked stages, of Cuthbert's sanctity through spiritual discipline and divine grace.[41] As such he is a saint that invites imitation in the journey towards perfection. Bede also reworks the *Life* to portray Cuthbert's kindness and equanimity. However, he also makes Cuthbert the guardian of orthodoxy. In the death scene, totally absent in the anonymous life, Bede has Cuthbert command: "Have no communion with those who depart from the unity of the Catholic peace, either in not celebrating Easter at the proper time or in evil living."[42]

Each of the three versions of Cuthbert's life has its literary and hagiographic merits, but those merits differ greatly. It is clear from manuscript history that Bede's prose life, which "reflects the ecclesiastical and national ambitions of Bede's mature years,"[43] won the palm in the Middle Ages: extant are seven manuscripts of the anonymous version, nineteen of Bede's metrical version, and thirty-six complete manuscripts of the prose version, not counting two containing extracts only and evidence for many more lost ones.[44] A comparison of the three lives tells a student much about Bede's qualities as an author of hagiography.[45]

Martyrology

> "A martyrology of the festivals of the holy martyrs, in which I have diligently tried to note down all that I could find out about them, not only on what day, but also by what sort of combat and under what judge they overcame the world" (*HE*, V.

---

[40] Alan Thacker, "Bede's Ideal of Reform," in *Ideal and Reality in Frankish and Anglo-Saxon Society*, ed. Patrick Wormald (Oxford, 1983), pp. 130–53 at 142.

[41] Newlands, "Bede and Images of Saint Cuthbert," pp. 82–85, and 106: "With his brilliant powers of organization and his eloquent Latinity, Bede in his prose vita reshaped the static character of the anonymous vita and the remote, mystical figure of the metrical vita into a powerful, coherent icon of English sanctity."

[42] Colgrave, *Bede's Life*, ch. 39, pp. 284–5.

[43] Newlands, "Bede and Images of Saint Cuthbert," p. 81.

[44] See Jaager, *Bedas metrische Vita Cuthberti*, pp. 24–32; Colgrave, *Two Lives*, pp. 17–50; Laistner, *Hand-List*, pp. 88–90.

[45] Whitney F. Bolton, *Anglo-Latin Literature* (Princeton, 1967), I: 136–38, provides without commentary a sample text and translation of the three accounts of the two sea otters wiping and warming Cuthbert's feet.

24). Bede, *Martyrology*, ed. and trans. Felice Lifshitz, in *Medieval Hagiography: An Anthology*, ed. Thomas Head, pp. 169–97.

Besides the four saints' lives and those he included as part of his histories, Bede made another, greater contribution to hagiography. From the pseudo-Jerome fifth-century martyrology, a liturgical calendar simply naming the martyrs and the places of their martyrdom, Bede composed between 725 and 731 what is termed an historical martyrology: it includes a brief account of each saint's life and death.[46] As Michael Lapidge and Rosalind Love note: "Bede ... was the greatest hagiographer of the Anglo-Saxon period: not simply for the quantity of his own surviving saints' lives, but for his sophisticated awareness of the hagiographer's duty and his exhaustive control of earlier hagiographal sources."[47] His martyrology served as a matrix and model for all future cumulative martyrologies produced in the Latin West, including Florus, Hrabanus, Usuard, and the later Baronius; it forms the basis of the Roman martyrology used by the Catholic Church today. For this project, Bede did a great deal of research, and the work is witness to an impressive number of sources, including some fifty lives of saints, ecclesiastical histories, writings of Fathers of the Church, and the *Liber Pontificalis*.[48] One of the more sensational entries is that for St. Cassian (the martyr, not the monk) on August 13:

> On the Ides of August. The birthday [into heaven] of St. Cassian, at Rome. When he had refused to adore idols, the persecutor demanded to know what his profession was. He answered that he taught students grammar (*notas*). Then, stripped of his clothes and bound with his hands behind his back, he was placed in the center. The boys to whom by his teaching he had become hateful were called, and permission was given them to destroy him. To the degree that they had suffered while learning, to that degree they enjoyed vengeance. Some beat him with their tablets and boards, others wounded him with their pens. In as much as their hands were weak, so much heavier by the extended death was the pain of his martyrdom. Prudentius the poet has written the life.[49]

Bede's martyrology contained 114 notices. This left a number of calendrical

---

[46] Dom Henri Quentin, *Les martyrologes historiques du moyen âge: Étude sur la formation du martyrologe romain*, 2nd ed. (Paris, 1908), ch. 2, pp. 17–119, in which Bede's contribution to the martyrological genre is explored. Lifshitz's translation is based on this edition, with consultation of the manuscripts in Sankt Gallen and Munich (p. 175). She notes that Bede "was an innovator who moved the Latin churches away from simple lists of saints and martyrs to the use of historical martyrologies" and his *Martyrology* is an example of his *Romanitas* (p. 171).

[47] M. Lapidge and R. C. Love, "The Latin Hagiography of England and Wales (600–1550)," in *Corpus Christianorum III, Hagiographies* (Turnhout, 2001), p. 213.

[48] The martyrology itself is conveniently available in the *Édition practique des martyrologes de Bède, de l'anonyme lyonnais et de Florus*, ed. Dom Jacques DuBois and Geneviève Renaud (Paris, 1976).

[49] Dubois and Renaud, *Édition pratique*, p. 149; cf. Quentin, *Les martyrologes*, p. 68. My translation.

spaces open. With the medieval *horror vacui* and the amplification of saints, editors filled Bede's work with supplemental entries.[50]

Sacred poems

> "A book of hymns in various meters and rhythms. A book of epigrams in heroic and elegiac meter" (*HE*, V. 24).

These two books did not survive the Middle Ages intact.[51] However, a number of individual poems have come down to us. Besides the metrical life of St. Cuthbert in almost a thousand lines of skillfully wrought hexameters, discussed above under hagiography, we have some two dozen poems of varying length and meter, some certainly by Bede and the rest quite probably so. One poem, in honor of St. Æthelthryth, we know is genuine because Bede includes it in the *Ecclesiastical History*, with the introductory remark: "It seems fitting to insert in this history a hymn on the subject of virginity which I composed many years ago in elegiac meter in honor of this queen and bride of Christ, and therefore truly a queen because the bride of Christ; imitating the method of holy Scripture in which many songs are inserted into the account and, as is well known, these are composed in meter and verse."[52] Bede's poem, a *tour de force*, begins:

> Alma Deus Trinitas, quae saecula cuncta gubernas,
>   adnue iam coeptis, alma Deus Trinitas.
> Bella Maro resonet; nos pacis dona canamus,
>   munera nos Christi; bella Maro resonet.

---

[50] The composite jumble is represented by the martyrology printed as Bede's work in Migne, PL 94: 799–1148.

[51] Laistner was misleading in the *Hand-List* where he states: "Neither of these collections of poems has survived as such, but, according to John Boston of Bury, the library of Bury St Edmunds early in the fifteenth century had a *Liber hymnorum* and a *Liber epigrammatum* bearing Bede's name" (p. 122). Richard H. Rouse, "Bostonus Buriensis and the Author of the *Catalogus Scriptorum Ecclesiae*," *Speculum* 41 (1966): 471–99, demonstrated that Bostonus Buriensis was only the scribe of the catalogue and that Henry of Kirkestede, subprior and librarian, was the author; but Rouse also made clear that Kirkestede's catalogue was not an actual catalogue of library holdings but a bio-bibliographic union catalogue which comprised a list of all the books by authoritative and approved authors that Kirkestede knew of and wished to acquire if they were not yet available (pp. 471–72, 493–94). It is clear that Kirkestede learned about Bede's works from Bede's own bibliography, which he copied in the same order and wording as found in *HE*, 5. 24. That neither Bury St Edmunds nor the Franciscan convents or neighboring monasteries possessed Bede's poems is manifest from the fact that Kirkestede was unable to supply an incipit and explicit for the works nor a reference number for their location (see p. 496, items 40 and 41). Laistner's misunderstanding of the nature of the list resulted in Michael Lapidge's statement in *English Historical Review* 90 (1975): 798, that a copy of the book of epigrams "was known to Henry of Kirkestede …"

[52] Bede, *Ecclesiastical History*, ed. Colgrave and Mynors, 4. 20, pp. 396–401, with Colgrave's facing-page translation. On the great and lasting influence of Bede's poem and *vita* of St. Æthelthryth, see Virginia Blanton, *Signs of Devotion: The Cult of St. Æthelthryth in Medieval England, 695–1615* (University Park, PA, 2007), and more on the tradition in my *Bedan Legacy*.

Carmina casta mihi, fedae non raptus Helenae;
  luxus erit lubricis, carmina casta mihi.
Etc.

[All-bounteous Three in One, Lord of all time,
  Bless mine emprise, all-bounteous Three in One.
Battle be Maro's theme, sweet peace be mine;
  Christ's gifts for me, battle be Maro's theme.
Chaste is my song, not wanton Helen's rape.
  Leave lewdness to the lewd! Chaste is my song.]

From this sample of the beginning lines, which instantiate Bede's topos of the superiority of Christian verse over pagan, the paean is not only abecedary (23 distichs each beginning with a following alphabetic letter, plus A, M, E, N for the *Amen*) but also epanaleptic (that is, the last quarter of the distich repeats the first; esteemed in the Middle Ages as reciprocal, echoic, or serpentine verse).[53]

Bede's poems, other than some single lines, distichs, and short poems inserted in his prose work, have been edited in the Corpus Christianorum series, but unfortunately not well.[54] Fraipont's edition goes by the title *Bedae venerabilis liber hymnorum, rhythmi, variae preces*. This is misleading, since there are no "rhythmi" in the collection that fit Bede's definition taken from late Latin grammarians in his *De arte metrica*, I. 24, where rhythmic poetry, as contrasted with metrical, means accentual verse. Thirteen of the fifteen hymns taken by Fraipont from Dreves' 1907 edition are properly ascribed to Bede; but two, IV and V, are most probably not, since they were never attributed to him even in the Middle Ages.[55]

Hymns I through XIII are in traditional Ambrosian hymn meter, iambic

---

53 On the alphabetic and reciprocal form, see Plummer, ed., *Bedae opera historica*, II, 241. Bede cites the well-known accentual alphabetic poem, "Apparebit repentina" in *De arte metrica*, ed. Kendall, CCSL 123A, I. 24, p. 139; Bede, *Libri II De arte metrica et de schematibus et tropis*, ed. and trans. Kendall, pp. 162–63. Ernst Robert Curtius, *European Literature and the Latin Middle Ages*, trans. Willard R. Trask (New York, 1953), pp. 235–36, identifies and describes the use of the topos as "the contrast between pagan and Christian poetry." Bede would be familiar with it from his reading in Juvencus, Paulinus of Nola, and Paulinus of Périgueux.

54 Bede, *Opera rhythmica*, ed. J. Fraipont, CCSL 122 (Turnhout, 1955), pp. 405–51. Anyone using the Fraipont edition should take note of Walther Bulst's scathing critique of it, "Bedae opera rhythmica," *Zeitschrift für deutsches Altertum und deutsche Literatur* 89 (1958–59): 83–91. My remarks on the form and contents of the CCSL edition draw on his expertise, as well as on that of Josef Szövérffy, *Die Annalen der lateinischen Hymnendichtung* (Berlin, 1966), I: 168–76. W. F. Bolton's list of Bede's poems in *History of Anglo-Latin Literature*, pp. 167–68, is inaccurate; for instance, he reports three elegiac couplets at the end of ch. 3 of *De locis sanctis* that simply are not there in any manuscript or edition; the four epitaphs in *HE* which he labels "some at least probably by Bede" are all by earlier authors duly credited by Bede.

55 G. M. Dreves, *Lateinische Hymnendichter des Mittelalters*, 50 (1907), p. 98, prints eleven hymns attributed to Bede in George Cassander's Renaissance collection, taken from a tenth-century manuscript. He adds another four (including the two hymns) from MS Bamberg B.II.10, which are amongst hymns without authorial ascription but found adjacent to hymns attributed to Bede. As Bulst asserts, pp. 88–89, that is not sufficient reason to ascribe these two to Bede, which he brands as "dürftig, plump und mühselig zusammengestückt."

dimeter.[56] Hymn I, *Primo Deus caeli globum*, is on a familiar topic in Bede, the six days of creation and the six ages of the world. After two introductory stanzas, the first line of one stanza becomes the last line of the next, up to stanza 19, which, after the sabbath rest of souls on the seventh day, deals with the extra-temporal eighth day of eternal bliss. On that day and age,

> Vultumque Christi perpetim
> Iusti cernent amabilem
> Eruntque sicut angeli
> Caelesti in arce fulgidi.
>
> [(Stanza 20). The just behold forever the lovable countenance of Christ; they will be as shining angels in the celestial citadel. (My translation.)]

Stanza 28 ends the poem with praise to the Trinity, following the common practice of concluding a hymn with a doxology. Fraipont unaccountably includes the spurious stanzas 29 to 33 (pp. 410–11), which are metrically defective and anticlimactic.

Hymn II, *Hymnum canentes martyrum*, is for the Feast of the Holy Innocents (December 28). Bede again uses the echoic stanza form, so that the first line of one stanza serves as the last line of the next. For example (stanzas 5 and 6):

> Bimos et infra paruulos
> Herodis ira perculit
> Finesque Bethlemiticos
> Sancto respersit sanguine.
> Praeclara Christo splenduit
> Mors innocens fidelium,
> Caelis ferebant angeli
> Bimos et infra paruulos.
>
> [The wrath of Herod struck down the babes under two years and splashed the regions of Bethlehem with their holy blood. The glorious and innocent death of the faithful gave splendor to Christ, as the angels bore to heaven the babes under two years. (My translation.)]

Though there is a repetition of the first line in the eighth, the meaning has changed radically, for the subject of the first line, *ira*, has changed to *angeli* in the last.

Hymn IX, *In natali SS. Petri et Pauli*, another alphabetic poem proceeding from A to Z, honors the two patron saints of Wearmouth and Jarrow (stanza 2):

> Bar Iona Simon Petrus
> Et doctor almus gentium

---

[56] For a description of the *hymni Ambrosiani*, see F. J. E. Raby, *A History of Christian-Latin Poetry, from the Beginnings to the Close of the Middle Ages*, 2nd ed. (Oxford, 1966), pp. 28–41 at 33.

Festiua saeclis gaudia
Suo dicarunt sanguine.

[Simon Peter, son of Jonah, and the nurturing teacher of the Gentiles have
by their blood consecrated the festive joys for the ages. (My translation.)]

Judging from the number of manuscripts extant, VI, *Hymnos canamus
gloriae*, on the Ascension, was Bede's most popular hymn.[57] The poem, with
its emphasis on Christ's harrowing of hell and royal entrance into heaven,
is an epitome of the early medieval theology of glory. It contains many of
the Scriptural and patristic motifs that will be used by Cynewulf in his Old
English poem, *Christ II (The Ascension)*.[58] After the beauty and regular meter
of the first seventeen stanzas, the interpolated and defective stanza 17a spoils
the flow, but 18 through 32 restore the reader's equilibrium.

Another hymn particularly interesting because of its use of the personifi-
cation frequently found in Old English vernacular literature is the second
hymn in honor of Saint Andrew, XIII, *Salue, tropaeum gloriae* (pp. 437–38).
In this poem, the first seven stanzas are Andrew's address to the cross. They
manifest Bede's literary debt to *The Passion of Saint Andrew the Apostle*
and use the device of prosopopoeia employed in the Old English poem, *The
Dream of the Rood*.[59]

A third poem, *De die iudicii* (XIV, pp. 439–44), is still more closely linked
with the vernacular, since the fine Old English poem of the late tenth century,
Judgment Day II, formerly called *Be Domes Dæge*, is a 304-line paraphrase of
it.[60] The dactylic hexameter Latin poem, *De die iudicii*, thought to have been
composed between 716 and 731, is not in the usual sense a hymn, though it
has been included in hymn collections, but a 163-line poem of meditation.
Although the authenticity of that poem has been questioned, the consensus
supports Bedan authorship. Thirty of the more than forty extant manuscripts

---

[57] See A. S. Walpole, ed., *Early Latin Hymns* (Cambridge, 1922, rpt. 1966), pp. 371–76. Walpole's
edition with its excellent introduction and notes remains the best introductory text for the early
hymns.

[58] See Daniel G. Calder, *Cynewulf*, Twayne English Authors Series 327 (Boston, 1981), ch. 3, pp.
42–74; and my "The Descent-Ascent Motif in *Christ II* of Cynewulf," *JEGP* 73 (1974): 1–12.
A. S. Cook suggested a relationship between Bede's and Cynewulf's poems in his edition of *The
Christ of Cynewulf* (Boston, 1909), pp. 116–18.

[59] M. Bonnet, ed., *Acta Apostolorum apocrypha*, II, 1 (Leipzig, 1898), pp. 24–26. See the notes,
particularly to verses 39a, 42a, 87–89a, of *The Dream of the Rood* in Frederick G. Cassidy and
Richard N. Ringler, eds., *Bright's Old English Grammar & Reader*, 3rd ed. (New York, 1971), pp.
309–17; also, Michael Swanton, ed., *The Dream of the Rood* (Manchester and New York, 1970),
pp. 42–78.

[60] The poem was edited with an English translation by J. Rawson Lumby with the title *Be Domes
Dæge, De die judicii*, for the Early English Text Society, Original Series 65 (London, 1876).
A recent edition of the poem by Graham D. Caie, *The Old English Poem 'Judgement Day II':
A Critical Edition with Editions of De die iudicii and the Hatton 113 Homily Be domes dæge*
(Cambridge, 2000) has been negatively reviewed by Mark Griffith (*Medium Ævum* 60.2 [2001]:
322–23) and Frederick Biggs (*Modern Language Review* 98.1 [2003]: 153–54). Between 1944
and 1972 Leslie Whitbread published a series of useful articles examining Bede's Latin text and
the Old English versions, but he never produced his proposed edition.

ascribe it to him; and the only other author to whom it was ascribed (once, without any justification) is Alcuin.[61] In Northumbrian manuscripts the poem has a personal address to Bede's patron, Bishop Acca, and his monks at Hexham. The theme of doomsday is consonant with Bede's other writings, such as chapter 70 of *De temporum ratione*;[62] Dryhthelm's account of his trip to the otherworld in *HE*, V. 12–13; Psalms 41 and 73, which Bede versified in Latin;[63] and the little prayer he recited on his deathbed.[64] It is difficult to identify the pious Bede with the sinful persona and reluctant repentant "lying in filth and full of crimes" ("Quid tu in sorde iaces, scelerum caro plena piaclis," line 39), and tarred with the vices catalogued in lines 114–123. However, the most serious objection to Bede's authorship is that the poem as edited in Corpus Christianorum contains a number of metrical faults, which Michael Lapidge has enumerated.[65] Lapidge, who notes that numerous phrases and words as well as metrical techniques in *De die iudicii* are shared with Bede's *Vita metrica S. Cuthberti*, concludes, "There can be no doubt that Bede composed both poems."[66] He then shows that most of the metrical errors in the printed edition are due to faulty readings either in manuscripts or in Fraipont's badly edited text. Nonetheless, there remain a small number of prosodic faults in the poem. These, surmises Lapidge, can be ascribed to an early redaction that Bede did not later correct, as he did the *Vita metrica S. Cuthberti*.[67]

The poem starts out with a line describing a pleasant glade, using the classical and medieval topos of the *locus amoenus*, but immediately wheels about in the second line with a description of a powerful wind that brings on the melancholic mood in line 4. The subject-matter of the poem, the separation of the just and unjust according to their merits, their rewards and punishment, naturally prompts a rhetorically contrastive treatment. The earthly flowery scene in the first line parallels the rosy aspect of heaven in lines 146–47; the list of hell's sufferings, lines 91–97, contrast with heaven's

---

[61] The attribution of the poem to Alcuin, often repeated in Old English scholarship from Lumby's remark in the preface to his edition and translation, *Be Domes Dæge, De die judicii*, Early English Text Society, Original Series 65 (London, 1876), pp. v–vi, is due to a chance juxtaposition of the poem next to one attributed to Alcuin in Vienna, MS 89. See Whitbread, "After Bede: The Influence and Dissemination of his Domesday Verses," *Archiv* 204 (1967): 250–66 at 251 and note 3.

[62] Bede, *De temporum ratione*, ed. Jones, CCSL 123B, c. 70, pp. 539–42.

[63] Bede, *Hymni et preces*, ed. Fraipont, CCSL 122, pp. 447–48, 449.

[64] As quoted in Cuthbert's *Epistola de Obitu Bedae*, in Bede, *Historia Ecclesiastica*, ed. Colgrave and Mynors, p. 582.

[65] Michael Lapidge, "Bede and the 'Versus de die iudicii,'" in *Nova de veteribus: Mittel- und neulateinsiche Studien für Gerhard Schmidt*, ed. Andreas Bihrer and Elisabeth Stein (Munich and Leipzig, 2004), pp. 103–11.

[66] Lapidge, "Bede and the 'Versus de die iudicii,'" pp. 105–108.

[67] See Lapidge, "Bede's Metrical Vita S. Cuthberti," in *St Cuthbert, his Cult and his Commmunity to AD 1200*, ed. G. Bonner, D. Rollason and C. Stancliffe (Woodbridge, 1989), pp. 77–93.

joys, lines 124–28, and "Nox ubi nulla," line 128, provides a verbal echo to "Nex vox ulla," line 93, as well. It is an artful and pious poem.[68]

Poem XV, *Oratio Bedae presbyteri*, is a twenty-six line prayer to God in elegiac couplets, in which he beseeches, "Remember me that am like an ash and wind and shadow!" ("Me similem cineri uentoque umbraeque memento!" [line 7]). The poems XVI, XVII, already discussed above, and XVIII, are poems based on Psalms 41, 83, and 112.

Bede occasionally inserted a brief poem, epigram, or epitaph before, within, or after a prose work. The form is usually the elegiac couplet. For instance, in the *Prose Life of St. Cuthbert*, Bede puts the prayer of Bishop Eadbert (d. 698), on the occasion of Cuthbert's elevation, into an eighteen-line elegiac couplet poem, which includes these highly alliterative lines (the second of which seems Aldhelmian):

> Mortua nunc tanto qui membra decorat honore,
> Pulchroque perpetuae pignore prestet opis   (lines 5–6)
>
> [The lord who now adorns these lifeless limbs with grace.
> Fair pledges of good things that know no end.][69]

Bede also composed another elegiac couplet poem of twenty-two lines as an attachment to his preface to the *Expositio Apocalypseos*.[70] It is a beautiful introduction in generally clear Latin, but in the second line it uses the recondite word "choico," a calque or loan translation from the Greek "of earth, clay," which caused later transcribers some trouble.

In ten lines before *De locis sanctis* Bede describes the geographic work and concludes with a prayer to Jesus.[71] Two elegiac couplets preface the *De natura rerum liber*, the first describing the work, the second a prayer.

Some remnants of Bede's lost *Liber epigrammatum* have been discovered. John Leland, commissioned by Henry VIII to search out British antiquities in ecclesiastical libraries, relates in his *Collectanea* that he inspected a very old collection of epigrams belonging to Milred of Worcester (bishop 745–775), of which five are attributed to Bede on good grounds. Leland transcribed two of them, which Michael Lapidge has published and discussed.[72] Although much of the manuscript that Leland saw perished along with many of the

---

[68] F. J. E. Raby, *A History of Christian-Latin Poetry from the Beginnings to the Close of the Middle Ages*, 2nd ed. (Oxford, 1953), pp. 145–49, who thinks little of Bede's poetry in general, is dismissive of this *Hymnus de die iudicii*: "Its merits are small and it displays nothing half so well as the piety of its author" (p. 148). Recent critics treat Bede's poetry with greater respect, even though it does not match the supreme quality of Venantius Fortunatus's poems.

[69] *Bede's Life of St. Cuthbert*, in *Two Lives of Saint Cuthbert*, ed. and trans. Bertram Colgrave (Cambridge, 1940 and 1985), pp. 294–95.

[70] *Bedae Expositio Apocalypseos*, ed. Roger Gryson, CCSL 121A (Turnhout, 2001), pp. 218–19. The verses appear before the Preface in most manuscripts, but after it in a half dozen others.

[71] Bede, *De locis sanctis*, ed. I. Fraipont, in *Itineraria et alia geographica*, CCSL 175 (Turnhout, 1965), p. 251.

[72] See Michael Lapidge, "Some Remnants of Bede's Lost *Liber epigrammatum*," *English Historical Review* 90 (1975): 798–820, with transcript of the epigrams on pp. 802–806. A notation by

texts of the Malmesbury monastery, a bifolium of the "ancient codex" has survived, now in the Library of the University of Illinois.[73] The last, acephalous three-line epigram in Milred's collection quoted by Lapidge may be from the concluding lines of Bede's own lost *Liber epigramatum*.[74]

As for vernacular poetry, there are apparently no extant Old English poems composed by Bede, but we have his own authority and that of his contemporary Cuthbert that he translated Latin into Old English, and Cuthbert also asserts that Bede was versed in Old English poetry.[75] From his account of Caedmon's poetic gift and career, we know that Bede was sensitive to the beauty and uniqueness of Old English verse and approved it as a medium for translating and embellishing the sacred text.[76] However there is no compelling evidence that he composed the five-line poem called "Bede's Death Song." The early and best manuscripts of Cuthbert's letter indicate only that Bede repeated the little poem as a favorite during his last days. Cuthbert's words are: "In nostra quoque lingua, ut erat doctus in nostris carminibus, dicens de terribili exitu animarum et corpore ..." ["In our own language also, for he was learned in our poetry, speaking of the soul's dread departure from the body ..."].[77]

Instructional letters

"Also a book of letters to various people: one of these is on the six ages of the world; one on the resting places of the children of Israel; one on the words of Isaiah, 'And they shall be shut up in the prison, and after many days shall

---

Leland, listed by Lapidge on p. 803, that part of the manuscript contained *Enigmata Bedae* suggests that Bede, like Aldhelm and Tatwin, may have authored *aenigmata* (learned riddles).

73 See Patrick Sims-Williams, "Milred of Worcester's Collection of Latin Epigrams and its Continental Counterparts," *ASE* 10 (1982): 21–38, rpt. as item IX in his *Britain and Early Christian Europe* (Aldershot, 1995); Michael Lapidge's Additional Notes in his *Anglo-Latin Literature 600–899* (London and Rio Grande, 1996), pp. 510-12; Dieter Schaller, "Bemerkungen zur Inschriften-Sylloge von Urbana," *Mittellateinisches Jahrbuch* 12 (1977): 9–21, rpt. with additions as item IX in *Studien zur lateinischen Dichtung des Frühmittelalter* (Stuttgart, 1995), with additional notes on pp. 423–24.

74 Patrick Sims-Williams,"Milred of Worcester's Collection of Latin Epigrams and its Continental Counterparts," *ASE* 10 (1982): 21–38 at 38, rpt. as item IX in his collection, *Britain and Early Christian Europe* (Aldershot, 1995). For more on Milred's *Sylloge*, see Patricia Lendinara, "Gregory and Damasus: Two Popes and Anglo-Saxon England," in *Rome and the North: The Early Reception of Gregory the Great in Germanic Europe*, ed. Rolf H. Bremmer, Jr., Kees Dekker, and David F. Johnson (Paris and Louvain, 2001), pp. 137-56 at 145–52.

75 "Letter to Cuthbert," *EHD*: 801; "Letter on the Death of Bede," *HE*, pp. 580–83.

76 *HE*, IV. 24, pp. 414–19.

77 *HE*, pp. 580–81, poem on 582–83. On this text Colgrave remarks, pp. 580–81, n. 4, "Only a comparatively small group of the MSS. of the Letter attribute the composition of the poem to Bede himself, and those the later ones." See E. V. K. Dobbie, *The Manuscripts of Cædmon's Hymn and Bede's Death Song* (New York, 1937). A. H. Smith's statement in his edition of *Three Northumbrian Poems*, rev. ed. (Exeter, 1978), p. 17, "On Cuthbert's testimony the Death Song is Bede's," is therefore unwarranted. On pp. 41–43 Smith includes with the Old English poem the surrounding Latin phrases of the Northumbrian (MS St Gall 254) and the later manuscript recension (MS Cotton Titus A II).

they be visited'; one on the reason for leap year; and one on the equinox, after Anatolius" (*HE*, V. 24).

From this catalogue it is obvious that Bede did not will to posterity a collection of familiar letters; these are all scholarly disquisitions. Although the book itself has not come down to us as such, we have all the five letters listed, in addition to two others, written after the *Ecclesiastical History* was finished, which two I discuss in connection with it.[78] Likewise, since each of the letters deals with a related Bedan treatise, I have included the discussion of each in connection with the related treatise. So the first letter on the six ages, *De sex aetatibus mundi*, is examined in connection with the *De temporibus* above in Chapter 2. The last two letters listed, *De ratione bissexti una* and *De aequinoctio iuxta Anatolium*, I also discuss in Chapter 2, because they treat computational questions put to Bede by colleagues, if in less controversial contexts. The second and third letters, *De mansionibus filiorum Israel una* and *Una de eo quod ait Isaias 'Et claudentur ibi in carcerem et post multos dies uisitabuntur,'* respond to questions of exegesis asked by Bede's patron, Bishop Acca, for whom he wrote so much, and for whom Bede interrupted his commentary on I Samuel to compose those letters. They are, like the *Eight Questions*, discussed in Chapter 3, though they are rather special because they take a particular biblical topic and treat it discursively rather than by Bede's usual method of verse-by-verse commentary.

---

[78] Migne, PL 94: 655–710, prints sixteen texts as Bede's *epistolae*, but, useful though it is to have all of them gathered together, most of these are Bede's prefaces to his exegetical works. I therefore do not discuss them here but in connection with the commentaries to which they were attached. *Epistola I* is the brief note to Albinus sent with the advance copy of the *HE* and *Epistola II* is the letter to Bishop Ecgbert. Both of these I treat in connection with *HE*.

5

The Histories

BEDE is known today principally as an historian, although throughout the Middle Ages he was renowned as a biblical interpreter and indeed spent most of his career commenting voluminously on Scripture. If medieval biblical exegesis owes much to his copious analyses, his exegetical works are only a portion of the hundreds of extant patristic and medieval commentaries. His histories, on the other hand, particularly *The Ecclesiastical History of the English People*, are unique. Without them whole centuries of early English history would be blank. And they are not only unique, they represent the highest quality writing of the period. These works are the mature products of Bede's scholarship and long career; *The Ecclesiastical History* is his last major work, supplemented by the *Letter to Egbert*, a final call for reform. His education, training, and talent culminate in the *History.* In it, his monastic vision of sacred and secular history and his reforming idealism, exemplified by his depiction of good and bad leaders and of faithful and faithless peoples, are combined. Although a cloistered monk living ascetic ideals, through his multiple contacts and extensive correspondence he knows better than anyone the complex realities of Anglo-Saxon society and he deals with the real, disorderly, and contentious factors of that life and politics.[1] Because of his insightful understanding of the unifying authority of the church of Canterbury and York as envisaged by Pope Gregory the Great, Bede precociously represented a single nation of a country that actually was and would remain long a collection of Anglo-Saxon tribal divisions. His treatment of Bernician and Deiran rivalries in Northumbria and of the Mercian polity, and his contentious treatment of the British and Irish as opponents, are understood and subsumed under his vision of the unity of the *gentis Anglorum*.

Like all great historians Bede marshals his materials in a carefully arranged presentation. He is a master of the overarching viewpoint as well as of the discreet silence, the omission that consigns a person or factions to oblivion.

---

[1] Bede's engagement in the life and politics of his age have now come to the fore; see, for instance, Alan Thacker, "Bede's Ideal of Reform," in *Ideal and Reality in Frankish and Anglo-Saxon Society*, ed. Patrick Wormald et al. (Oxford, 1983), pp. 130–53; Scott DeGregorio, "Literary Contexts: Cædmon's Hymn as a Center of Bede's World," in *Cædmon's Hymn and Material Culture in the World of Bede*, ed. Allen J. Frantzen and John Hines (Morgantown, 2007), pp. 51–79 at 74–76; Walter Goffart, "Bede's History in a Harsher Climate," in *Innovation and Tradition in the Writings of the Venerable Bede*, ed. Scott DeGregorio (Morgantown, 2006), pp. 203–26; Alan Thacker, "Bede and the Ordering of Understanding," in *Innovation and Tradition*, pp. 37–63 at 54–63.

His chapters, sections, and sentences are adroitly structured, with rhetorical hypotaxis and emphasis.[2] His many years as a teacher and writer of postclassical Latin, coupled with his impressive natural endowments, enabled him to write a well structured, long and coherent treatise. His many years as an exegete had honed his interpretative skills; the commentaries on the Gospels and Acts had especially practiced his talents for narrative, artistic selectivity, and the reconciliation of real and seeming contradictions. His work as a computist developed his special abilities for chronology, for fixing and relating events, and for understanding temporal sequence and relationships. His works of biography and hagiography had trained him to incorporate detail and sign into the larger fabric, to utilize reports, data, popular accounts, and miracle stories for studied effect. His expertise in poetry as well as rhetorical prose allowed him to use both forms effectively within the text, and his editorial expertise allowed him to edit and use letters and quotations effectively. The fact that many of his works were digests, revisions, or summaries of earlier materials also served his development as an historian. All his training as grammarian, exegete, literary artist, and chronologer was brought to bear on history. Conversely, his historical work boldly and candidly manifests the means and ends of each of those disciplines, so that literature and its devices, hermeneutics both in its literal and allegorical manifestations, saints' lives and miracles, and modes of ecclesiastical and secular history are presented and amalgamated.

The Lives of the Abbots of Wearmouth and Jarrow

"A history of the abbots of this monastery in which it is my joy to serve God, namely Benedict, Ceolfrith, and Hwætberht, in two books" (*HE* V. 24). Bede, *Historia abbotum*, in *Opera historica*, ed. Plummer; translation by J. F. Webb in *The Age of Bede*, ed. D. A. Farmer, pp. 185–208.

As in his saints' lives, Bede's succinct and reverent account of the lives of the first abbots of Wearmouth-Jarrow had in part a previous written source. In this case, *The Life of Ceolfrith* (*Vita Ceolfridi*, titled by Plummer *Historia abbatum auctore anonymo* – although it is mostly about Ceolfrith) was no mean prototype.[3] Indeed, *The Life of Ceolfrith* has been convincingly demonstrated

---

2 For some of Bede's techniques as an historical writer see Judith McClure, "Bede and the Life of Ceolfrid," *Peritia* 3 (1984): 71–84, esp. 74–80. A full analysis of Bede's style is yet to be done, but see W. Wetherbee, "Some Implications of Bede's Latin Style," in *Bede and Anglo-Saxon England: Papers in Honour of the 1300th Anniversary of the Birth of Bede, Given at Cornell University in 1973 and 1974*, ed. R. T. Farrell, British Archaeological Reports 46 (Oxford, 1978), pp. 23–31, esp. 23; George Hardin Brown, "Bede's Style in his Commentary on I Samuel," in *Text, Image, Interpretation*, ed. Alistair Minnis and Jane Roberts (Turnhout, 2007), pp. 233–51.
3 Charles Plummer edited both the anonymous and Bede's life in *Venerabilis Baedae opera historica* (Oxford, 1896): *Historia Abbatum Auctore Anonymo*, I: 388–404; *Historia Abbatum*, I: 364–87. Translations of the former have been published by Douglas Boutflower, *The Life of Ceolfrid* (Sunderland, 1912), Clinton Albertson, in *Anglo-Saxon Saints and Heroes* (New York, 1967), pp. 247–71; and Dorothy Whitelock in *English Historical Documents* I, no. 155. Translations of the

by Judith McClure to be by Bede himself, and subsequently incorporated by him into the fuller *Lives of the Abbots of Wearmouth and Jarrow*.[4] The *Life*, extant in only two manuscripts (which also contain the *Lives of the Abbots*),[5] was apparently intended as a homily or exhortation specifically for the Wearmouth-Jarrow community. This concise while expressively pious biography begins with a Scriptural text and ends with a doxology and contains many internal, personal references (e.g., "de memoria reuerentissimi patris et praepositi *nostri* Ceolfridi," par. 1; "qui nos abundanter ordinem cantandi ... edocuit," par. 10). The *Life* contains in its thirty-nine paragraph-chapters invaluable data about the Northumbrian monastery and its leader and describes the internal workings of the monastery and its cultural relationships with Gaul and Rome. It also includes a transcription of the dedicatory page of the Codex Amiatinus, the earliest surviving manuscript of the complete Bible, written in the Wearmouth-Jarrow scriptorium.[6] Like *The Lives of the Abbots* it is straightforwardly historical, delaying any account of miraculous wonders until the apparitions at Ceolfrith's tomb related at the end of the last chapter. Events are recorded by the year of the Incarnation (the methodology of dating BC and AD was used first by Bede in the Middle Ages, eventually becoming universal) as well as by indictions and by the regnal years of the Northumbrian kings.[7] Bede quotes from this *Life* in the Chronicle he attaches to the end of *De temporum ratione*, rather than from his *Lives of the Abbots*, which shows that his *Lives of the Abbots* postdates both the *Life of Ceolfrith* and the Chronicle.

Besides editing and freely incorporating this *Life of Ceolfrith* into his *History of the Abbots of Wearmouth and Jarrow*,[8] Bede adds items of traditional material and personal experience to the institutional history. Bede presents the life and career of the great founder of his monastery, Benedict

---

latter have been made by J. A. Giles, in *The Ecclesiastical History of the English Nation* (London, 1900), pp. 349–66; D. H. Farmer, in *The Age of Bede* (London, 1983), pp. 185–208; J. E. King, in *Bedae Opera Historica*, Loeb Classical Library (London and New York, 1930), 2: 392–445 (unsatisfactory); and J. Campbell, in *The Ecclesiastical History of the English People and Other Selections* (New York, 1967), pp. 371–96. Although Bede titles the work "history," most modern editors call it "lives," to conform to contemporary designation of genre.

4   Judith McClure, "Bede and the Life of Ceolfrid," *Peritia* 3 (1984): 71–84.

5   London, British Library, MS Harley 3020, s. x, transcribed with additions and corrections in Oxford, Bodleian Library, MS Digby 112, s. xii. See Plummer, ed., *Bedae opera historica*, I: cxxxii–cxxxiv, cxl–cxli.

6   The precious transcription gives the original text of which lines 1, 2, and 5 were erased and overwritten after the manuscript arrived on the Continent. See ch. 1 for details on the production of the Codex Amiatinus.

7   Although Dionysius Exiguus (c. 470 – c. 544) is credited with inventing the *Anno Domini* time-reckoning, he did not use it to date historical events but only to fix the date of Easter. The use of AD became dominant after Bede used it for the *HE*. See George Declercq, *Anno Domini: The Origins of the Christian Era* (Turnhout, 2000), esp. pp. 169–88.

8   Plummer helpfully notes parallel passages of the *Hist. Anon.* (=*Vita Ceolfridi*) in the margins of his edition of the *Historia Abbatum* with verbal borrowings placed in italics. It is worth noting that, just as Bede in his biblical commentaries often restates his sources with variations in syntax and structure, he does the same in re-using his own work.

Biscop (Book I, chs. 1–14), which supplements his homiletic eulogy of that dynamic leader.[9] Benedict, descended from noble lineage, "refused to become the father in the flesh of mortal children, being foreordained by Christ to bring up in spiritual learning immortal children for Him in the heavenly life" (ch. 1).[10] In his journeys to Gaul and Rome "he brought back a large number of books relating to the whole of sacred learning" (ch. 4) and founded under King Ecgfrith's auspices the monastery of St. Peter at Wearmouth. He established the rule, distilled from the best of seventeen monasteries he had visited (ch. 11), and obtained a letter of papal sponsorship guaranteeing the monastery's independence. At his request the pope sent his archcantor to teach the monks proper liturgical chant and liturgy. He brought stone masons and glaziers to construct the church, and furnished the church with books, relics, and pictures from the Continent (chs. 6, 9, 11). After dealing with Benedict's life, Bede describes his holy death and his last testament to his monks (chs. 12–14). In this first part of the *Lives* he also intersperses the histories of Benedict's subordinate abbots, Ceolfrith, Eosterwini, and Sigfrid. The eighth chapter, a separate eulogy on Eosterwini, contains a particularly moving account of that nobleman's monastic humility in performing menial tasks.

After a summary chapter of the abbots' lives (ch. 14), Book II constitutes the history of Ceolfrith's reign, emphasizing his own contributions ("He doubled the size of the library for both monasteries," ch. 15) and his piety (ch. 16) before recounting his resignation and the installation of his elected replacement, Bede's coeval Hwætberht. The history ends with Ceolfrith's pious death at Langres on his way to Rome with another reference to the pandect, the Codex Amiatinus, as a gift of homage to the pope.

Significantly, Bede in *The Lives of the Abbots* attributes no miracles to any of the five holy abbots. This could be interpreted as Bede's honest reluctance to ascribe miracles to men whose lives he knew had caused none. But he omits even the modest account of the miraculous apparitions at Ceolfrith's tomb in the last chapter of *Life of Ceolfrith*. Thus he does not make Ceolfrith's afterlife more extraordinary than that of his other abbots. Bede's venture into historical biography in *The Lives of the Abbots* anticipates the later local monastic chronicles, widespread from the eleventh century on, which factually describe the foundation, leadership, patronage, and possessions of abbeys.

The Chronicles

To his treatises, the early *De temporibus* and the later *De temporum ratione*, Bede attached chronicles as final chapters.[11] As a brief summary of major events the chronicle serves as a sort of historical index. Each entry presents a

9 *Opera homiletica 13, In Natale s. Benedicti Biscopi*, CCSL 122, pp. 88–94.
10 Campbell's translation of *The Ecclesiastical History and Other Selections*, p. 372.
11 *Chronica minora*, ed. Jones, CCSL 123C, pp. 601–11; *Chronica maiora*, ed. Jones, CCSL 123B, pp. 461–538.

concise reference to an historical incident, so the chronicle differs from history, which as a literary form has material arranged and developed according to a sustained theme. Both forms, chronicle and history, were bequeathed to the Middle Ages by Eusebius of Caesarea (c. 260 – c. 340). Eusebius's *Chronicle*, based on the time scheme of the Septuagint, was translated intact by Jerome and copied by Isidore. In recording the most important events in what was considered world – that is, Roman and ecclesiastical – history, Bede generally follows the Eusebian-Jerome calculations but revises the overall time scheme according to his reckoning of the six ages of the world, using dates derived from the Vulgate Bible. The earlier chronicle is attached to the *De temporibus*, and like it, it is much briefer than the second version in the *De temporum ratione*. Since the calculation of calendrical time is related to dating, the chronicle of major world events serves as an appendix to the treatises on computus, even though to many, even among the first readers, the chronicles have seemed adventitious to the treatises.[12] So these chapters often circulated as historical records separately from the two treatises to which Bede attached them. The two chronicles themselves display major differences. The first, shorter chronicle attached to the *De temporibus* is structured according to the six ages of the world, subsuming all events under one or other of the ages. The individual entries are usually no more than a half dozen words, all of them culled from earlier sources without explanation, such as the curious "Egypt barks with the error of Dioscorus," from Isidore of Seville;[13] like the earlier work, its dating ends some years before that of the *Chronica maiora*, the longer, more detailed and useful chronicle.[14] Entries for the latter range from three or four lines to more than a dozen.

As Faith Wallis points out, "These chronicles are not a history like the *Ecclesiastical History*; they are universal, not national, and based on *annus mundi* rather than *annus Domini* reckoning."[15] The world-chronicle integrates portions of historical events in Britain and Ireland within world history, particularly the Roman conquest of Britain and the collapse of post-Roman Britain by Irish, Pictish, and Anglo-Saxon onslaughts.[16] However, Bede does not couple events in England with Rome as extensively and integrally as he does in the *Ecclesiastical History*. Although the world-chronicle has entries on Gregory the Great and major English figures such as King Edwin, Abbess Æthelthryth, Cuthbert, Abbot Ceolfrith and the missionaries Willibrord and Egbert, it omits many local persons, such as Abbess Hild, Bishop Chad and

12 Bede, *The Reckoning of Time*, trans. Wallis, p. 363.
13 "Aegyptus errore Dioscuri latrat," Isidore, *Chronica minora*, ed. Th. Mommsen, MGH Auctores antiquissimi, XI, B 247, p. 381, referring to the antipope Dioscurus (d. 530).
14 Bede, *Chronica maiora*, CCSL 123B, pp. 463–544. To envisage how greatly expanded the second chronicle is over the first, compare the two as printed in parallel in Mommsen's edition (MGH, Auctores antiquissimi, XIII, pp. 247–327).
15 Bede, *The Reckoning of Time*, trans. Wallis, p. lxviii.
16 See Diarmuid Scully, "Bede's *Chronica maiora*: Early Insular History in a Universal Context," in *Anglo-Saxon/Irish Relations before the Vikings, Proceedings of the Royal Irish Academy/ British Academy Symposium, London, 12th–14th October 2005* (London, forthcoming), pp. 1–29.

even Bishop Wilfrid, and many Anglo-Saxon events, such as the Irish mission to Northumbria, that are included in the *Ecclesiastical History*.

After the last entries, for the year 4679, recalling Ceolfrith's pilgrimage and demise, and 4680, recording the Saracen invasions, the *Chronica maiora* has additional theological chapters concerning the end of the sixth age, the time of the Second Coming, the arrival of Antichrist, and beyond world-time the seventh and eighth ages. The addition of this eschatological element to the world chronicle became traditional after Bede. As Friedrich Ohly points out:

> For almost thirteen centuries, the genre of the world chronicle, richly represented in over a hundred works from Orosius (AD 417) to the end of the seventeenth century, usually started with the Creation and then proceeded to follow the progress of the six ages of the world. From the time of Bede, who was stimulated by Augustine, to Hartmann Schedel (AD 1493) and down to the seventeenth century, it was customary to close the chronicle with the end of history in the eschatology to which Otto von Freising, Joachim di Fiore, and Vincent de Beauvais – to name just three of the more well-known figures among many others in the East and West – had paid especial attention.[17]

By insisting on the open-ended date of the end of the world ("To be sure, all the saints wait attentively for the hour of His coming and long for it to arrive quickly. But they behave rather dangerously if any of them presumes to speculate or to teach that this [hour] is near at hand or far off"),[18] Bede also confutes the belief that ages of the world are exactly 1000 year-days each. In this he agrees with Augustine, who posited the humanly indeterminate seventh age as the Church Expectant.[19] For dating in the chronicles Bede follows Isidore's scheme of the *annus mundi* (the year of the world according to biblical reckoning) and indictions, which apply to "the continuity and pattern of general providence throughout time," that is, throughout the history of the world from its inception, rather than to "the particular providence of God with regard to the English," in the Christian era of *The Ecclesiastical History*.[20]

---

[17] Friedrich Ohly, *Sensus Spiritualis*, ed. Samuel P. Jaffe, trans. Kenneth J. Northcott (Chicago, 2005), p. 37.

[18] Bede, *The Reckoning of Time*, trans. Wallis, ch. 68, pp. 240–41.

[19] See Bede, *The Reckoning of Time*, trans. Wallis, commentary on chs. 66–71, pp. 353–75. Wallis, while giving an accurate account of the two heterodox beliefs, unfortunately labels them chiliasm and millenarianism, but the two terms are usually understood as synonyms (with only an etymological – Greek vs. Latin – difference).

[20] Bede, *The Reckoning of Time*, trans. Wallis, p. lxx, pp. 357–58. Bede discusses the AD years of the Lord's Incarnation in ch. 47 of *De temporum ratione*, ed. Jones, CCSL 123B, pp. 427–33; Wallis, trans., pp. 126–29; see also n. 7 above.

The Ecclesiastical History of the English People

"The history of the Church of our island and race, in five books" (*HE*, V. 24). Bede, *Ecclesiastical History of the English People*, ed. Bertram Colgrave and R. A. B. Mynors, Oxford, 1969; *Storia degli Inglesi (Historia ecclesiastica gentis Anglorum)*, ed. Michael Lapidge, trans. di Paolo Chiesa, vol. 1 (Milan, 2008).

With a brief entry Bede lists his famed masterwork that has provided posterity with the only link – although a superb one – for much about England in its earliest history. Bede constructs a national identity that sets the norm for medieval English history; he writes of England as a nation from the very first chapter rather than of a particular ethnic or regional group, even though as a Northumbrian his emphasis is on that area. The work is so beautifully crafted with its overall thematic structure and use of selected evidence and chronology that it has shaped historiography not only of England but also of the Western world. It was immensely successful from the outset. A multitude of extant manuscripts from the Middle Ages (over 150), both in England and on the Continent, indicate its early renown.[21] Since the Renaissance it has often been printed, edited: quite well by John Smith (d. 1715) published by his son (1722), using the Moore manuscript, still better by Plummer in the splendid – although not making use of the eighth-century St. Petersburg (formerly Leningrad) Bede manuscript – scholarly edition, of 1896,[22] and then by Mynors with Colgrave in 1969, incorporating the St. Petersburg manuscript readings. Now it is being edited superbly by Michael Lapidge (volume 1, Books I–II, in 2008), who in the introduction has provided a detailed and carefully argued relationship of the early manuscripts of the *History*, and has established the transmission of the text. The Moore manuscript (Cambridge University Library Kk. 5. 16 = M) is close to Bede's autograph; the St. Petersburg (*olim* Leningrad, Publichnaja Biblioteka Q. v. I. 18) and British Library (London, British Library, Cotton Tiberius A. XIV) are once removed *via* a lost exemplar from the archive of Wearmouth-Jarrow. The Kassel manuscript (Kassel, Gesamthochschulbibliothek, Qu. Theol. 2), with the closely related British Library (London, British Library, Cotton Tiberius C. II) and Oxford (Bodleian Library, Hatton 43) manuscripts, form a third group. The latter group, called the c-type recension, originated from

---

[21] "The popularity of the *HE* on the European Continent is very striking and makes the view sometimes expressed, that this work interested only the English, look very foolish," remarks Laistner, *Hand-List*, p. 94. To the 159 manuscripts of the whole work listed by Laistner, pp. 94–102, should now be added at least half a dozen more. Joshua Westgard is now compiling a more accurate and complete survey. See also David Dumville, "The Two Earliest Manuscripts of Bede's *Ecclesiastical History?*" *Anglo-Saxon* 1 (2007): 55–108.

[22] In *Opera historica*. When Mynors described the codex in 1969, p. xlv, St. Petersburg still had its Revolutionary name of Leningrad (1924–1991).

a redaction at Canterbury, brought there most likely by Albinus or Nothelm, who received the copy from Bede in 731 or perhaps 732.[23]

Numerous editions have preceded those of Plummer, Mynors, and Lapidge. The *History* has also been translated and commented upon many times.[24] The text constantly challenges medievalists to analyze, augment, revise, correct, or validate Plummer's commentary and those of subsequent editors, though it would prove difficult to fault any of Lapidge's work. Although our world-view and historiography differ from Bede's, the grounds for this interest and re-evaluation are apparent to every serious student of the Middle Ages.

The title of the work tells us what in fact it actually is, an ecclesiastical history. It is not like the classical histories of Herodotus, Thucydides, Livy, Caesar, or Tacitus; indeed, there is no evidence that Bede or his contemporaries even knew those ancient historians. Rather, it belongs to the genre and tradition established by Rufinus's translation of Eusebius's *Ecclesiastical History*.[25] In technique as in content, ecclesiastical history differs from pagan historiography, which frequently uses fictional quotations and data to arrive at verisimilitude; however, it too has its conventions. An ecclesiastical history, based on biblical rather than classical concepts of time and event, presupposes a theocentric universe in which primary concern is focused on the sacred, and the secular is understood in terms of the sacred. Like Eusebius Bede includes documents and gives references to sources. Bede's *History* traces the development of the church through conversion and the spread of the faith as it advances in time and geography to "the ends of the earth" (Acts 1: 8) and finishes on a guardedly optimistic note, without emphasizing the troubles and problems described in his admonitory *Letter to Bishop Egbert*.[26]

Although in the *History* Bede shows special admiration for some persons, such as Bishop Cuthbert and King Oswald, throughout his narrative he demonstrates an objectivity and balance that made him an ideal model for the historians of the twelfth century and later. Bede gives even-handed and sober

---

[23] Michael Lapidge, ed., *Storia degli Inglesi (Historia ecclesiastica gentis Anglorum)*, vol. 1 (Milan, 2008), "Introduzione," ch. 2, "Per un'edizione critica," pp. XCIV–CXXVI.

[24] For an excellent survey of preceding editions see Lapidge, *Storia degli Inglesi*, ch. 3, "Edizioni precedenti," pp. CXVI–CXXVI.

[25] See Arnaldo Momigliano, "Pagan and Christian Historiography in the Fourth Century AD," in *The Conflict between Paganism and Christianity in the Fourth Century*, ed. Momigliano (Oxford, 1963), pp. 79–99; J. Campbell, "Bede," in *Latin Historians*, ed. T. A. Dorey (London, 1966), pp. 159–90 at 162–65; R. A. Markus, *Bede and the Tradition of Ecclesiastical Historiography*, Jarrow Lecture 1975, rpt. in *Bede and his World*, ed. Lapidge, I: 385–403.

[26] *Epistola Bede ad Ecgbertum episcopum*, in *Opera historica*, ed. Plummer, I: 404–23; trans. McClure and Collins, *Bede's Letter to Egbert*, in Bede, *The Ecclesiastical History of the English People, The Greater Chronicle, Bede's Letter to Egbert* (Oxford, 1994), pp. 343–57; for more on the Letter see above, Ch. 2. For a complete guide to the *HE* the reader is encouraged to refer to the full text along with the fine notes of Plummer, ed., *Baedae opera historica*, supplemented by J. M. Wallace-Hadrill's *Historical Commentary* (Oxford, 1988), and the translation by McClure and Collins, which incorporates much of Wallace-Hadrill's commentary in the notes. On some details N. J. Higham's *(Re-) Reading Bede* (London, 2006) is also helpful.

treatment to historical personages: with both his generosity and restraint in the presentation of bishops who pursued different ideals and models, such as Cuthbert and Wilfrid; of princes with good and bad qualities, such as Edwin and Oswiu; and with his judicious selectivity of events and balanced structure. "Bede's account of the Church in the *Ecclesiastical History*," writes James Campbell, "is distinguished by great discretion. ... He clearly did not think it appropriate to enlarge on the deficiencies of the clergy in a work such as the *Ecclesiastical History* which was intended for a fairly wide audience."[27] The vast majority of modern historians, following Plummer, such as Mayr-Harting, Bonner, Meyvaert, Wallace-Hadrill, Bullough, and a host of others, see Bede as an ideal ecclesiastical historian writing with the charity and prudence he so extolled in his theological works. However, a few contemporary historians, such as Goffart and Higham, see in Bede's method a subtle manipulation of facts, and the use of guile for the purpose, according to Goffart, of denigrating Wilfrid and his party and advancing the Cuthbertan Northumbrians.[28]

In the preface Bede expressly defines his work as an ecclesiastical history "gentis Anglorum" ["of the English people"], which marks it off from Eusebian universal history because it presents local history within world history. He signals his intention to record the history of one people (nationhood was an operative concept only later in the Middle Ages), as Gregory of Tours did in the *History of the Franks*. Bede's accomplishment of melding Eusebian historiography with local history stands in sharp contrast to Gregory's "untidy and unreflexive" record.[29] In showing that the English Church developed according to the Eusebian model, Bede sees the people of England, and especially of his beloved Northumbria, as one of God's chosen tribes.[30] Following the lead of Gregory the Great, Bede refers to the whole race as "Angli." As Patrick Wormald notes:

> Bede, as it happens, was himself an Angle. But that is not why he wrote about a *'gens Anglorum.'* Among the various English churches whom he thanked in his preface for their guidance, Canterbury was clearly pre-eminent; and his conception of the 'Angles' was that of the Canterbury church and of its papal founder. But behind Bede's vision of the English lurked a deeper and weightier inspiration. He came to the writing of his own people's history after a lifetime

---

[27] James Campbell, "Bede," in *Latin Historians*, ed. T. A. Dorey (London, 1966), pp. 159–90 at 176–77; see also Clare Stancliffe, "Cuthbert and the Polarity between Pastor and Solitary," pp. 21–44 at 27 and 33.

[28] Walter Goffart, *The Narrators of Barbarian History (AD550–800): Jordanes, Gregory of Tours, Bede, and Paul the Deacon* (Guildford, 1988), pp. 235–328.

[29] *The Oxford Dictionary of the Christian Church*, ed. F. L. Cross and E. A. Livingstone (Oxford, 1997), p. 714.

[30] While Bede refers to the whole race as "Angli," many others afterwards, including Boniface and Alcuin continued to use the name "Saxones"; however, Bede's authority ultimately fixed the name in perpetuity. See Michael Richter, "Bede's *Angli*: Angles or English?" *Peritia* 3 (1984): 99–114.

of studying that of Israel as told in the Old Testament. The pattern of God's dealings with his original Chosen People remains Bede's underlying theme.[31]

Bede was sensitive to the remoteness of his country geographically and temporally from the Mediterranean centers of Christianity, Jerusalem and Rome; but he is asserting in his history that in these days the converted English, whom he calls "our people" in the letter to Abbot Albinus,[32] are a tribe of the new Israel even at the ends of the earth.

The preface to the *History* is, like much of Bede's writing, at once conventional and quite original. It is constructed of exordial topoi that entered Christian historiography from classical literature: it addresses a leader with a formula of submission by which a subject presents himself as a servant (*famulus*) seeking his benevolence, artfully intermixed with a devotional formula, *famulus Christi*.[33] However, in the salutation the immediate juxtaposition of the names of King Ceolwulf and of Bede, "Gloriosissimo regi Ceouulfo Beda famulus Christi et presbyter," as well as the personal if formal tone that follows, places the "servant" Bede on a level of authoritative equality with or even superiority to that of the royal recipient.[34] Drawing on other topoi to his purpose, Bede expresses in the preface the moral usefulness of history, and then turns to his readers, requesting with authorial modesty their indulgence.

The greater part of this extensive preface is taken up with the acknowledgement of sources. In this Bede goes far beyond the conventional appeal to compelling witnesses. As in his commentaries on the gospels, and in remarkable contrast to the practice of other early medieval authors, Bede is at pains to list his authorities with their credentials. However, for the remoter background information on the history of the Church in England,

---

31 Patrick Wormald, "*Engla Lond*: The Making of of an Allegiance," *Journal of Historical Sociology* 7: 1 (March 1994): 1–24 at 14.

32 Bede refers to his "ecclesiastica gentis nostrae historia," in his "Letter to Albinus." Plummer, ed., *Bedae opera historica*, I: 3, first published by Jean Mabillon in his *Vetera Analecta* (Paris, 1723) from a now-lost manuscript. Perhaps the exiguous transcription history led McClure and Collins to doubt the letter's authenticity (Bede, *Ecclesiastical History*, p. 359), even though the letter is so characteristically Bedan in style and content. Now Joshua Westgard has discovered manuscript copies of the letter in manuscripts of Bede's *De Templo*, between the prologue and the main text. The letter tells us something of Bede's publishing procedures: he says he sent out drafts, *schedulae*, for verification and correction, then a fair copy, *membranulae*, for final approval and copying. Since the manuscript was publicized and copied in various degrees of revision, different versions, or editions, naturally ensued. See Bede, *Opera historica*, ed. Plummer, II, 1–2; Levison, "Bede as Historian," in *Bede: His Life, Times and Writings*, ed. Thompson, p. 128; and especially Meyvaert, "Medieval Notions of Publication," *Journal of Medieval Latin* 12 (2002): 78–89 at 80–81.

33 On exordial topoi see Roger Ray, "Bede's *Vera lex historiae*," *Speculum* 55 (1980): 1–21 at 11–12 and n. 51. For Bede's artful collocation of a "formula of submission" with a "devotional formula," see Calvin Kendall, "Bede's *Historia Ecclesiastica*: The Rhetoric of Faith," in J. J. Murphy, ed., *Medieval Eloquence: Studies in the Theory and Practice of Medieval Rhetoric* (Los Angeles and Berkeley, 1978), pp. 145–72, at 152.

34 Such an egalitarian stance has led some to surmise that Bede was nobly born. On Bede's "self-positioning" see Higham, *(Re-)Reading Bede*, pp. 11–12.

that is, for the period from the beginnings up to the arrival of Augustine, Bede remarks only that he got the "material from here and there, chiefly from the writings of earlier writers."[35] So for Book I, chapters 1–22, Bede fashions this historical prelude from neatly assembled bits from late antique and British authorities: Pliny, Solinus, Orosius, Eutropius, Vegetius, Basil, Prosper, the *Liber Pontificalis*, the lives of St. Alban and of St. Germanus, and especially the invective *De excidio Britanniae* by the Romano-British Gildas.[36] For the period from the conversion to the present (particularly the recent past), Bede is more explicit about his sources of information. Such a procedure makes sense even to a modern reader: the preliminary material is treated as common knowledge derived from traditional authorities; but the core of the history is verified by certified sources. These sources, written and oral, include: for Canterbury, Kent, and relations with Rome and with English sees, Abbot Albinus through the intermediary of Nothelm from London, who examined the archives in Rome as well; for the West Saxons, South Saxons, and Wight, Bishop Daniel; for Mercia and the East Saxons, the monks of Lastingham; for East Anglia, oral and written tradition and Abbot Esi; for Lindsey, Bishop Cynebehrt and others; for Northumbria, "the faithful testimony of innumerable witnesses" and the lives (his own and the anonymous) of St. Cuthbert. As Bede summarizes at the end of the *History* (5. 24) the material was assembled "either from ancient documents or from tradition or from my own knowledge."[37] But the result is totally his own art.

Bede concludes his summary of sources with a plea: "I humbly implore the reader that he not impute it to me if in what I have written he finds anything other than the truth. For, in accordance with a true law of history (*uera lex historiae*), I have tried to set down in simple style what I have collected from common report, for the instruction of posterity."[38] The loaded phrase, *uera lex historiae*, which Bede also used in his commentary on Luke 2: 33–34,[39] means that in human history, as opposed to theological revelation, common perception is a valid criterion. Although he has tried to use only trustworthy data, he has of necessity had to rely on much oral tradition and hearsay for which he cannot be held unreasonably accountable; the probable truth of the material urges its inclusion.[40]

In the last paragraph of the preface Bede points out that what he has recorded for the various provinces should be pleasing, "grata," to their inhabitants.

---

35 *HE*, Preface, pp. 4–5.
36 On Bede's sources, see *HE*, p. xxxi; Campbell, "Bede," pp. 163–64; Levison, "Bede as Historian," pp. 134–37.
37 *HE*, pp. 566–67.
38 *HE*, pp. 6–7.
39 Bede, *In Lucae ev.*, I, 2: 33–34, CCSL 120, lines 1905–12.
40 Bede takes the term "uera lex historiae" from Jerome, who uses it in his defense against Helvidius concerning the Evangelists' calling Joseph the father of Jesus, asserting that they were simply "expressing the common opinion, which is the true law of history." See Walter Goffart, "Bede's *uera lex historiae* Explained," *ASE* 34 (2005): 11–16; Roger Ray, "Bede's *vera lex historiae*," *Speculum* 55 (1980): 1–21.

This is consonant with the generally positive thrust of the narrative, which includes frequent interspersion of pleasing story and anecdote with historical record. It is nonetheless clear from the narrative and architectonic thrust of the *History* that the main aim of the whole work is to expound the development of God's plan for the English as a chosen people and the development of one unified Church in a violent and feuding land. It tells of the coming of the faith to the beautiful but remote island described in chapter 1, of the failures of the Britons to missionize the Anglo-Saxons but the successes of the Roman missionaries, of the Anglo-Saxon church's progress and its setbacks, and of its present positive but not entirely roseate position.

The only work of Bede honoring a layman, the *History* is clearly intended for an educated lay as well as a clerical audience. The dedication to the prince presages one important thematic interest in the *History*, that of royal conduct.[41] It carefully records the succession and genealogy of kings. It is in part an early form of the mirror for princes, so prominent in the later Middle Ages and Renaissance. In his accounts of the careers of Æthelbert, Edwin, St. Oswald, Oswiu, Oswine, Sigebert of the East Saxons, Cenwealh of Wessex, and others, Bede illustrates the role of Christian kings, to protect and defend their people and the Church, to observe its teachings, and to foster it. He shows how rulers prosper when observing Christian law and virtue, and how the Church avails them and they the Church. The earthly power of Edwin and Oswald magnified after their conversion (II. 9 and III. 6), and Oswiu and Aldfrith because of their faith overpowered superior forces in war (III. 24). Bede also provides negative examples of divine retribution for royal infidelity and backsliding. But Bede is a Christian monk who knows from the psalms and prophets that the wicked often prosper in this life as a test of faith and as penance for sins, so the narrative of royal events is not naively or perversely skewed to fit a simple thesis of virtue immediately rewarded in this life. Virtue is not always to a king's earthly advantage as the prophecy of St. Aidan shows: as King Oswine humbled himself before Aidan, he exclaimed "I know the king will not live long; for I never before saw a humble king; therefore I think he will very soon be snatched from this life; for this nation does not deserve to have such a ruler" (III. 14).

If Bede intended the *History* to serve at least in part as a *speculum principis* for King Ceolwulf and other Anglo-Saxon rulers, why did he write it in Latin, the language of the Church and not of the laity? The answer in part is that Ceolwulf like his predecessor Aldfrith, whom Bede calls "most

---

41 On this theme see N. J. Higham, *(Re-)Reading Bede*, pp. 131–34; James Campbell, *Bede's Reges et Principes*, Jarrow Lecture 1979, and his "Bede" in *Latin Historians*, ed. T. A. Dorey (London, 1966), pp. 168–72; J. M. Wallace-Hadrill, "Bede," in *Early Germanic Kingship in England and on the Continent* (Oxford, 1971), pp. 72–97, and his "Gregory of Tours and Bede: Their Views on the Personal Qualities of Kings," *Frühmittelalterliche Studien* 2 (1968): 31–44; Hans-Joachim Diesner, "Incarnationsjahre, 'Militia Christi' und anglische Königsporträts bei Beda Venerabilis," *Mittellateinisches Jarhbuch* 16 (1981): 17–34; Antonia Gransden, *Historical Writing in England c. 550 to c. 1307* (Ithaca, 1975), pp. 13–28.

learned in all respects" (V. 12), had received education in Latin, the common language of culture in Europe. Bede sent advance drafts of the *History* to Ceolwulf for his perusal and criticism, as he had done for Abbot Albinus. Furthermore, after a reign "filled with so many and such serious commotions and setbacks" that Bede was unwilling as he finished the *History* to predict the results (V. 23), Ceolwulf retired as a monk to Lindisfarne in 737. That fact does not necessarily bespeak his literacy, but it does associate him with the culture of literacy.

Another reason why Bede wrote the *Historia* in Latin is that it also, and in greater part, is directed to the clergy in the language of the Church, as the correspondence with Abbot Albinus of Canterbury reveals. As an ecclesiastical history, it is in large measure about the clergy and their activity. It catalogues and discusses episcopal succession (II. 3–9). It not only describes the work of saintly prelates such as Gregory the Great, Augustine of Canterbury, Paulinus, and Theodore, but also adroitly includes the chequered career of Wilfrid.[42] Walter Goffart has argued that Bede artfully composed the *History* to counter Wilfrid's power and his partisans by diluting Wilfrid's prestige and ideally counterpoising the Northumbrian monastic clergy, such as John of Hexham, Aidan, and especially Cuthbert.[43] Cuthbert was already eulogized by Bede in his prose life, a saint who was both monk and prelate, Irish in training but Roman in his respect for the Rule of Benedict and the reckoning of the date of Easter. He stands as a model for the clergy as Oswald does for the lay leader. On the other hand, Bede is obviously too sincere in his honoring Wilfrid's disciple and Bede's diocesan, Aidan, to be condemning all of Wilfrid's clergy. Bede has words of unfeigned praise for other prelates trained by Wilfrid, such as Chad (IV. 3), and indeed for Wilfrid himself as loyal spokesman for Roman Catholicism at the Synod of Whitby and even as a missionary during his exile from his see (IV. 13). It is clear, on the other hand, that Bede sees in the humble and dedicated pastoral apostles of the Lindisfarne model the ideal for the English church. These apostles exemplify the Acts of the Apostles and Pope Gregory's *Pastoral Care* better than do the lives of the grand potentates such as Wilfrid, who accumulate power, wealth, and territory. True to his monastic and didactic vocation, Bede honors the pastoral apostolate in the *History* and especially in his *Letter to Egbert*, while in the *History* holding up as moral incentives the examples of good and bad for both cleric and layman (Preface, *Historia*).

The five books trace the history of England and the English chronologically, except for some necessary displacements and backtracking for historical

---

[42] On Bede's complex attitude toward Wilfrid, see N. J. Higham, *(Re-)Reading Bede*, pp. 64–66, taking issue with Walter Goffart, *The Narrators of Barbarian History (AD 550–800): Jordanes, Gregory of Tours, Bede, and Paul the Deacon* (Guildford, 1988), pp. 235–328.

[43] Walter Goffart, *Narrators of Barbarian History*, pp. 235–328, and his two subsequent articles, "The *Historia Ecclesiastica*: Bede's Agenda and Ours," *Haskins Society Journal* 2 (1990): 29–45, and "Bede's History in a Harsher Climate," in *Innovations and Tradition in the Writings of the Venerable Bede*, ed. Scott DeGregorio (Morgantown, 2006), pp. 203–26.

narrative, thematic groupings, and concurrent events and personages of the different kingdoms. Bede deftly inserts short biographies into the chronological narrative, usually in the form of a summary memorial after recording the person's death. Although as the most reliable and practiced chronographer of his age Bede strives for accuracy about dates, times, and events, he sometimes makes a mistake. He had to work with a vast quantity of unmanageable, lacunose, and discordant oral and written records, variously dated by memory and disparate regnal and indictional records. The marvel is that he got so much right and set so much straight.[44]

The first three books deal primarily with the Christianization of the English; the last two books describe the way in which the Christian life developed among them. Although each of the books is about equal in size, the first book sweeps through 650 years, whereas each of the remaining four covers about a generation. Each of the books and its parts manifests an artistic organizational symmetry. Following the account of the triumphant Synod of Whitby in Book III, the events of Book IV, as Benedicta Ward and Scott DeGregorio have noted, present the vibrant proselytizing developments in the English church.[45] Book V presents the positive results of the apostolate, with missionizing in Germany, fruitful preaching among the South and West Saxons and the establishment of bishops, Abbot Ceolfrith's sending church builders to the king of the Picts, and the monks of Iona and their subject monasteries' accepting the Roman canonical dating of Easter through the instruction of the Irish monk Ecgbert. Historians have noticed, however, that Bede discusses the recent past much more completely than his own immediate period. Although he deals with his own times to some extent in his troubled Letter to Bishop Ecgbert, he seems reluctant to explore some of the contemporary negative issues in a work that sets out to express the theme of the victorious Christianization in Britain, optimistically climaxed in the last chapter, V. 23.

Besides ordering his material chronologically and geographically, Bede also arranges it in clusters by association with a certain person, place, or event. For instance, as Donald Fry has observed, "Bede's *Ecclesiastical History* contains fifty-one miracles, most of them grouped into clusters, usually around a person, such as Cuthbert, a subgenre, such as visions of hell,

---

44 On chronological and factual errors detectable in *HE* see Campbell, "Bede," in *Latin Historians*, ed. Dorey, pp. 165–67; D. P. Kirby, "Bede and Northumbrian Chronology," *English Historical Review* 78 (1963): 514–27, and his "Bede's Native Sources for the *Historia Ecclesiastica*," *Bulletin of the John Rylands Library* 48 (1966): 341–71; Patrick Sims-Williams, "The Settlement of England in Bede and the *Chronicle*," *ASE* 12 (1983): 1–41. On the other hand, Kenneth Harrison in *The Framework of Anglo-Saxon History to AD 900* (Cambridge, 1976), pp. 76–98, examines Bede's dating and concludes, p. 96, that "the main sequence of dates from 596 to 729 appears to be reliable and free of systematic error."

45 Benedicta Ward, *The Venerable Bede* (Kalamazoo, 1998), p. 124; DeGregorio, "Literary Contexts," pp. 75–76.

or a place, such as the double monastery at Barking."[46] Within the clusters, Bede unifies by use of particular images and symbols. Thus in the Barking series (V. 7–11), he unifies by "complicated patterns of diction and imagery invoking light and fearful confinement."

Book I first provides the geographical and historical background for the coming of the Anglo-Saxons, their arrival as mercenaries to assist the British and remaining as the Britons' masters (I. 15), and the neglect on the part of the indigenous corrupt Celts to missionize them.[47] "Nevertheless God in his goodness did not reject the people whom he foreknew" (I. 22), so Pope Gregory sent Augustine to win the English for Christ (I. 23–26). The English are saved not by imperial Rome but by papal Rome. As Diarmuid Scully points out, Bede in contrast to Orosius and Gildas, "locates Rome's greatness not in its imperial past but in its petrine present as the capital of Christ's empire on earth."[48] The long chapter containing the purportedly verbatim responses of Gregory to Augustine's pastoral questions reveals Bede's respect for his documentary sources, especially those by the ecclesiastical hero of the Anglo-Saxon Church, Pope Gregory; Bede does not correct even obvious grammatical errors in the Canterbury copy of the *Libellus responsionum*.[49] Book I does not end with an account of the spread of Christianity in southeastern England and the deaths of the first archbishop of Canterbury, Augustine, and his first abbot, Peter (ch. 33); rather, it ends with a chapter on the career of the pagan king, Æthelfrith of Northumbria (ch. 34). Through its exultant tone that comes close to the bravura of *The Battle of Brunanburh* and through its biblical allusion to King Saul ("but with this exception, that Æthelfrith was ignorant of the divine religion"), the chapter combines the Old Testament militarism of the Book of Joshua and the Old English heroic boast: "No ruler or king had subjected more land to the English race or settled it, having first exterminated or conquered the natives." It concludes with the vaunt, "From that time no Irish king in Britain has dared to make war on the English race to this day" (I. 34). The book thus comes to a close about the year 605 with the initial spiritual conquest of the English by the

---

46 Donald K. Fry, "Bede Fortunate in his Translator: The Barking Nuns," in *Studies in Earlier Old English Prose*, ed. Paul E. Szarmach (Albany, NY, 1986), pp. 345–62 at 345–46.

47 See *HE*, II. 22, pp. 204–5, and V. 22, pp. 554–55; Barbara Yorke, "Anglo-Saxon Origin Legends," in *Myth, Rulership, Church and Charters*, ed. Julia Barrow and Andrew Wareham (Aldershot, 2008), pp. 15–29. T. M. Charles-Edwards, "Bede, the Irish and the Britons," *Celtica* 15 (1983): 42–52, on Bede's hostility to the Britons for failing to preach to the Anglo-Saxons and Bede's sympathy for the Irish for preaching to them, even though they initally were in error on Easter dating; Higham, *(Re-)Reading Bede*, pp. 134–42.

48 Diarmuid Scully, "Bede, Orosius and Gildas on the Early History of Britain," in *Bède le Vénérable entre Tradition et Postérité*, ed. S. Lebecq, M. Perrin, O. Szerwiniack (Lille, 2005), pp. 31–42 at 42.

49 See Paul Meyvaert, "Bede's Text of the *Libellus responsionum* of Gregory the Great to Augustine of Canterbury," in *England before the Conquest: Studies in Primary Sources Presented to Dorothy Whitelock*, ed. P. Clemoes and K. Hughes (Cambridge, 1971), pp. 15–73. On Bede's respect for Gregory see Meyvaert, *Bede and Gregory the Great*, Jarrow Lecture 1964, both reprinted in *Benedict, Gregory, Bede and Others* (London, 1977), selections VIII and X.

missionaries and the physical overthrow of the Irish by a Northumbrian king, anticipating the expansive Northumbrian history in the next books.

In the first chapter of Book II, at the end of the short biography of Gregory the Great done in loving tribute to that monastic pope for his service to the English Church, Bede adds the legend about the pope and the English slave boys, in which the Angles are described as having "the face of angels" (II. 1). The famous account of the conversion of King Edwin takes up chapters 9–14, including, in chapter 13, the tale of the self-seeking pagan high priest Coifi, whose cynical speech is matched by a counselor's famous words comparing man's life to the flight of a sparrow flying swiftly through the hall from and then into the winter storm. King Edwin, "with all the nobles of his race and a vast number of the common people," agrees to be baptized (II. 14). Afterwards Edwin proselytizes by converting Eorpwold of the East Angles to the faith (II. 15). But the book ends negatively at the year 633, with Edwin falling in battle against Cædwalla, and Paulinus, who had converted Edwin and the Northumbrians, having to flee from the North with Edwin's queen, Æthelburh. A positive note is sounded even here, by the report of Paulinus's becoming bishop of Rochester (II. 20).

Book III treats mainly the subsequent development of the Church in Northumbria under Irish influence. But first chapter 2 narrates how King Oswald erected a large cross at Heavenfield and commanded his army to kneel and pray before it. Then, although greatly outnumbered, he advanced victoriously on Caedwalla, "the abominable leader of the Britons together with the immense force which he boasted was irresistible," who had slain Edwin and his successors, the apostate kings Osric of the Deiri and Eanfrith of the Bernicians (III. 1). Although Bede does not expressly call attention to the typology, the reader of Christian history cannot but notice the similarity drawn between Oswald and the battlefield cross and Constantine and the vision of the cross before the battle at the Milvian bridge – the event in 312 that led to the conversion of the Roman Empire to Christianity. Chapter III tells how the saintly King Oswald asked the Irish elders for a bishop and received Aidan from Iona to become bishop of Lindisfarne (III. 3). Chapters 25 and 26, however, describe the rejection of the Iona-Lindisfarne Irish tradition when the Roman-Canterbury faction, under the youthful leadership of the eloquent Wilfrid, triumphed over the Irish at the Council of Whitby, settling the questions of Easter reckoning and of the style of clerical tonsure, bonding the English Church with the Continent and Rome.[50]

The first part of Book IV recounts Archbishop Theodore's apostolate of great consequence, in 668: "he was the first of the archbishops whom the whole English Church consented to obey" (IV. 2). He and his abbot Hadrian purveyed learning "in sacred and secular literature" at Canterbury, giving Latin and Greek "instruction not only in the books of holy Scripture but

---

[50] On the importance of the issue of correct clerical tonsure, see Edward James, "Bede and the Tonsure Question," *Peritia* 3 (1984): 85–98.

also in the art of meter, astronomy, and ecclesiastical computation" (IV. 2). Theodore, despite his advanced age, energetically organized the Church, conducted official visitations, held the important synods of Hertford (IV. 5) and Hatfield (IV. 15), and brought about peace between the warring kings Ecgfrith and Æthelred.

Chapter 23 (earlier version, chapter 21)[51] tells about the royal lady Hild, who became the abbess of the double monastery of men and women at Whitby, a superior so successful in training and fostering the religious life that five from her establishment became bishops. And she was politically potent. She was Archbishop Theodore's formidable confederate against the ambitious Wilfrid.[52] In chapter 24 (22) Bede relates the precious story about her subject, the herdsman Cædmon, who was originally so intimidated by poetic recitation that he fled the hall to avoid it but following the empowering command of a visitor in his dream became the first known Anglo-Saxon *scop*. Cædmon's first little poem in Old English has been inserted in the margins of the Latin text in a number of early manuscripts of the *Historia*. Literary historians have analyzed Cædmon's verse for what it can tell us about oral composition, poetic rumination – "like some clean animal chewing the cud" – and Old English versification (IV. 24).[53] Bede provides a Latin paraphrase with the perceptive note: "This is the sense but not the order of the words which he sang as he slept; for it is not possible to translate verse, however well composed, literally from one language to another without detriment to

---

[51] The present chapter numbering of Book IV, 15–30, is the result of dividing the original chapters in German manuscripts of the ninth century, and thence into the printed editions. So I give the earlier chapter numbers in parentheses. See textual note c in *HE*, p. 380; *Baedae opera historica*, ed. Plummer, I: xciv.

[52] Since Bede is the major (and sometimes only) source of information about the important aristocratic abbesses such as Hild and Ælfflaed of Whitby and of their contributions to Anglo-Saxon ecclesiatical history, it seems ironic that contemporary feminist historians such as Stephanie Hollis, Clare Lees and Gillian Overing blame him severely for marginalizing or limiting his report of these women. On the other hand, Sarah Foot and Barbara Yorke acknowledge Bede's greatly positive contribution to the history of Anglo-Saxon women, abbesses and nuns. See Stephanie Hollis, *Anglo-Saxon Women and the Church* (Woodbridge, 1992); Clare A. Lees and Gillian R. Overing, "Birthing Bishops and Fathering Poets: Bede, Hild, and the Relations of Cultural Production," *Exemplaria* 6.1 (Spring 1994): 35–64; and, for the opposing assessment, Sarah Foot, *Veiled Women*, 2 vols. (Aldershot, 2000), esp. I: 20–21; Barbara Yorke, *Nunneries and the Anglo-Saxon Royal Houses* (London, 2003), chs. 1–2. See also Joan Nicholson, "*Feminae gloriosae*: Women in the Age of Bede," in *Medieval Women*, ed. Derek Baker (Oxford, 1978), pp. 15–29; and David Pelteret, "Bede's Women," in *Women, Marriage and Family in Medieval Christendom*, ed. Constance M. Rousseau and Joel T. Rosenthal (Kalamazoo, 1998), pp. 19–46.

[53] Bruce Holdinger, "The Parable of Caedmon's Hymn: Liturgical Invention and Literary Tradition," *JEGP* 106 (2007): 149–75 (which is excellent except for a misunderstanding of Anglo-Saxon poetic meter); Daniel Paul O'Donnell, *Cædmon's Hymn: A Multimedia Study, Archive, and Edition*, with cd-rom (Cambridge, 2005); Allen Frantzen and John Hines, eds., *Cædmon's Hymn and Material Culture in the World of Bede: Six Essays* (Morgantown, 2007); Stanley B. Greenfield and Daniel Calder, *A New Critical History of Old English Literature* (New York, 1986), pp. 227–31. On rumination see Gernot Wieland, "Caedmon, the Clean Animal," *American Benedictine Review* 35 (1984): 194–203; André Crépin, "Bede and the Vernacular," in *Famulus Christi*, ed. Bonner, pp. 172–73; Philip J. West, "Ruminations in Bede's Account of Cædmon," *Monastic Studies* 12 (1976): 217–36.

its beauty and dignity" (IV. 24). Bede anticipates by centuries the saying by Robert Frost, "Poetry is what gets lost in translation." Cædmon afterwards spent the rest of his life composing Old English poems about biblical and doctrinal themes.

Bede devotes the last chapters of Book IV, chapters 27–30, to the monk and bishop Cuthbert. As the great Theodore appears as the model of a Roman prelate, Cuthbert is the exemplar of the monastic preacher in the Irish tradition, but in full union with Rome. For these chapters Bede depends on both the anonymous life and his own prose life of the saint.

The fifth book brings the *History* from the time of Cuthbert's successor (after 687) up to the present (mid-731), with some backtracking to trace developments of earlier events. In Chapter 20 Bede speaks of his admired friends Abbot Albinus, to whom he wrote the discussed letter, and Bishop Acca, to whom he warmly dedicated most of his theological works. In Chapter 23 he considers the state of the Church in the present period of smiling peace and serenity. The last sentence of the chapter incorporates Psalms 96: 1 and 29: 3 in a hymn of thanks but also on a subtle eschatological note, because the spread and acceptance of the faith among "the multitude of isles" at the ends of the earth are signs of the final days. But Bede, who in his exegesis of apocalyptic texts is always careful to note that "of that day and hour no one knows" (Matt. 24: 36),[54] prudently says no more. His subsequent Letter to Egbert sounds, as we have seen, a more ominous but still idealistic note.

Bede completed his history almost 1300 years ago. With such a temporal and cultural gulf, it should not seem odd that modern students, even while recognizing its clarity, order, literary and historical value, should be puzzled and troubled by some of its qualities.[55] Secular events and data form our modern sense of history; Bede's was formed by the Bible, the Fathers, and the Church with its liturgy. Bede came to history as an exegete who had learned his trade from immersion in the hermeneutics of Ambrose, Jerome, Augustine (particularly), and Gregory. He spoke that idiom.[56] His biblical Christian view holds that there is a continuous and close bond between eternity and time, that time at once creates a distance between past and present but also links the two, and that time marks the continuity of the people of God on the way

---

[54] Also Matt. 25: 13 and Rev. 3: 3; Bede, *De temporum ratione*, ch. 67, ed. Jones, CCSL 123B, pp. 535–37.

[55] J. Robert Wright's *A Companion to Bede* (Grand Rapids, 2008) is designed to assist "the intelligent and enquiring reader" (p. 5). The slender volume helpfully explains complex historical and religious issues in the *History*. Its misleading title is elucidated by the subtitle, *A Reader's Commentary on The Ecclesiastical History of the English People*, which reveals that it is meant to be a companion to Bede's *History* and not to his many other works.

[56] For the influence of exegesis on Bede's historiography, see Jan Davidse, "The Sense of History in the Works of the Venerable Bede," *Studi Medievali* 23 (1982): 664–70; Roger D. Ray, "Bede, the Exegete, as Historian," in *Famulus Christi*, ed. G. Bonner, pp. 125–40, and his "Augustine's *De consensu evangelistarum* and the Historical Education of the Venerable Bede," *Studia Patristica* 16 (1984): 555–61; Robert W. Hanning, *The Vision of History in Early Britain* (New York, 1966), pp. 62–90.

to God's future. Bede's choice for his history of the time reckoning from Christ's Incarnation is absolutely fitting, for it allows him to express the linearity of time linked to the central event of Christ's birth and also to link events and personages of the Old Testament who prefigure, foreshadow, and explain the meaning of the New Testament, as well as the present state of historical development. Because the Incarnation also marks the beginning of Christian salvation history, it serves as the fulcrum for Bede's history, with his hope for reform and his idealistic assurance that, despite all setbacks, God and man will be victorious. Bede's historical outlook is therefore at once achronological (typical, symbolic, allegorical, timeless) and temporal (continuous, distinct, unique). Such a religious historicity is strange to the reader today.

Furthermore, Bede's sense of history encompasses both human and divine causality, the ordinary working out of God's plan, man's contribution to history for good and ill, and the miraculous. The recounting of the miraculous in the *Ecclesiastical History* is most likely to cause the modern reader to balk or be amused. Historians of a former generation, even great ones who convinced the academic world of Bede's eminent qualities as an historian, rejected the religious and theological elements as foreign to the writing of true history; they considered that Bede's inclusion and use of miracle stories detracted from a work which in other places manifested accuracy, attention to eyewitnesses and reliable sources, and great synthetic analysis.[57] In recent years scholars have begun to recognize and study Bede as part of his own cultural milieu and have gained a new sympathy for the whole of his historiography. Bede believed in miracles as part of his world and of his history. History and hagiography are not different categories. God could work miracles and did, though with Gregory and Augustine Bede believed that physical miracles were more frequent because more necessary in the early days of the Church, and that God worked greater miracles in the souls of men than he did in palpable wonders. But he also knew of latter-day occurrences, which he used for his purposes in the *History*. Of the fifty-one accounts of miracles and the miraculous he relates, most (twenty-eight) appear in the last two books, that is, after the conversion of the Anglo-Saxons. The miracles are not demonstrations of force or magic; Bede usually calls them *signa* as in the Bible (especially in John's Gospel), not *miracula*, for they are indications, signs of an inner meaning, not marvelous fireworks. They encourage, enrich, and confirm those who already have faith. Particularly for the later miracles Bede takes care to identify sources. Except for the wonder he experienced while writing the life of Cuthbert, he does not record the miracles as an

---

[57] Henry Mayr-Harting pointed out in his review of the collection *Famulus Christi* in *Journal of Ecclesiastical History* 29 (1978): 363–65 at 363, that "one of the significant advances of 1976 over 1935 is the appreciation of how Bede's scriptural scholarship affected, indeed permeated, his work as an historian." See also Davidse, "Sense of History," pp. 648–49.

eyewitness. But they form part of the ecclesiastical history of his nation, the account of the workings of God amongst his people.

The *Ecclesiastical History* is Bede's most notable and publicized work, intended for a wide public, as Bede indicates in his preface.[58] It presents a great and generally optimistic overview of the English and in particular of the Northumbrians. Its audience was and continues to be widespread. *The Letter to Egbert*, however, was sent on 5 November 734 as a private admonition to his former pupil, who was to become archbishop of York the following year.[59] It presents a grim view of the Northumbrian church and land, and calls for reform. Though in failing health and destined to die within a year, Bede energetically admonishes the prelate to carry out much-needed reforms. The tone is that of a prophet exhorting a high priest.[60] Although all of the principal works of his later years deal to some extent with reform (see, for instance, Homily I. 7),[61] the letter is the most severely critical of Church and state, and the most concrete in its proposals for change.[62] In the letter, he begins by urging the prelate to live holily, to avoid gossip and unrestrained speech, to follow the instructions of Pope Gregory on pastoral responsibilities, and to teach. He censures bishops for setting bad examples, giving in to the seductions of the soft life and failing to meet the needs of their remote flocks.

> And because the places in the diocese under your authority are so far apart that it would take you more than the whole year on your own to go through them all and preach the word of God in every hamlet and field, it is clearly essential that you appoint others to help you in your holy work; thus priests should be ordained and teachers established who may preach the word of God and consecrate the holy mysteries in every small village, and above all perform the holy rites of baptism wherever the opportunity arises.[63]

He criticizes the bishop who associates with "those who are given to laughter, jests, tales, feasting, and drunkenness" (recall Bede's censure of Bishop Wilfrid's court in his letter to Plegwin), and the avaricious bishop "who, urged on by love of money, takes under his authority a larger portion of the population than he could visit and preach to in the course of a year"

---

[58] "... uel tibi [i.e., regi] uel ceteris auditoribus siue lectoribus huius historiae ..."; "... ad instructionem posteritatis ...," *HE, Praefatio*, ed. Colgrave and Mynors, pp. 2, 6.

[59] *EHD* I: 799–810; *Baedae opera historica*, ed. Plummer, I: 405–23; II: 378–88.

[60] Compare Bernard of Clairvaux's admonitions in *De consideratione* to his former pupil, Pope Eugenius II, and the *sermo ad clerum* genre represented by Colet and Latimer in the English Renaissance. As Patrick Sims-Williams remarks, *Religion and Literature in Western England, 600–800* (Cambridge, 1990), pp. 126–27, "Bede's letter should not however, be taken at face value. Historians have insufficiently realized that the *Epistola* belongs to a tradition of monastic polemic that goes back at least as far as Cassian ... and St. Fructuosus ..."

[61] *Homilia* I. 7 in *Opera homiletica*, CCSL 122, p. 48; Homily I. 7 in Bede, *Homilies on the Gospels*, trans. Martin and Hurst, pp. 68–69.

[62] Alan Thacker, "Bede's Ideal of Reform," pp. 130–53.

[63] "Bede's Letter to Egbert," in Bede, *Ecclesiastical History*, trans. McClure and Collins, p. 345; "Epistola Bede ad Ecgbertum episcopum," ed. Plummer, I: 408.

(in a clear allusion to the practice of a prelate like Wilfrid).[64] He insists that the populace be taught the essentials of their faith and their prayers, in Latin for those educated and in the native tongue for the unlearned.

Bede denounces the laymen who give money to kings to obtain lands for pseudo-monasteries, which are established to avoid military service and taxation.

> There are ... laymen who have no love for the monastic life nor for military service, who commit a graver crime by giving money to the kings and obtaining lands under the pretext of building monasteries, in which they can give freer rein to their libidinous tastes; these lands they have assigned to them in hereditary right through written royal edicts, and these charters, as if to make them really worthy in the sight of God, they arrange to be witnessed in writing by bishops, abbots, and the most powerful laymen.[65]

Bede suggests abrogating such contractual deeds as bogus.[66] At the end of the *Ecclesiastical History* Bede said, "In these favorable times of peace and prosperity, many of the Northumbrian race, both noble and simple, have laid aside their weapons and taken the tonsure, preferring that they and their children should take monastic vows rather than train themselves in the art of war" (*HE*, V. 23). Here, however, he insists that lands handed over for pseudo-monasteries deprive the king of men and revenue for the defense of the land.

Bede's ardent plea was neither successful in having more bishops consecrated nor in establishing diocesan headquarters at monasteries, after the Irish model. Although Bede's moral authority was the greatest of any contemporary, Egbert was limited in his ability to implement the specific proposals for reform called for in the *Letter*. However, Bede's influence on the Anglo-Saxon clergy, especially the missionaries on the Continent and particularly on Alcuin, who furthered the Carolingian reforms, made Bede *nostri didasculus aevi*, "the teacher of our age."[67] Bede was the unquestioned teacher of all ages for hundreds of years. Medieval historians simply accepted his data and his writings as accurate and objective. It is only in our age that medieval historians such as Walter Goffart, N. J. Higham, Roger Ray, Patrick Wormald, Andrew Scheil, and others have argued that Bede was sophisticated, subtle, biased, subjective, and programmatic. They note how devastating his silences were on certain topics and how subtle was his calculated treatment of Bishop Wilfrid, who represented Roman orthodoxy but also autocratic

---

64 "Letter to Egbert," p. 248; Plummer, ed., I: 411–12.

65 "Letter to Egbert," p. 351; Plummer, ed., I: 415.

66 On the undermining of the charters' purposes, see McClure and Collins' note on p. 428 and Patrick Wormald's *Bede and the Conversion of England: The Charter Evidence*, Jarrow Lecture 1984, pp. 19–23, rpt. *Bede and his World*, ed. Lapidge, II: 631–35.

67 MGH, Poetae II, p. 665, cited by Thacker, "Bede's Ideal," p. 153, also citing J. M. Wallace-Hadrill, *Early Medieval History* (Oxford, 1975), p. 182.

triumphalism.[68] In various ways they point out that Bede the historian was, like all historians, manipulative, even if especially adroit. Now scholars, such as Alan Thacker and Scott DeGregorio, are also exploring his homilies for personal themes and emphasis on reform.[69]

---

[68] Goffart, *Narrators of Barbarian History*; Higham, *(Re-)Reading Bede*; Ray, "Bede's *Vera lex historiae*," *Speculum* 55.1 (1980): 1–21; Wormald, *The Times of Bede*; Scheil, *Footsteps of Israel*.

[69] Thacker, "Bede's Ideal," pp. 130–53; DeGregorio, "'Nostrorum socordiam temporum': The Reforming Impulse of Bede's Later Exegesis," *Early Medieval Europe* 11 (2002): 107–22; and "Bede's *In Ezram et Neemiam* and the Reform of the Northumbrian Church," *Speculum* 79 (2004): 1–25.

6

A Brief History of Bede's Works through the Ages

FROM the time of Bede's death in the eighth century until the present, his widely disseminated works have been read, studied, cited, and analyzed, but in each age in a different way and with different purposes and emphases.[1] In general, history has been remarkably kind to Bede's writings as to him, even if not all of his works have received the same attention in each age.

Although Bede says at the end of the *Ecclesiastical History* that he wrote for his own benefit and for that of his monastic brothers, it is clear from his practice of sending out his works to various authorities for their instruction, comments, and suggestions, that his audience even in his lifetime extended far from Wearmouth-Jarrow. His works circulated widely in England, and he was scarcely in his grave when the demand for his works on the Continent overwhelmed the manuscript copyists at his Wearmouth-Jarrow monastery.[2] "Now Bede lived hidden away in the extreme corner of the world," wrote Symeon of Durham, "but after his death he lived on in his books and became known to everyone all over the world."[3] Dorothy Whitelock remarks of his importance and influence:

> He has been called "the teacher of the whole Middle Ages"; his writings on orthography, rhetoric and metrics, intended in the first place for his own scholars, were for centuries the basic school-books on these subjects; similarly, all subsequent teaching on computation, chronology and science was based on his writings, which handed on the learning of antiquity, until the dawn in early modern times of new methods of scientific study; his commentaries on the Bible caused him to be regarded on a level with the Catholic Fathers and were in constant use throughout centuries, until the method of allegorical interpretation of the Scriptures went out of fashion; his historical work has been read continuously ever since it was written, and has formed a model for later writers.[4]

---

[1] For a more detailed and extensively cited account of Bede's *Nachleben* and *Nachlaß* see my *The Bedan Legacy: The Influence of the Venerable Bede's Works from the Eighth Century to the Present* (Turnhout), in preparation.

[2] See Malcolm Parkes, *The Scriptorium of Wearmouth-Jarrow*, Jarrow Lecture 1982 (Jarrow), rpt. in *Bede and his World*, ed. M. Lapidge, II: 555–86, at 569–71.

[3] Symeon of Durham, *Libellus de exordio atque procursu istius, hoc est Dunhelmensis, Ecclesie/ Tract on the Origins and Progress of this the Church of Durham*, ed. and trans. D. W. Rollason (Oxford and New York, 2000), p. 65.

[4] Dorothy Whitelock, *After Bede*, Jarrow Lecture 1960 (Jarrow), rpt. in *Bede and his World*, ed. Michael Lapidge (Aldershot, 1994), I: 37–49.

By the end of the eighth century Bede's works were frequently transcribed on the Continent and widely distributed.[5] Bernhard Bischoff has argued the Moore Bede (Cambridge University Library, MS Kk. 5. 16) was in the court library of Charlemagne, perhaps brought there by Alcuin, where it "spawned a large family of texts on the Continent."[6]

The Carolingians ranked Bede with the Fathers; he served as monastic mediator and continuator of the patristic legacy to the later ages.[7] Considered the most expert commentator after Gregory the Great ("peritissimi post Gregorium tractatoris"),[8] Bede was so admired that in the eighth century no writer in all of Europe could compare in the number and range of works. Hence, because of his contributions in every field, his continuation of the patristic exegetical tradition, and his absolute orthodoxy, he has been honored since Carolingian times, both as a monastic exegete and as a Father of the Church.[9] Bede would not want to be identified as singular and apart from his patristic tradition, but Amalarius of Metz (c. 780–850), the renowned liturgist, discussing an interpretation, baldly asserts "mihi sufficit ejus auctoritas" ["his authority is sufficient for me"].[10] Michael Allen calls attention to further testimonials to Bede's stature:

> Bede was a literary giant in the judgment of Notker Balbulus (d. 912), and he remained a looming presence in the copywork and scholia of an unsung, but alert thirteenth-century scholar who left his mark on history in the shape of his annotations in the St. Gallen copy of the *Historiae* of Frechulf of Lisieux. (fl. 835)[11]

---

5   As Joshua Westgard has noted in "Bede and the Continent in the Carolingian Age and Beyond": "Within a few generations of his death, not only were his works known throughout Britain and Ireland, but they also had made their way to Continental Europe, where they became a central component of the educational and literary flowering under the Carolingians. It was among the Carolingians that Bede's reputation as an authority figure was firmly and permanently established, and ultimately it was in the Carolingian scriptoria and libraries that his works were carefully copied and preserved, and from which some of them had to be re-imported into Britain in the wake of the ninth-century disruption and neglect that led to the loss of the many early manuscripts of his works that undoubtedly had existed in the libraries of eighth-century Northumbria."

6   Bernhard Bischoff, *Manuscripts and Libraries in the Age of Charlemagne*, trans. Michael Gorman (Cambridge, 1994), p. 67.

7   See Scott DeGregorio, "Bede, the Monk, as Exegete: Evidence from the Commentary on Ezra-Nehemiah," *RB* 115 (2005): 343–69.

8   Monk of St. Gall, *De gestis Caroli magni*, lib. 1, PL 100: 121D: Alcuinus "ut pote discipulus doctissimi Bedae, peritissimi post Gregorium tractatoris."

9   See, e.g., Hincmar of Reims, *De praedestinatione dissertatio posterior*, PL 125: 353C, where Bede is lauded as the English authority among patristic authorities on predestination.

10 Amalarius of Metz, *De ecclesiasticis officiis*, IV. I (PL 105: 1164C), "mihi sufficit ejus auctoritas," quoted by Hill in "Carolingian Perspectives," p. 227. On Bede's less impressive ranking in liturgical texts, see Richard W. Pfaff, "Bede among the Fathers?" *Studia Patristica* 28 (1993): 225–29; rpt. as no. 10 in Richard W. Pfaff, *Liturgical Calendars, Saints, and Services in Medieval England* (Aldershot, 1998).

11 Michael Idomir Allen, "Bede and Frechulf at Medieval St. Gallen," in *Beda venerabilis: Historian, Monk and Northumbrian*, ed. L. A. J. R. Houwen and A .A. MacDonald (Groningen, 1996), pp. 61–80 at p. 62.

Bede's works were influential and authoritative, for religious both men and women. Just as Bede provided one of his most challenging commentaries, on the Canticle of Habakkuk, for a nun, so the finest medieval convents, such as those of Gandersheim, Essen, and Quedlinburg, owned and used his biblical commentaries.[12] An example of a convent's active interface with Bede's works is the poem "De muliere forti" ["On the valiant woman"], dedicated to the nun Hadewiga (Hadwig), a poetic paraphrase of the last part of Bede's *In Proverbia Salomonis* (CCSL 119B: 149–163). [13]

Bede's insertion into the mainstream of patristic sources by the Carolingian scholars assured his place throughout the later periods. As Westgard notes,

> The wide availability of Bedan works in the Carolingian period in turn made possible their even greater multiplication and spread during the course of the twelfth century, when they continued to be copied frequently for both new and established monastic communities and when Bede's popularity seems to have peaked. To judge by their position in surviving medieval library catalogues, Bede's works ranked in importance with the works of the Latin Fathers in a typical twelfth-century book collection. The numerous copies of his works that were made in the twelfth century, moreover, were probably, at least for the most part, still in circulation as copying slowed in the thirteenth and fourteenth centuries. His scientific works in particular were neglected in the late Middle Ages, but his exegetical works and the *Ecclesiastical History* continued to be copied, though not as frequently as before, right up to the arrival of printing in the fifteenth century.[14]

A major indicator of the prevalence of Bede's works in the Middle Ages is the number and location of known manuscripts of his works. Two main sources provide information: medieval library catalogues listing Bedan manuscripts (though many of them have since disappeared) and medieval manuscripts still extant and catalogued in modern library collections. Although many manuscripts were lost or destroyed during extended periods of regional warfare and the tumult of the Viking invasions, Bede's works had been disseminated to the Continent and were reintroduced into England from the eleventh century onwards. Then the dissolution of the monasteries in the sixteenth century and the dispersal of their libraries brought about the destruction of many of these copies. In 1943 Max Laistner, incorporating earlier published lists, provided a handlist of Bede's works in medieval catalogues, without claiming

---

[12] Katrinette Bodarwé, *Sanctimoniales litteratae* (Münster, 2004), pp. 241, 260, 280, 295 n. 392, 312, 319, 337, 383, 403, 408, 451, 465–66. See also Alison I. Beach, *Women as Scribes* (Cambridge, 2004), pp. 21, 56, 105.

[13] "De muliere forti," MGH, *Poetae latini medii aevi*, V, 3rd part (Munich, 1979), pp. 601–19. The dedicatee (named in the introductory *metrum*, line 14) is most likely Hadwig, Abbess of the Canonesses of Lindau (s. xi fin.).

[14] Joshua Westgard, "Bede and the Continent in the Carolingian Age and Beyond," in *The Cambridge Companion to Bede*, ed. Scott DeGregorio (Cambridge, forthcoming 2010).

completeness in his enumeration.[15] Since Laistner's day much progress has been made in printing and annotating medieval library catalogues with Bedan holdings, both in England and on the Continent. For England, a survey of the yet incomplete series (twelve of eighteen extant catalogues), the Corpus of British Medieval Library Catalogues, identifies hundreds of manuscripts containing Bede's works, many now lost.[16] For some idea of the great number of manuscripts that were lost or destroyed in the Renaissance and after, a perusal of the catalogue entries on Bede in the fourteenth-century union catalogue *Registrum Anglie de libris doctorum et auctorum veterum*, in the same series, reveals that about eight out of every ten manuscripts have disappeared.[17] For the Continent, the recently constituted online databank of medieval manuscripts in the German-speaking territories, *Manuscripta mediaevalia*, records over a thousand Bedan manuscripts located in hundreds of libraries.[18] Within the Netherlands the *Bibliotheca Neerlandica manuscripta* in Leiden lists nineteen Bede manuscripts in the library itself, primarily in the Vossian, Scaliger, and Public Library collections, but in the entry that encompasses all extant Dutch manuscripts it provides information for sixty-five.[19] For Germany and Switzerland many manuscripts are recorded in the print series Mittelalterliche Bibliothekskataloge Deutschlands und der Schweiz.[20] Rosamond McKitterick lists 112 manuscripts of Bede's works in the East Frankish territory alone during the Carolingian period.[21] The two-volume *Handschriftencensus Rheinland* records nearly fifty manuscripts of Bede.[22] The series Veröffentlichungen der Kommission für Schrift- und Buchwesen published by the Österreichische Akademie der Wissenschaften has produced

15 Max Laistner with the collaboration of H. H. King, *A Hand-List of Bede Manuscripts* (Ithaca, 1943).
16 See Richard Sharpe's online *British Medieval Library Catalogues*, List of Identifications, http://www.history.ox.ac.uk/sharpe/index.htm#catalogues, pp. 133–40.
17 *Registrum Anglie de libris doctorum et auctorum veterum*, ed. Richard H. Rouse, Mary A. Rouse, R. A. B. Mynors, Corpus of British Medieval Library Catalogues (London, 1991).
18 Consult the Handschriftendatenbank with the query "Beda" at the website manuscripta-mediaevalia.de.
19 See the website of Bibliotheca Neerlandica manuscripta: http://bnm.leidenuniv.nl.
20 *Mittelalterliche Bibliothekskataloge Deutschlands und der Schweiz*, Bayerische Akademie der Wissenschaften, 4 vols. with 3 supplements to date (Munich, 1969–); from St. Gallen, I. 75, lines 5–20; Reichenau, I. 249, lines 25–35.
21 Rosamond McKitterick, "Kulturelle Verbindungen zwischen England und den fränkischen Reichen in der Zeit der Karolinger: Kontexte und Implikationen," in *Deutschland und der Westen Europas im Mittelalter*, ed. Joachim Ehlers (Stuttgart, 2002), pp. 121–48, esp. 125–32 and Tabelle I, pp. 145–46. For numerous other references to manuscripts of Bede's works in Frankish territories, see her articles: "The Diffusion of Insular Culture in Neustria between 650 and 850: the Implications of the Manuscript Evidence," in *La Neustrie. Le pays au nord de la Loire de 650 à 85*, ed. Hartmut Atsma (Sigmaringen, 1989), pp. 395–432, at 397, 403–404, 409; "Anglo-Saxon Missionaries in Germany: Reflections on the Manuscript Evidence," *Transactions of the Cambridge Bibliographic Society*, IX.4 (1989): 291–329; "Carolingian Book Production: Some Problems," *The Library*, 6th series, 12 (1990): 1–33, at 9, 11, 28.
22 *Handschriftencensus Rheinland: Erfassung mittelalterlicher Handschriften im rheinischen Landesteil von Nordrhein-Westfalen mit einem Inventar*, ed. Günter Gattermann, Heinz Finger, et al. (Wiesbaden, 1993).

five volumes of catalogues and inventories of manuscripts once or still in Austrian libraries: in the series many Bede manuscripts are registered as in the libraries.[23] Geneviève Nortier's catalogue of medieval Norman libraries records more than sixty works of Bede.[24] While these select catalogues report only a portion (if indeed a large one) of the Bedan manuscripts extant during the medieval period, they do provide some idea of the extent and impact of Bede's writings on that period.

The complementary source for information about the scope of Bede's influence is the lists of Bedan manuscripts now extant in various collections. Unfortunately, the only attempted survey of all these manuscripts is that by Max Laistner, published during World War II when access to European libraries was impossible. Despite the stature of Laistner as a scholar, and indeed excellence as editor of Bede's *Expositio Actuum Apostolorum et retractatio*, his *Hand-List* is incomplete, lacunose, and often inaccurate, but currently the only one available. The catalogue is more complete for early manuscripts (of the eighth and ninth centuries) than for later ones. Many more manuscripts of Bede's works from the mid- and late Middle Ages than are included in the census are known to exist. Neil Ker in turn in his review of Laistner critcizes his work, calling attention to numerous omissions and wrongly dated and falsely identified manuscripts.[25] Other scholars have since augmented Ker's additions and emendations, and Ker himself has provided further information about Bedan materials in his meticulously recorded catalogue of *Medieval Manuscripts in British Libraries*.[26] A valuable resource for information about Bedan manuscripts in Northumbria is R. A. B. Mynors' *Durham Cathedral Manuscripts to the End of the Twelfth Century*, supplemented by Anne Lawrence-Mathers' commentary in *Manuscripts in Northumbria in the Eleventh and Twelfth Centuries*.[27]

On the mainland, though some good catalogues were available at the beginning of the twentieth century, it is only since 1945 that many European libraries have issued more accurate and detailed catalogues of their medieval manuscript collections, with the result that we now know of hundreds more extant manuscripts of Bede's works than Laistner lists. For manuscripts of his works from the early period (eighth and ninth centuries) we have two

---

23 Renate Schipke, *Scriptorium und Bibliothek des Benediktinerklosters Bosau bei Zeitz: die Bosauer Handschriften in Schulpforte* (Wiesbaden, 2000), Register, p. 134. Besides the snippet from *De Tabernaculo* most of the texts are from Bede's homilies.

24 Geneviève Nortier, *Les bibliothèques médiévales des abbayes bénédictines de Normandie. Fécamp, Le Bec, Mont St. Michel, St. Evroul, Lyre, Jumièges, Saint-Wandrille, St. Ouen* (Paris, 1971).

25 Neil R. Ker, review of Laistner and King, *Hand-List of Bede Manuscripts*, in *Medium Aevum* 13 (1944): 36–40.

26 Neil R. Ker, *Medieval Manuscripts in British Libraries*, 5 vols., vol. 5 with indexes and addenda edited by C. Cunningham and A. G. Watson (Oxford, 1969–2002).

27 R. A. B. Mynors, *Durham Cathedral Manuscripts to the End of the Twelfth Century* (Oxford, 1939); Anne Lawrence-Mathers, *Manuscripts in Northumbria in the Eleventh and Twelfth Centuries* (Woodbridge, 2003).

excellent sources: E. A. Lowe's twelve volumes of *Codices Latini Antiquiores* inform us of eighth-century manuscripts of Bede,[28] and Bernhard Bischoff's extensive catalogues of Carolingian manuscripts and of ninth-century Continental manuscripts, though highly compressed, provide an astounding inventory of Bedan manuscripts:[29] a preliminary list of these ninth-century manuscripts totals 390.[30]

Some years ago Hubert Silvestre produced an impressive catalogue of manuscripts of Bede's works for the Royal Library of Belgium.[31] In a review of Silvestre's catalogue, Élisabeth Pellegrin supplied a substantial list of manuscripts in various European collections missed by Laistner's *Hand-List*.[32] Michel Popoff's inventory of manuscripts in public libraries of France lists more than seventy works by Bede.[33] For Italian holdings there is G. Mazzatinti's *Inventari*, which in its 111 volumes to date records a multitude of Bede's works in Italian libraries.[34] Michael Gorman has identified a number of Bedan manuscripts formerly belonging to the now dispersed collection of the great monastery of Monte Amiata and of other monasteries that also escaped Laistner's notice.[35]

The facts that an exhaustive index of medieval manuscripts containing Bede's works is far from complete, that the catalogues of medieval libraries are still being assembled for publication, and that scholars such as Gorman are still finding manuscripts of Bede in various collections mean that an inventory at the present time is provisional and incomplete; nonetheless, such a tentative inventory gives an idea of Bede's authority and presence in the medieval and modern intellectual sphere. Because of the number of Carolingian and later manuscripts of Bede's works, most of his works have survived to the present day.

---

[28] E. A. Lowe, ed., *Codices latini antiquiores: a Palaeographical Guide to Latin Manuscripts Prior to the Ninth Century*, 12 vols. (Oxford, 1934–71), and the revised *Part II: Great Britain and Ireland* (Oxford, 1972).

[29] Bernhard Bischoff, *Die südostdeutschen Schreibschulen und Bibliotheken in der Karolingerzeit*, 2 vols. (Wiesbaden, 1960); also, *Katalog der festländischen Handschriften des neunten Jahrhunderts (mit Ausnahme der wisigotischen)*, 2 vols. to date (Wiesbaden, 1998–).

[30] I am grateful to Birgit Ebersperger of the Bavarian Academy of Sciences for providing me with the preliminary list of manuscripts containing Bedan works before publication of the third, final volume of Bischoff's *Katalog*, which she is editing.

[31] Hubert Silvestre, *Les manuscrits de Bède à la Bibliothèque Royale de Bruxelles*, Studia Universitatis "Lovanium," Faculté de philosophie et lettres 6 (Leopoldville, 1959); see also his "À propos de quelques manuscrits de Bède," *Scriptorium* 17 (1963): 110–13.

[32] É. Pellegrin, review of Silvestre's *Les manuscrits de Bède*, in *Bibliothèque de l'école des chartes* 117 (1959): 284–86.

[33] Michel Popoff, *Index général des manuscrits décrits dans le Catalogue général des manuscrits des bibliothèques publiques de France*, 3 vols. (Paris, 1993).

[34] G. Mazzatinti, *Inventari dei Manoscritti delle Biblioteche d'Italia*, 111 vols. to date (Florence, 1890–).

[35] Michael M. Gorman, "Manuscript Books at Monte Amiata in the Eleventh Century," *Scriptorium* 56 (2002): 225–93 at 269–70. Gorman in "Bernhard Bischoff's Handlist of Carolingian Manuscripts," *Scrittura e Civiltà* 25 (2001): 89–112, notes in reviewing Vol. I of Bischoff's *Katalog* on p. 89 that "We would perhaps not have imagined that the second most popular author [after Augustine] was Bede, with 120 items ..."

A further index to the popularity and actual use of Bede's works, especially the educational treatises, is the number of known manuscripts of those works that received extensive glosses and commentaries, particularly during the Carolingian period.[36] In England, too, in addition to adding Latin glosses, students glossed some manuscripts in their native Anglo-Saxon.[37] However, of far greater importance than those Old English glosses for the vernacular tradition is the anonymous translation of most of the *Ecclesiastical History*, freely rendered into Old English roughly during the period of King Alfred (sometime between the ninth and tenth centuries). The Old English version exists in five manuscripts and three excerpts copied from the early tenth to the eleventh century. The Latin source for the translation is the C-type of *HE*. Sharon Rowley in her extensive soon-to-be published study has compared the Old English text to the original and concludes that "the Old English translator transformed his text as he worked, mostly by abbreviating his source."[38] The complete Old English version has been edited four times, first by Abraham Wheloc (1643, reprinted 1644), then included in the fine edition of the Latin by Smith (1722), then by Jacob Schipper in the fourth volume of Grein's *Bibliothek der angelsächsischen Prosa* (1899), and finally by Thomas Miller for the Early English Text Society (1890, reprinted 1959), who gives a facing page English translation without the Latin.[39] Although the EETS volume is now the most accessible, of all the editions Schipper's is the preferable because he provides the Latin text on the same page and the versions in the manuscripts with their variants, many of which are diverse and interesting. The generic Old English version of Miller's edition is well known to modern students of Old English because the chapter on Abbess Hild and the miracle of Cædmon's gift of vernacular poetry (*HE*, IV. 24) is usually given in Old English readers. The Old English version with its numerous important editorial changes to the spirit and arrangement of the Latin text no doubt influenced medieval English readers, as it does readers today.

To complete the survey of Bede's influence we must include his works used outside the central areas of England and the Continent. Bede's works were prominent in Ireland at an early date. As Joseph Kelly notes:

---

36 Charles W. Jones, "Bede's Place in Medieval Schools," in *Famulus Christi: Essays in Commemoration of the Thirteenth Centenary of the Birth of the Venerable Bede*, ed. Gerald Bonner (London, 1976), pp. 271–77.

37 Arthur S. Napier, ed., *Old English Glosses, Chiefly Unpublished* (Oxford, 1900), nos. 29–34.

38 Sharon M. Rowley, *Reading the Old English Version of Bede's Historia ecclesiastica in its Manuscript Contexts*, to be published, typescript introduction, p. 2.

39 Bede, *Historia ecclesiastica gentis Anglorum libri v, cui accessere Leges Anglo-Saxonicae*, ed. Abraham Wheloc (London, 1644); Bede, *Historiae ecclesiasticae gentis Anglorum libri quinque*, ed. John Smith (Cambridge, 1722); *König Alfreds Übersetzung von Bedas Kirchengeschichte*, ed. Jacob Schipper, in Bibliothek der angelsächsischen Prosa, ed. Christian Grein (Leipzig, 1899); Bede, *The Old English Version of Bede's Ecclesiastical History of the English People*, ed. and trans. Thomas Miller, Early English Text Society, Original Series 95, 96, 111 (Oxford, 1890, 1898, rpt. 1959, 1963).

At least four Irish texts which date no later than 790 use Bede's exegesis, and two may date as early as 750, that is, only fifteen years after Bede's death. Later, i.e., ninth-century, Irish texts regularly make use of of Bede, although by that time he was widely accepted as an *auctoritas* in much of Western Europe. An Irish commentary on Luke, dated c. 785, depends heavily upon Bede's Lukan commentary. This is particularly significant because the two oldest extant manuscripts of Bede's work, one complete, one fragmentary, are both dated to the second half of the eighth century, which means this Irish text is contemporaneous with them. To my knowledge, this Irish commentary represents the earliest known use of Bede's commentary on Luke.[40]

In the Irish *Commentarius in epistolas catholicas Scotti anonymi* Bede's commentaries on the Catholic Epistles is used to explain numerous verses.[41] Próinséas ní Chatháin remarks: "There is ample evidence that the Irish knew several of Bede's works and glossed some of them, quoted them in glosses and annals, and translated them into the vernacular."[42] Among those works are *De natura rerum, De arte metrica, De temporum ratione, De locis sanctis,* the *Chronica maiora,* and of course the *Historia ecclesiastica.*[43]

Welsh scribes were responsible for copying the *De natura rerum* and *De orthographia,* and there are Welsh glosses to the *De natura rerum* and the *De temporum ratione.* Besides Breton glosses of the *De temporum ratione,* there are also Breton glosses of the *Historia.* In the modern era, the Welsh collector Robert Vaughan (1592–1667) owned the fine twelfth-century manuscript of the *Historia ecclesiastica* (now at Aberystwyth, National Library of Wales, Peniarth 381), and Sir Thomas Mostyn (d. 1692) owned a thirteenth-century copy of the *Historia.*[44]

In Scandinavia and Iceland Bede's historical and chronologic works were often referenced. For instance, the prologue to the *Landnámabók (Book of*

---

40 Joseph F. T. Kelly, "The Venerable Bede and Hiberno-Latin Exegesis," in *Sources of Anglo-Saxon Literary Culture,* ed. Paul E. Szarmach (Kalamazoo, 1986), pp. 65–75 at 69.

41 See Robert E. McNally, ed., *Scriptores Hiberniae minores,* pars 1: *Commentarius in epistolas catholicas Scotti anonymi,* CCSL 108B (Turnhout, 1973), Index Scriptorum, pp. 253–54.

42 Próinséas ní Chatháin, "Bede's *Ecclesiastical History* in Irish," *Peritia* 3 (1984): 115–30, at 120; Francis John Byrne, "*Ut Beda boat:* Cuanu's Signature?" in *Ireland and Europe in the Early Middle Ages: Texts and Transmission = Irland und Europa im früheren Mittelalter,* edited by Próinséas ní Chatháin and Michael Richter (Dublin; Portland, OR, 2002), pp. 45–67.

43 See V. Hill, "The Middle Irish Version of Bede's *De locis sanctis,*" *Zeitschrift für Celtische Philologie* 17 (1927): 225–40 at 226. The Irish glosses to Bede's *De temporum ratione* in Karslruhe, Cod. Augiensis CLXVII, and Vienna, Suppl. MS 15298 (Reichenau MSS), are printed in *Thesaurus Palaeohibernicus,* ed. Whitley Stokes and John Strachan (Cambridge, 1901–03), II: 10–30, 31–37; see also Strachan's "The Vienna Fragments of Bede," *Revue Celtique* 23 (1902): 40–49; and Pierre-Yves Lambert, "Les Commentaires celtiques à Bède le Vénérable," *Études Celtiques* 20 (1983): 119–43, and his "Gloses en vieux-breton, 1–5," *Études Celtiques* 26 (1990): 81–93. For the Irish use of the *Historia,* see the articles by Próinséas ní Chatháin and Byrne referred to in the preceding note, and Steven B. Killion, "Bedan Historiography in the Irish Annals," *Medieval Perspectives* 6 (1991): 20–36.

44 See Daniel Huws, *Medieval Welsh Manuscripts* (Aberystwyth, 2000), ch. 15, p. 295; ch. 16, p. 319, no. 16. The former manuscript, not noted by Laistner or Colgrave, is listed as no. 2 and the latter as no. 1 by Westgard, "Dissemination and Reception of Bede's *Historia ecclesiastica*" in Appendix A, p. 134.

the Settlement of Iceland) cites the *De temporum ratione*, as does, twice, the *Ólafs Saga Tryggasonar en Mesta (History of King Olaf Tryggvason).*[45] The *Historia* was known by at least a few in Iceland, as were Bede's commentaries on Genesis and on the Acts of the Apostles.[46] Although there is an Icelandic version of the Life of St. Oswald, it is only indirectly derived from Bede's *Historia*, by way of an elaborating German version.[47]

In the South, in Italy, with its many manuscripts of Bede's works, and particularly in Spain (and to a lesser extent Portugal), especially during the Renaissance and Reformation, Bede's works were prominent among the revered theologians and historians. The Jesuits were responsible for the popularity of the works of Bede especially in Spain. Cited were his *Historia, De locis sanctis, De sex aetatibus, Martyrologium, De temporum ratione, De arte metrica, De Tabernaculo, In Lucam,* and *Retractatio.*[48]

An odd tribute to Bede's authority is the great number of inauthentic works ascribed to him in the medieval and early modern periods, something that he shares with the other Fathers of the Church.[49] It is worth noting that most of the catalogues listed above contain one or more spurious works attributed to Bede.

Bede's place in the early modern period is substantiated by print editions of his works.[50] Josse Bade's three volumes (1521–36) are the "editio princeps" of Bede's opera.[51] Those volumes were reprinted by Jean de Roigny in 1544–45. In 1563 Johann Herwagen the Younger published in Basel the big eight-volume complete works, which is essentially de Roigny's edition augmented by numerous inauthentic texts;[52] this was reprinted in 1622, 1682, and 1688. Then in 1843–44 J. A. Giles reproduced Herwagen's edition,

---

[45] *The Book of Settlements: Landnámabók*, trans. Hermann Pálsson and Paul Edwards (Manitoba, 1972), p. 15; *Ólaf Saga Tryggsonar en Mesta*, ed. Ólafur Halldórrson, Editiones Arnamagnæanæ, series A, vol. 3 (Copenhagen, 2000), III: 69–70, 75–76.

[46] See Benedikt S. Benedikz, "Bede in the Uttermost North," in *Famulus Christi*, ed. Bonner, ch. 18, pp. 334–41 at 334–35, 340.

[47] See Marianne E. Kalinke, ed. and trans., *Oswald of Northumbria* (Tempe, 2005), pp. 31–39, 101.

[48] See Helmut Heidenreich, "Beda Venerabilis in Spain," *Modern Language Notes* 85:2 (1970): 120–37, esp. at 122: the Jesuits "had taken a special liking for Bede." Heidenreich's reference (incorrect as to volume, year, and pages) on p. 120, n. 2, to J.S., "El llibre de les Homilies del venerabile Beda de Giron," *Vell i Nou* 4, no. 96 (1919): 287–89, seems actually, despite its title, not to be to a manuscript of Bede but of a homiliary.

[49] For an indication of the number of pseudo-Bedan biblical commentaries that emerged during the Middle Ages, see Friedrich Stegmüller, *Repertorium biblicum medii aevi* (Madrid, 1950–80), 2: 186–193, nos. 1647–88; 8: 346–47, nos. 1647–1651, 1652–1688, 1.

[50] See Wilhelm Levison, "Modern Editions of Bede," *The Durham University Journal* 37, n.s. 6 (1945): 78–85; Roger Gryson, ed., *Bedae presbyteri Expositio Apocalypseos*, CCSL 121A (Turnhout, 2001), Les éditions, pp.130–32; Michael Gorman, "The Canon of Bede's Works and the World of Ps. Bede," *Révue Bénédictine* 111 (2001): 399–445.

[51] Vol. 2 in 1521, vol. 3 in 1522, but vol. 1 only after Bade's death, 1536, by his son-in-law, Jean de Roigny, and Michel Vascosan. See Gorman, "Canon," p. 407, n. 18. The libraries of Syon possessed the 1521 and 1522 volumes, and King's College, Cambridge, had all three volumes: Sharpe, List of Identifications, p. 133.

[52] *Opera Bedae venerabilis presbyteri anglosaxonis*, ed. Johann Herwagen, 8 vols. in 4 (Basel, 1563). On this edition see Gorman, "Canon," pp. 399–400, 409–11.

performing a positive deed by correcting some of the more blatant errors but also doing a disservice by curtailing the lemmata, the biblical passages being commented upon.[53] This flawed text was reprinted by J-P. Migne in his *Patrologia latina* series, volumes 90–95. Editions of Bede's works printed before 1536 have been listed by Michael Gorman.[54] Various works of Bede other than his frequently published *Ecclesiastical History* have been printed since the sixteenth century, such as Henry Wharton's *Bedae opera quaedam theologica* (1693).[55] Now most of Bede's works are produced by the publisher Brepols in the Corpus Christianorum series, and those editions, though varying in editorial reliability, are a genuine improvement.[56] A sign of Bede's continuing importance not just in the field of history is the ever-increasing number of editions and translations of his exegetical works.[57]

Bede's fame and authority were the result of both the widespread dissemination of his works and the frequent citation of his name and works by authors of the early and high Middle Ages. Following the example of Alcuin many Carolingian missionaries, such as the Frisian Liudger, used Bede and stocked his works in the monasteries they founded. In the ninth century at least the major works of Bede were available in cultural centers, as the testimonies by Hrabanaus Maurus, Smaragdus, Notker Balbulus, Lupus of Ferrières, and Hincmar of Reims affirm.[58] Florus of Lyons (d. c. 860) cites from a number of works of Bede in his *Expositio missae*;[59] and Paschasius Radbertus (786 – c. 865) shows a knowledge of Bede's works, especially in his *Vita Adalhardi*, where he cites him by name, and in his *Epitaphium Arsenii* (i.e, *vita Walae abbatis*).[60] Even the highly individualist scholar John Scottus Eriugena (c. 810 – c. 877) was influenced by Bede.[61] In Carolingian ecclesiastical

---

[53] *The Complete Works of the Venerable Bede, in the Original Latin*, ed. J. A. Giles, 12 vols. (London, 1843).

[54] Gorman, "Canon of Bede's Works," pp. 443–45, Appendix 2.

[55] *Bedæ venerabilis opera quædam theologica*, ed. Henry Wharton (London, 1693), available electronically as part of Early English Books Online. On later editions of Bede's works, see Wilhelm Levison, "Modern Editions of Bede," *Durham University Journal*, 37.2, n.s. 6.2 (1944–45): 78–85.

[56] A website by Stephen Harris, devoted to Bedan scholarship, lists editions and secondary works at http://bede.net/; Scott DeGregorio is responsible for a bibliography (only up to 1995).

[57] A list of English translations of Bede's works are at the Bede.Net website, http://bede.net/bib/trans.html/. The list needs some updating, but the reader will find information about recent translations in the chapters above dealing with individual works.

[58] Whitelock, *After Bede*, pp. 7–10.

[59] Jean-Paul Bouhot, "Fragments attribués à Vigile de Thapse dans *l'Expositio missae* de Florus de Lyon," *Revue des Études Augustiniennes* 21.3–4 (1975): 302–16. The quotations are from Bede's *De Tabernaculo*, *In Lucam*, and *In primam epistolam Petri*.

[60] Paschasius Radbertus, *Opera, Vita S. Adalhardi*, PL 120: 1507–1556, at 1531B; *Epitaphium Arsenii (vita Walae abbatis)*, PL 120: 1557–1650; see E. Ann Matter, "The Bible in Early Medieval Saints' Lives," in *The Study of the Bible in the Carolingian Era*, ed. Celia Chazelle and Burton Van Name Edwards (Turnhout, 2003), pp. 155–65, at 162–64.

[61] John J. Contreni, "John Scottus and Bede," in *History and Eschatology in John Scottus Eriugena and his Time*, ed. James McEvoy and Michael Dunne (Leuven, 2002), pp. 91–140.

councils Bede is cited as authority: Mainz in 813, Aachen in 816, Paris in 825 and in 829 (six times), and Aachen in 836.[62]

After the Viking invasions Bede's works saw a resurgence during the Benedictine reform movement of the tenth and eleventh centuries. Examples of Bede's influence in the tenth and eleventh centuries in England are, besides Asser and Lantfred of Winchester, Ælfric's extensive citations from thirteen of Bede's works, and Byrhtferth of Ramsey's use of thirteen works, mostly different from Ælfric's citations.[63] From the twelfth century on Bede's works appear in most libraries in England and even more on the Continent.[64] Although Bede continues to be cited frequently and favorably throughout the period, he is often but one of many authorities. His interpretations show up frequently in the form of glosses to biblical texts as well as in theological compendia, and his authority is called upon in other disciplines as well, such as liturgy. Although Bede's method is monastic, exegetical, and discursive, his explanations and positions were used by practically all the major and minor Scholastics in their categorical adversarial methodology of questions, objections, statements, and responses.[65] The *Glossa ordinaria*, the medieval commentary on the Bible in the form of marginal and interlinear glosses, contains among the extracts from the Fathers a plethora of Bedan quotations, though sometimes they are slightly modified.[66] Bede "is the primary source of the glossed Song of Songs, appearing in every verse and contributing about 450 glosses."[67] By means of the great compendium that became the standard biblical interpretation of the high Middle Ages, Bede was so universally known to the Schoolmen that they often cite Bede by way of the *Glossa* as well as directly from his works. Among the twelfth-century theologians, Peter Abelard (1079–1142/3) cites Bede more than thirty times in his *Sic et non*,[68] and in his theological works even provides extended quotations.[69]

---

62 Joyce Hill, "Carolingian Perspectives," pp. 235–39, citing *Concilia Ævi Karolini* I, MGH, Legum III, Concilia II, I, pp. 266, 409, 517, 620, 653, 662, 664, 666, 759, 762.

63 See Michael Lapidge, *The Anglo-Saxon Library* (Oxford, 2006), Appendix E: Latin Books Cited, pp. 238, 239–40, 254–57, 268–69.

64 For examples, see Sharpe, List of Identifications, pp. 133–39, for England, and for the Continent, see the entries in *Mittelalterliche Bibliothekskataloge Österreichs*, vols. 1–5 with suppl. (Vienna, 1915; Aalen, 1974), and in *Mittelalterliche Bibliothekskataloge Deutschlands und der Schweiz*, 4 vols. in 8 with 3 supplements (Munich, 1969).

65 For a concise but superb summary history of Scholasticism with bibliography see *The Oxford Dictionary of the Christian Church* (1997), s.v. For bio- and bibliographic information for the period, consult the website Alcuin: Regensburger Infothek der Scholastik, at http://www.alcuin. de/.

66 On the *Glos(s)a ordinaria*, its importance and its complex history, with bibliography, see *The Oxford Dictionary of the Christian Church* (1997), s.v. The best text available is *Biblia latina cum glossa ordinaria: Facsimile Reprint of the Editio princeps Adolph Rusch of Strassburg 1480/81*, ed. Karlfried Froehlich and Margaret T. Gibson, 4 vols. (Turnhout, 1992).

67 Mary Dove, trans. *The Glossa ordinaria on the Song of Songs* (Kalamazoo, 2004), pp. xvi–xix at xvi.

68 See the Index in Peter Abelard, *Sic et non: A Critical Edition*, ed. Blanche B. Boyer and Richard McKeon (Chicago, 1977), p. 63.

69 See the particularly long quotation from Bede's *Commentary on Acts* in Abelard's *Opera theologica*, ed. E. M. Buytaert et al., CCCM 11 (Turnhout, 1969), p. 328, lines 60–70.

Peter Lombard (c.1095–1160), whose *Sentences* became the basic textbook of theology to be glossed and expanded by every major Scholastic theologian, shows a predilection for Bede, citing him by name and quotation some seventy times (mostly by way of the *Glossa Ordinaria*) from a wide variety of his works.[70] Since the Scholastic method involved the citing of authoritative opinions, it is not unexpected that Peter Lombard would cite Bede; however, even more tellingly, he favors him over most medieval writers – as Marcia Colish has pointed out, "among the post-patristic writers his favorites are Bede and Remigius."[71] Consequently, the many commentators on the *Sentences* follow Lombard's lead by likewise giving Bede prominence. For example, Peter Comestor (d. 1178/9), Lombard's disciple, in his commentary on the Book of Genesis, cites not only Bede's Commentary on Genesis a dozen times but also the *De temporibus liber* and the *Retractatio in actus Apostolorum*.[72] Although the Victorines Hugh (1096–1141) and Andrew (c. 1110–1175) call on Bede rarely, Peter Cantor (d. 1197) is more indebted, with thirty-six citations in his great *Summa de sacramentis*, fifteen in his *Verbum abbreviatum*, and several in his *Glossae super Genesim*.[73]

In the thirteenth century, the Scholastic Franciscans regularly refer to Bede's works, using entries from the *Glossa ordinaria* as well as directly from his works.[74] Alexander of Hales (c. 1186–1245), who was largely responsible for the adoption of Peter Lombard's *Sententiae* instead of the Bible as the basic text for the university theological curriculum, calls on Bede's authority more than fifty times in his *Glossa in quatuor libros sententiarum Petri Lombardi*.[75] Alexander cites Bede (mostly from the Commentaries on Luke and Mark) even more in his *Quaestiones disputatae "Antequam esset frater"* (i.e., before his Franciscan career).[76] In the *Summa theologica*, which Alexander began but which William of Middleton (Guillelmus de Melitonia, 1245 – c. 1260) and others completed, nearly all of Bede's works are cited, some, particularly the New Testament commentaries, numerous times.[77] Bonaventure (c. 1217–1274) in his *Commentary on the Sentences*,

---

[70] Peter Lombard, *Sententiae in IV libris distinctae* in the excellent critical edition of Spicilegium Bonaventurianum 4–5 (Grottaferrata, 1971, 1981), Indices 2 (Auctoritates citatae) I, pt. 2, 594 and II, 568 (Auctores et scripta) II, 576.

[71] Marcia Colish, *Peter Lombard* (Leiden, 1994), I: 165.

[72] Peter Comestor, *Scholastica historia, Liber Genesis*, ed. Agneta Sylwan, CCCM 191 (Turnhout, 2005), Index, pp. 200–201.

[73] Peter Cantor, *Summa de Sacramentis et animae consiliis*, ed. Jean Albert Dugauquier (Louvain, 1954), Table des citations, I: 188; II: 496; III: 800–01; *Verbum abbreviatum: textus conflatus*, ed. Monique Boutry (Turnhout, 2004), Index fontium, pp. 950–51; *Glossae super Genesim: Prologus et captula 1–3*, ed. Agneta Sylwan (Göteborg, 1992), nominatim on p. 18 and refs. pp. 96–97.

[74] For confirmatory details see the authorial indices of the volumes of the Bibliotheca Franciscana Scholastica Medii Aevi, 28 vols. to date (Grottaferrata, 1904–).

[75] Alexander of Hales, *Glossa in quatuor libros sententiarum Petri Lombardi* (Rome, 1951).

[76] Alexander of Hales, *Quaestiones disputatae "Antequam esset frater,"* 3 vols. (Florence, 1960).

[77] Alexander of Hales, *Doctoris irrefragabilis Alexandri de Hales Ordinis Minorum summa theologica*, ed. Bernardin Klumper, 4 vols. in 5 (Florence, 1924).

in his commentaries on Scripture, and in his other theological works uses Bede extensively, especially the commentaries on Mark and Luke, and in his *Sermones dominicales*.[78] William of Middleton in his *Quaestiones de Sacramentis* cites Bede's commentaries on both the Old and New Testaments and his homilies some fifty times.[79] William de la Mare, who wrote the *Correctorium fratris Thomae* (1278), a critique of the writings of Thomas Aquinas, cites Bede fifteen times.[80] Matthew of Aquasparta (d. 1302), prolific composer of *quaestiones*, cites Bede in his works, mostly from the *Glossa ordinaria*.[81] In his *Compotus* Roger Bacon (c. 1214–c. 1292) names both Bede's works on time and quotes from *De temporum ratione*.[82]

Among the Dominican Scholastics Albertus Magnus and Thomas Aquinas are the most renowned representatives, both of whom use Bede extensively. Albertus Magnus (c. 1193–1280), while not referencing theologians in his volumes on *Physica*, does cite Bede among the respected authorities in his exegetical, doctrinal, and sacramental works.[83] Thomas Aquinas cites Bede by name either in quotation or by reference well over a hundred times. Although Thomas usually refers to Bede's New Testament commentaries, he also cites the commentaries on Genesis, on the Tabernacle, and on other works.[84] His *Catena aurea*, a running commentary on the four Gospels from the works of the Fathers, frequently and extensively quotes from Bede's works, especially the commentaries on Luke (216 citations) and Mark (376 citations).[85] Unlike the typical Scholastic treatises and the *Glossa ordinaria*, the *Catena* usually provides substantial chunks from patristic texts, and the quotations from Bede are sometimes two or three to a page. It is ironic that even the excommunicated opponent of papal primacy and supporter of the

---

78 Bonaventure, *Opera omnia*, vol. 10 (Rome, 1882), Index locorum ss. Patrum, p. 270; *Sancti Bonaventurae sermones dominicales* (Grottaferrata, 1977), *sermones* 45, 46.

79 William of Middleton (Guilelmus de Miltona), *Quaestiones de sacramentis*, ed. Caelestinus Pian and Gál Gedeon (Florence, 1961), Index II: Auctores, p. 1098.

80 William de la Mare (William de Mara), *Scriptum in primum librum Sententiarum*, ed. Hans Kraml (Munich, 1989), pp. 38, 197; *Scriptum in secundum librum Sententiarum*, ed. Hans Kraml (Munich, 1995), pp. 29, 31, 37, 50, 95, 97, 129, 170, 249, 263.

81 Matthew of Aquasparta, *Quaestiones disputatae de incarnatione et de lapsu* (Florence, 1957), pp. 112, 236, 237; *De fide et de cognitione* (Florence, 1957), pp. 67, 108; *De anima* (Florence, 1959), pp. 14, 393, 507, 564.

82 *Compotus Fratris Rogeri, opera hactenus inedita Rogeri Baconi*, Fasc. 6, ed. Robert Steele (Oxford, 1926), pp. 32–33, 85, 101, 190.

83 Albertus Magnus, *Opera omnia ad fidem codicum manuscriptorum edenda, apparatu critico, notis, prolegomenis*, vols. 1–26, in parts (Westfalia, 1951–). This new edition of the *opera omnia* of Albertus is still being edited and there are gaps among the parts, so many of Albert's references to Bede's works are not yet noted. Also, on occasion Albert simply cites the name Bede without reference to a work (e.g., 19: 172, 174; 25 pt. 2: 167).

84 Thomas Aquinas, *Opera omnia*, Editio leonina, 50 vols. (Rome, 1882–1976), Index; *Super IV libros sententiarum*, ed. Roberto Coggi, 10 vols. (Bologna, 1999); Charles H. Lohr, ed., *St. Thomas Aquinas, Scriptum super Sententiis: An Index of Authorities Cited* (Avebury, 1980).

85 Thomas Aquinas, *Catena aurea in quatuor Evangelia*, ed. Angelico Guarienti (Turin, 1953).

power of the Emperor and state, Marsilius of Padua (c. 1275–1342), uses Bede from Thomas's *Catena* as an authority in his *Defensor pacis*.[86]

Thomas's Dominican opponent, Robert Kilwardby (c. 1215–1279), archbishop of Canterbury, in his *Quaestiones in libros Sententiarum* cites some of the usual Bedan references that occur in other commentaries of the *Sentences*, but also occasionally from Bede's homilies.[87] Like the Franciscans many of the greater and lesser Dominican *magistri*, such as Baldwin of Maflix, Godefroid de Blenau, Guerric of Saint-Quentin, Hannibaldus, Hugh of Saint Cher, John of Treviso, Jean Pointlasne, John de Moussy, Roland of Cremona, and Stephen of Venizy, crafted commentaries on the *Sentences*, or *quodlibetales* and *summae* that typically included references to Bede's work.

Non-fraternal Masters (i.e., secular clerics or members of other religious communities) likewise draw on Bede's works. The Augustinian canon Alexander Nequam (Neckham, d. 1217) in his *Speculum speculationum* refers to Bede's *De Tabernaculo* and *In epistulam Iacobi*.[88] The work ascribed on dubious grounds to Prepositinus (Prévostin) of Cremona (fl. 1190–1210), the *Summa contra haereticos*, cites Bede but always *via* the *Glossa ordinaria*.[89] William of Auxerre (Guillelmus Altissiodorensis, d. 1231) in his magisterial *Summa aurea* cites Bede's works twenty-six times (mostly by way of the *Glossa ordinaria*).[90] Robert Grosseteste cites Bede in his new scientific treatises as well as in his theological works, especially the *Hexaëmeron,* where he associates him with the Fathers without distinction, e.g., "Beda, Ambrosius, et Basilius, et Ieronimus" (p. 68) or "Augustinus et Beda et Basilius et Ambrosius" (p. 175).[91] Grosseteste neglects his scholastic predecessors in favor of those Fathers; as R. W. Southern notes, "He went first to the Bible, then to its main expositors – Augustine, Jerome, Gregory,

---

86 Marsilius of Padua, *Defensor pacis*, ed. Joannes de Janduno and Richard Scholz (Hanover, 1932), pp. 288, 312, 318.

87 See the *Indices auctorum et scriptorum* in each of the volumes of Robert Kilwardby's *Quaestiones in libros Sententiarum*, ed. Gerhard Leibold et al., 5 vols., Bayerische Akademie der Wissenschaften 10, 12, 13, 16, 17 (Munich, 1982–93).

88 Alexander Nequam, *Speculum speculationum*, ed. Rodney M. Thomson (Oxford, 1988), Index scriptorum, p. 474.

89 Ascribed to Prepositinus, *Summa contra haereticos*, ed. Joseph N. Garvin and James A. Corbett (Notre Dame, 1958), Index citationum et nominum, p. 300.

90 William of Auxerre, *Summa aurea*, ed. Jean Ribaillier, 4 vols. in 6 (Paris and Rome, 1980), Indices II: Auctores et scripta, I: 391, II: 787, III: 1080, IV: 563.

91 Robert Grosseteste, *De cessatione legalium*, ed. Richard C. Dales and Edward B. King (London, 1986), citing *De temporum ratione* and *Expositio Apocalypseos; De decem mandatis*, ed. Dales and King (London, 1987), citing *De templo Salomonis*; in *De anima*, in *Die philosphischen Werke*, ed. Ludwig Baur (Münster, 1912), from *In Genesim* and *In Lucam*. Although Grosseteste in the *De anima* lists Bede among theologians after the Greek and Latin Fathers but above the "moderniores scriptores," p. 285, and among the major historians, p. 289, in the *Hexaemeron* he associates him with other Fathers: see *Hexaemeron*, ed. Richard C. Dales and Servis Gieben (London, 1982), pp. 58, 63, 68, 88, 89, 90, 92, 175, 248, 256. On the linking of Jerome with Bede see the editors' remarks on p. xxiii. See also Robert Grosseteste, *On the Six Days of Creation*, trans. C. F. G. Martin (Oxford, 1996), Index, p. 356.

Ambrose, Bede, John Chrysostom, John of Damascus, Origen."[92] Although William of Auvergne (c. 1180–1249) names Bede only once in *De virtutibus*,[93] Guido of Orchelles (fl. 1217 – c. 1230) in his *Tractatus de sacramentis* cites him a number of times, thrice by name.[94]

When other authors in turn copy and excerpt writers such as Peter Comestor, they include those authors' imbedded Bedan citations. Thus Peter Comestor's commentaries on the Gospels and the Acts of the Apostles in his *Historia scholastica* are found complete with Peter's Bedan references in Albert Behaim's *Brief- und Memorial Buch*.[95]

Chroniclers and historians owe a huge debt not only to Bede's *Ecclesiastical History* but to many of his other works as well. Ordericus Vitalis (1075 – c. 1142) in his *Ecclesiastical History*, for instance, besides modeling his history on Bede's and drawing extensively on it especially in the first books, also uses the *Chronica maiora* (= *De temporum ratione*, ch. 26), the homilies, the commentaries on Luke, Mark, and the Acts of the Apostles. Frechulf of Lisieux (fl. 825–52), mentioned earlier, while using the *Historia* and Bede's other works rather sparingly, draws plentifully (seventy-three times) upon the *Chronica maiora* in his *Historiae*.[96] Just as the English historian Bede used and cited the Spaniard Isidore, so during the thirteenth century the Spanish historian Rodrigo Jiménes (d. 1247), author of the *Historia de rebus Hispanie*, used and cited the Englishman Bede.[97]

As noted above, Bede's influence as an historian was potent and vital for historiography from soon after his death through the Carolingian period, but it became particularly strong again in the Benedictine reform of the tenth and eleventh centuries, and then especially, as Antonia Gransden has noted, in the late eleventh and twelfth centuries: "Perhaps at no time in medieval England were Bede's historical works more intensively studied than in the Anglo-Norman period."[98] At the brilliant resurgence of historiography in England during the twelfth century, the great historians, particularly William

---

92 R. W. Southern, *Robert Grosseteste* (Oxford, 1986), p. 187.
93 William of Auvergne, *De virtutibus et de moribus*, 2. *De moribus*, II. 10.
94 Guido of Orchelles (de Orchellis), *Tractatus de sacramentis ex eius Summa de sacramentis et officiis Ecclesiae*, ed. Damien and Odulphus van den Eynde (St. Bonaventure, NY, 1953), Index III, Citationes, p. 325.
95 Peter Comestor, *Scholastica historia, liber Genesis*, ed. Agneta Sylwan, CCCM 191 (Turnhout, 2005) Index fontium, pp. 200–201, and *Historia scholastica*, PL 198: 1054–1721; Albert Behaim, *Brief- und Memorial Buch*, MGH, Briefe des späteren Mittelalters, 1 (Munich, 2000), no. 167: 516. 11; 522. 14; 524. 16; 535. 5 and 7; 569. 6; 584. 7.
96 *Frechulfi Lexoviensis episcopi opera omnia*. Prolegemona and Indices, ed. Michael I. Allen, CCCM 169, 169a (Turnhout, 2002), pp. 280*–82*, 202*: "Frechulf quotes extensively from Bede's *Greater Chronicle*, and not only for the period after Eusebius-Jerome ... from AD 378."
97 Rodrigo Jiménez de Rada (Rodericus de Ximenes), *Historia de rebus Hispanie sive Historia gothica*, part 1, ed. Juan Fernández Valverde, CCCM 72 (Turnhout, 1987), *Breviarium historie Catholice*, Index fontium, pp. 637–38.
98 Antonia Gransden, "Bede's Reputation as an Historian in Medieval England," *Journal of Ecclesiastical History* 32 (1981): 397–425 at 403; reprinted in *Legends, Traditions and History in Medieval England* (London and Rio Grande, 1992), pp. 1–29 at 7.

of Malmesbury, Henry of Huntingdon (who also uses Bede's *Chronica maiora*), and John (alias Florence) of Worcester, all drew heavily upon Bede for the Anglo-Saxon past, not only on his *Ecclesiastical History* but on his other works, such as the *Lives of the Abbots of Wearmouth-Jarrow*, the works on time, chronology, geography, hagiography, and his biblical commentaries.[99] During the Reformation both Protestants and Catholics called on Bede for apologetic purposes. Thomas Stapleton published his translation of the *Ecclesiastical History* dedicated to Queen Elizabeth as a defense of the Catholic faith against the Protestant Reformation.[100]

Citations of Bede to add weight to argument are found not only in exegetical, homiletic, philosophical, and historical works but even, rather surprisingly, in canon law; and a wide range of Bede's works appears in the *Collectio canonum in v libris* and *Decretum Gratiani*.[101] Iacobus de Voragine (Iacopo da Varazze, c. 1230–1298) in his popular *Legenda aurea* cites Bede numerous times.[102]

During the early modern period Bede is referred to by a number of philosophers and theologians. For instance, Nicholas of Cusa (Nikolaus Kryffs, Nicolas von Cues, 1404–1464) cites Bede's grammatical, temporal, and exegetical works.[103] One might not expect the monk Bede to show up in the writings of the Reformers, but John Hus (c. 1372–1415) in his *Tractatus de ecclesia* cites him, though only to refute papal claims to unique divine guidance.[104] Bede is cited by name at least once in Martin Luther's works, and, although he is not cited by Jean Calvin, his exegetical influence shows up in Calvin's Commentary on Acts, via the *Glossa ordinaria*, despite his

---

[99]   William of Malmesbury, *Gesta regum Anglorum: The History of the English Kings*, ed. R. A. B. Mynors, Rodney M. Thomson, Michael Winterbottom, 2 vols. (Oxford, 1998), and *The Deeds of the Bishops of England (Gesta pontificum Anglorum)*, trans. David Preest (Woodbridge, 2002); Henry of Huntingdon, *Historia Anglorum (The History of the English People)*, ed. Diana Greenway (Oxford, 1996); John of Worcester, *Chronicle*, ed. Reginald R. Darlington and P. McGurk, 2 vols. of 3 (Oxford, 1995). See below for more details about these historians' use of Bede's individual works.

   On the advances in the study and understanding of Anglo-Saxon history made by these historians before the nineteenth century, see James Campbell, "Some Twelfth-Century Views of the Anglo-Saxon Past," *Peritia* 3 (1984): 131–50.

[100]   Thomas Stapleton, trans., *The History of the Church of England, Compiled by Venerable Bede, Englishman* (Antwerp, 1565), Preface. Note that the 1930 Shakespeare Head Press edition of Stapleton's translation lacks the second part (seven pages) of the 1565 apologetic preface. Stapleton's translation also forms the basis of J. E. King's translation in the Loeb edition, *Baedae opera historica*, 2 vols. (Cambridge, 1930).

[101]   *Collectio canonum in v libris*, ed. M. Fornasari, CCCM 6 (Turnhout, 1970), *lib.* 1, *praef.*, *cap.* 64, 189, *lib.* 3, *cap.* 188, 227; and extensively in *Decretum Gratiani* in *Corpus iuris canonici*, vol. 1, ed. Aemilius Ludwig Richter and Emil Albert Friedberg (Leipzig, 1879).

[102]   Jacobus de Voragine, *Legenda aurea*, ed. Giovanni Paolo Maggioni, 2nd rev. ed., Società Internazionale per lo Studio del Medioevo Latino (SISMEL), Millennio Medievale (MM) 6, 2 vols. (Florence, 1998), Indice delle fonti, II: 1304.

[103]   Nicholas of Cusa, *Opera omnia*, ed. Ernst Hoffmann, Raymond Klibansky, et al., 19 vols. in parts, to date (Hamburg, 1959–).

[104]   John Hus, *Tractatus de ecclesia*, ed. Samuel Harrison Thomson (Boulder, 1956), pp. 127, 136, 156.

opposition to allegorical exegesis.[105] Ulrich Zwingli does not cite Bede, but he requested from Kasper Hedio (1494–1552) a Bedan reference.[106] Given Bede's patristic tradition and monastic orthodoxy, he is more appropriately given as an authority by Counter-Reformation apologists: Hieronymus Emser (1478–1527), Johann Eck (1486–1543) (especially in his *Enchiridion locorum communiorum adversus Lutherum*), Johann Dietenberger (c. 1475–1537), the Dominican accused of plagiarizing Luther's translation of the Bible, Hieronymus Dungersheim (1465–1540), Nicholas Ellenbog (1504–1543), and others edited in the Corpus Catholicorum series.[107] The Dominican Thomas de Vio Cajetan (1469–1534) cites Bede's homilies in defending the papal primacy.[108] King Henry VIII (1491–1547) in the *Assertio septem sacramentorum* affirmed Catholic orthodoxy, and gained the papal title of "Defensor Fidei" before his defection from Rome; in the *Assertio* Bede is quoted on Luke's Gospel, as mediated by the *Glossa ordinaria*.[109] Although Robert Bellarmine (1542–1621) does not use Bede in his *Apologiae*, he has an analysis of Bede's writings in *De scriptoribus ecclesiasticis*.[110] In Spain, even though Bede's works were not generally prevalent there before the Reformation, he becomes a prime apologist for the Catholic view of history and the faith, and is particularly cited by the Spanish Jesuits.[111] So although Bede is less a presence among the Reformers, he remains a prime authority among the Catholics. Since the Reformation, every historian dealing with

[105] Martin Luther, *D. Martin Luthers Werke* (Weimar, 1883–1999), 2: 666; John Calvin, *Opera omnia*, ed. B. C. Armstrong, Helmut Feld, et al. (Geneva, 1992–): *Opera Exegetica, Commentariorum in Acta Apostolorum liber primus*, ser. 2, v. 12. 1, pp. 15. 4, 50. 15, 108. 27, 257. 54; *Commentariorum in Acta Apostolorum liber posterior*, p. 232. 11.

[106] Ulrich (Huldreich) Zwingli, *Sämtliche Werke*, ed. Emil Egli, George Finsler, et al., in Corpus Reformatorum 97 (Leipzig, 1929), 10: 646, Letter 1051 (27 June 1530).

[107] Hieronymus Emser, *De disputatione Lipsicensi* (1519), ed. Franz Xavier Thurnhofer, Corpus Catholicorum 4 (Münster, 1921), pp. 36, 66, and *Schriften zur Verteidigung der Messe*, ed. Theobald Freudenberger, Corpus Catholicorum 28 (Münster, 1959), pp. 67, 70, 82, 84; Johannes Eck, *Disputatio Viennae Pannoniae habita (1517)*, ed. Therese Virnich, Corpus Catholicorum 6 (Münster, 1923), p. 53, and his *Enchiridion locorum communium adversus Lutherum et alios hostes ecclesiae (1525–1543)*, ed. Pierre Fraenkel, Corpus Catholicorum 34 (Münster, 1979), where Eck cites eight of Bede's works: see Zitate, p. 432, and his *De sacrificio Missae libri tres* (1526), ed. Erwin Iserloh, et al., Corpus Catholicorum 36 (Münster, 1982), p. 110; Johann Dietenberger, *Phimostomus scripturariorum, Köln 1532*, ed. Erwin Iserloh and Peter Fabisch, Corpus Catholicorum 38 (Münster, 1985), pp. 134, 147, 204; Hieronymus Dungersheim, *Schriften gegen Luther*, ed. Theobald Freudenberger, Corpus Catholicorum 39 (Münster, 1987), pp. 115, 230; Nicholas Ellenbog, *Briefwechsel*, ed. Andreas Bigelmair and Friedrich Zoepfl, Corpus Catholicorum 19/21 (Münster, 1938), p. 162.

[108] Thomas de Vio Caietanus, *De divina institutione pontificatus Romani pontificis (1521)*, ed. Friedrich Lauchert, Corpus Catholicorum 10 (Münster, 1925), pp. 54, 98.

[109] Henry VIII, *Assertio septem sacramentorum adversus Martinum Lutherum*, ed. Pierre Fraenkel, Corpus Catholicorum 43 (Münster, 1992), p. 167.

[110] Robert Bellarmine, *Roberti Bellarmini politiani opera omnia*, ed. Justinus Fèvre (Paris, 1874; rpt. Frankfurt, 1965), 12: 419–21. Bellarmine had Herwagen's eight-volume edition of Bede's works, but he correctly and astutely rejected the spurious works in that edition, and showed also that Cardinal Baronius was wrong to deny Bede's authorship of the transcription of Paul's letters cited in Augustine (the minor work listed by Bede in *HE*, V. 4).

[111] Heidenreich, "Beda Venerabilis in Spain," esp. pp. 122–26.

Anglo-Saxon England must perforce rely on Bede for information of the period, and so Bede's *History* is both the subject and object of numerous contemporary works.

This sampling of references should suffice to indicate Bede's widespread influence through the ages. As emblematic of his universal status, he is the only Englishman to appear in the *Paradiso* of Dante's *Divina Commedia* (canto 10, line 131). Bede's influence now on contemporary thought and scholarship is demonstrated by the numerous references to his works in books, articles, and the media, by the many recent editions of his works, by the modern translations of his works, especially the *Ecclesiastical History* in a number of languages.[112]

For twelve centuries Bede's writings, including his histories, were accepted as straightforward accounts given with equanimity and charity. It is only in our age that critics, led by Walter Goffart and Stephanie Hollis, Clare Lees, and Gillian Overing, have begun to analyze and question Bede's motives and rhetorical techniques.[113] Goffart proposed a political agenda that few have accepted in its totality, and most have found Lees and Overing's critique of Bede's treatment of Abbess Hild's marginality unconvincing, but many others have now begun to analyze Bede's writings for thematic and subtextual elements. Patrick Wormald and Clare Stancliffe have delved into Bede's historical and hagiographic techniques, and Alan Thacker has admirably surfaced major themes, especially of reform, in Bede's homiletic writings.[114] I hope that this book, which tries to encompass all Bede's life and writings, will likewise contribute to a deeper understanding and appreciation of Bede's artistry, his cultural and historical contributions, and his impact on Western culture.

---

[112] For a survey of specific use and influence of Bede's individual works, the reader should consult the second part of my monograph, *The Bedan Legacy: The Influence of the Venerable Bede's Works from the Eighth Century to the Present*, publication of the *Journal of Medieval Latin* (in press).

[113] Walter Goffart, *The Narrators of Barbarian History*, pp. 235–328; "Bede's History in a Harsher Climate," in *Innovation and Tradition in the Writings of the Venerable Bede*, ed. Scott DeGregorio (Morgantown, 2006), pp. 203–26; Stephanie Hollis, *Anglo-Saxon Women and the Church: Sharing a Common Fate* (Woodbridge, 1992); Clare A. Lees and Gillian R. Overing, "Birthing Bishops and Fathering Poets: Bede, Hild, and the Relations of Cultural Production," *Exemplaria* 6. 1 (Spring 1994): 35–64.

[114] Patrick Wormald, *The Times of Bede: Studies in Early English Christian Society and its Historian*, ed. Stephen David Baxter (Malden, 2006); Clare Stancliffe, "St Cuthbert and the Polarity between Pastor and Solitary," in *St Cuthbert, his Cult and his Community*, ed. Gerald Bonner, David Rollason, and Clare Stancliffe (Woodbridge, 1989), pp. 21–44; Alan Thacker, "Bede's Ideal of Reform," in *Ideal and Reality in Frankish and Anglo-Saxon Society*, ed. Patrick Wormald, Donald Bullough, and Roger Collins (Oxford, 1983), pp. 130–53.

Works Cited

CLASSICAL AND MEDIEVAL

Medieval authors in this section are listed in the pre-modern manner according to their Christian (fore-) names, e.g. "Robert Grosseteste," not "Grosseteste, Robert."

Albert Behaim. *Brief- und Memorial Buch*. MGH. Briefe des späteren Mittelalters, 1. Munich, 2000.

Albertus Magnus. *Opera omnia ad fidem codicum manuscriptorum edenda, apparatu critico, notis, prolegomenis*. Vols. 1–26, to date. Westphalia, 1951– .

Alcuin. *The Bishops, Kings, and Saints of York*, ed. and trans. Peter Godman. Oxford, 1982.

_____. *Vita Willibrordi archiepiscopi Traiectensis*, ed. W. Levinson. MGH Scriptores rerum Merovingicarum, VII (1920): 81–141.

Alexander of Hales. *Doctoris irrefragabilis Alexandri de Hales Ordinis Minorum Summa theologica*, ed. Bernardin Klumper. 4 vols. in 5. Florence, 1924.

_____. *Glossa in quatuor libros sententiarum Petri Lombardi*. Bibliotheca Franciscana scholastica medii aevi, vols. 12–15. Rome, 1951.

_____. *Quaestiones disputatae "Antequam esset frater."* 3 vols. Bibliotheca Franciscana scholastica medii aevi, vols. 19–21. Florence, 1960.

Alexander Nequam. *Speculum speculationum*, ed. Rodney M. Thomson. Oxford, 1988.

Amalarius of Metz, *De ecclesiasticis officiis libri quattuor*, IV. I, PL 105: 985–1258.

Augustine. *Contra academicos, De beata vita, De ordine, De magistro, De libero arbitrio*, ed. W. M. Green. CCSL 29. Turnhout, 1970.

_____. *De doctrina christiana*, ed. Joseph Martin. CCSL 32. Turnhout, 1962.

_____. *Excerpts from the works of Saint Augustine on the Letters of the Blessed Apostle Paul*, trans. David Hurst. Cistercian Studies 183. Kalamazoo, 1999.

_____. *In Ioannis epistulam ad Parthos tractatus x*. PL 25: 1977–2.

_____. *On Christian Doctrine*, trans. D. W. Robertson, Jr. Indianapolis, 1958.

Bede, Venerable. *The Abbreviated Psalter of the Venerable Bede*, trans. Gerald M. Browne. Grand Rapids, 2002.

_____. *A Biblical Miscellany*, trans. Trent Foley and Arthur G. Holder. Liverpool, 1999.

_____. *Canticle of Bede the Priest on the Canticle of Habakkuk*, trans. Seán Connolly. Dublin, 1997. Pp. 65–95.

_____. *Chronica maiora*, ed Charles Jones. CCSL 123B. Turnhout, 1977. Pp. 461–538.

_____. *Chronica minora*, ed. Charles Jones. CCSL 123C. Turnhout, 1980. Pp. 601–11.

135

_____. *Collectio psalterii Bedae Venerabili adscripta*. Munich and Leipzig, 2001.

_____. *Commentary on the Acts of the Apostles*, trans. Lawrence T. Martin. Kalamazoo, 1989.

_____. *Commentary on the Seven Catholic Epistles*, trans. D. Hurst. Kalamazoo, 1985.

_____. *The Complete Works of the Venerable Bede, in the Original Latin*, ed. J. A. Giles. 12 vols. London, 1843.

_____. "Concerning Figures and Tropes," trans. Gussie Hecht Tannenhaus. In *Readings in Medieval Rhetoric*, ed. Joseph H. Miller, Michael H. Prosser, Thomas W. Benson. Bloomington, 1973. Pp. 76–80.

_____. *De arte metrica et De schematibus et tropis*, ed. Calvin Kendall. In *Opera didascalia pars 1*. CCSL 123A. Pp. 59–171.

_____. *De natura rerum*, ed. Charles W. Jones. In *Opera didascalia, pars 1*. CCSL 123A. Turnhout, 1975. Pp. 173–234.

_____. *De orthographia*, ed. Charles W. Jones. In *Opera didascalia, pars 1*. CCSL 123A. Turnhout, 1975. Pp. 1–57.

_____. *De locis sanctis*, ed. I. Fraipont. In *Itineraria et alia geographica*. CCSL 175. Turnhout, 1965. 245–80.

_____. *De schematibus et tropis*. In *De arte metrica et De schematibus et tropis*, ed. Calvin Kendall. In *Opera didascalia pars 1*. CCSL 123A. Pp. 59–171.

_____. *De Tabernaculo*, ed. D. Hurst. In *Opera exegetica pars II*. CCSL 119A. Turnhout, 1969.

_____. *De Templo*, ed. D. Hurst. In *Opera exegetica pars II*. CCSL 119A. Turnhout, 1969.

_____. *De temporum ratione*, ed. Charles W. Jones. In *Opera didascalia, pars 2*. CCSL 123B. Turnhout, 1977.

_____. *The Ecclesiastical History of the English People, The Greater Chronicle, Bede's Letter to Egbert*, ed. Judith McClure and Roger Collins. Oxford, 1994.

_____. *The Ecclesiastical History of the English People and Other Selections*, trans. J. Campbell. New York, 1967.

_____. *Ecclesiastical History of the English People*, ed. Bertram Colgrave and R. A. B. Mynors. Oxford, 1969.

_____. *Explanation of the Apocalypse by Venerable Beda*, trans. Edward Marshall. Oxford and London, 1878.

_____. *Expositio Actuum Apostolorum et retractatio*, ed. M. L. W. Laistner. In CCSL 121. Turnhout, 1983.

_____. *Expositio Actuum Apostolorum et retractatio*, ed. M. L. W. Laistner. Cambridge, MA, 1939.

_____. *Expositio Apocalypseos*, ed. Roger Gryson. CCSL 121A. Turnhout, 2001.

_____. *Historia abbatum auctore Baeda*. In Charles Plummer ed., *Baedae opera historica*. Oxford, 1896, rpt. 1975.

_____. *Historia ecclesiastica gentis Anglorum libri v, cui accessere leges Anglo-saxonicae*, ed. Abraham Wheloc. London, 1644, Ann Arbor, microfilm, 1966.

_____. *Historiae ecclesiasticae gentis Anglorum libri quinque*, ed. John Smith. Cambridge, 1722.

_____. *The History of the Church of England, compiled by Venerable Bede, Englishman*, trans. Thomas Stapleton. Antwerp, 1565.

_____. *The History of the Church of England, compiled by Venerable Bede,*

Englishman, trans. Thomas Stapleton. Shakespeare Head Press edition. Oxford, 1930.

———. *Homilies on the Gospels*, trans. Lawrence T. Martin and David Hurst. Kalamazoo, 1991.

———. *In Cantica canticorum*, ed. D. Hurst. In *Opera exegetica pars II*. CCSL 119B. Turnhout, 1983. Pp. 165–375.

———. *In Canticum Habacuc Prophetae*, ed. J. E. Hudson. In *Opera exegetica pars II*. CCSL 119B. Pp. 377–409.

———. *In epistulas VII catholicas*, ed. M. L. W. Laistner and D. Hurst. CCSL 121. Turnhout, 1983. Pp. 179–342.

———. *In Ezram et Neemiam libri III*, ed. Hurst. In *Opera exegetica pars II*. CCSL 119A. Turnhout, 1969. Pp. 235–392.

———. *In Habacuc*, ed. J. E. Hudson. In *Opera exegetica pars II*. CCSL 119B. Turnhout, 1983.

———. *In librum beati patris Tobiae*, ed. D. Hurst. In *Opera exegetica pars I*. CCSL 119A. Turnhout, 1969. Pp. 1–19.

———. *In Lucae evangelium expositio*, ed. D. Hurst. In *Opera exegetica pars III*. CCSL 120. Turnhout, 1960. Pp. 5–425.

———. *In Marci evangelium expositio*, ed. D. Hurst. In *Opera exegetica pars III*. CCSL 120. Turnhout, 1960. Pp. 427–648.

———. *In Principium Genesis, usque ad natiuitatem Isaac et electionem Ismahelis, libros IIII*, ed. C. W. Jones. CCSL 118A. Turnhout, 1967.

———. *In proverbia Salomonis*, ed. D. Hurst. In *Opera exegetica pars II*. CCSL 119B. Turnhout, 1983.

———. *In Regum librum xxx quaestiones*, ed. D. Hurst. In *Opera exegetica pars I*. CCSL 119. Turnhout, 1962. Pp. 289–322.

———. *In I Samuhelem*, ed. D. Hurst. In *Opera exegetica pars I*. CCSL 119. Turnhout, 1962.

———. *In Tobiam*, ed. D. Hurst. In *Opera exegetica pars II*. CCSL 119B. Turnhout, 1983.

———. *König Alfreds Übersetzung von Bedas Kirchengeschichte*, ed. Jacob Schipper, in Bibliothek der angelsächsischen Prosa, ed. Christian Grein. Leipzig, 1899.

———. *Libri II De arte metrica et de schematibus et tropis/ The Art of Poetry and Rhetoric*, trans. Calvin Kendall. Bibliotheca Germanica, series nova 2. Saarbrucken, 1991.

———. *Libri quatuor in principium Genesis*, ed. Charles W. Jones. *Opera exegetica* 1. Turnhout, 1967.

———. *The Life of Ceolfrid*, trans. Douglas Boutflower. Sunderland, 1912.

———. *The Lives of the Abbots of Wearmouth and Jarrow*, trans. D. H. Farmer. In *The Age of Bede*. Harmondsworth, 1965, rpt. 1986.

———. *Magnus circulus seu tabula paschalis, kalendarium sive martyrologium, de temporibus liber, epistola ad Pleguinam, opuscula fortassis genuina*, ed. Charles W. Jones. *Opera didascalia* 3. CCSL 123C. Turnhout, 1980.

———. *Martyrology*, ed. and trans. Felice Lifshitz. In *Medieval Hagiography: An Anthology*, ed. Thomas Head. New York and London, 2000. Pp. 169–97.

———. *Nomina regionum atque locorum de Actibus Apostolorum*, ed. M. L. W. Laistner. In CCSL 121. Turnhout, 1983. Pp. 165–78.

———. *The Old English Version of Bede's Ecclesiastical History of the English*

People, ed. and trans. Thomas Miller. Early English Text Society, Original Series 95, 96, 111. Oxford, 1890, 1898, rpt. 1959, 1963.

_____. *On Ezra and Nehemiah*, trans. Scott DeGregorio. Liverpool, 2006.

_____. *On Genesis*, trans. Calvin B. Kendall. Liverpool, 2008.

_____. *On the Song of Songs*, trans. Arthur Holder. In press.

———. *On the Tabernacle*, trans. Arthur G. Holder. Liverpool, 1994.

_____. *On the Temple*, trans. with notes by Seán Connolly, with an Introduction by Jennifer O'Reilly. Liverpool, 1995.

_____. *On Tobit and on the Canticle of Habakkuk*, trans. Seán Connolly. Dublin, 1997

_____. *Opera Bedae venerabilis presbyteri anglosaxonis*, ed. Johann Herwagen. 8 vols. in 4. Basel, 1563.

_____. *Opera de temporibus*, ed. Charles W. Jones. Cambridge, MA, 1943.

_____. *Opera historica*, trans. J. E. King. Loeb Classical Library. 2 vols. London and New York, 1930.

_____. *Opera historica*, ed. Charles Plummer. 2 vols. Oxford. 1896, rpt. 1975.

_____. *Opera homiletica*, ed. D. Hurst. CCSL 122. Turnhout, 1955. Pp. 1–403.

_____. *Opera quædam theologica*, ed. Henry Wharton. Early English Books Online. London, 1693.

_____. *Opera rhythmica*, ed. J. Fraipont. Published with *Opera homiletica*, ed. D. Hurst. CCSL 122. Turnhout, 1955. Pp. 405–70.

———. *Retractatio*. In *Expositio Actuum Apostolorum et retractatio*, ed. Laistner.

_____. *The Reckoning of Time*, trans. Faith Wallis. Liverpool, 1988, rpt. with corrections 2004.

_____. *Storia degli Inglesi (Historia ecclesiastica gentis Anglorum)*, ed. Michael Lapidge, trans. di Paolo Chiesa. Vol. 1. Milan, 2008.

_____. *Vita Cuthberti. Bedas metrische Vita Cuthberti*, ed. Werner Jaager. Leipzig, 1935.

_____. *Vita Felicis*, ed. Thomas W. Mackay in his "Critical Edition of Bede's *Vita Felicis*." Ph.D. diss., Stanford University, 1971. Ann Arbor: University Microfilms International, 1972.

Biblia latina cum glossa ordinaria: Facsimile Reprint of the editio princeps Adolph Rusch of Strassburg 1480/81, ed. Karlfried Froehlich and Margaret T. Gibson. 4 vols. Turnhout, 1992.

Bibliotheca Franciscana Scholastica Medii Aevi. 28 vols. to date. Grottaferrata, 1904– .

Bibliotheca Neerlandica Manuscripta. http://bnm.leidenuniv.nl.

Bonaventure. *Opera omnia*. 10 vols. Rome, 1882–1902.

_____. *Sancti Bonaventurae sermones dominicales*. Bibliotheca Franciscana scholastica medii aevi, vol. 27. Grottaferrata, 1977.

Bonnet, M., ed. *Acta Apostolorum apocrypha*. 2 vols. in 3 parts. Leipzig, 1891–1903.

The Book of Settlements: Landnámabók, trans. Hermann Pálsson and Paul Edwards. Manitoba, 1972.

Brenton, Lancelot C. L., ed. *The Septuagint with Apocrypha: Greek and English*. London, 1851, rpt. Peabody, MA, 1986.

Bright, Pamela. *The Book of Rules of Tyconius: its Purpose and Inner Logic*. Notre Dame, 1988.

Bruckner, Albert. *Die vier Bücher Julians von Aeclanum an Turbantius: Ein Beitrag zur Characteristik Julians und Augustins.* Berlin, 1910, rpt. Aalen, 1973. Pp. 113–16.

Caie, Graham D., ed. *The Old English Poem 'Judgement Day II': A Critical Edition with Editions of De die iudicii and the Hatton 113 Homily Be domes dæge.* Cambridge, 2000.

Cassidy, Frederick G., and Richard N. Ringler, eds. *Bright's Old English Grammar and Reader.* New York, 1971.

Colgrave, Bertram, ed. and trans. *Two Lives of Saint Cuthbert: A Life by an Anonymous Monk of Lindisfarne and Bede's Prose Life.* Cambridge, 1940, 1985.

Collectio canonum in v libris, ed. M. Fornasari. CCCM 6. Turnhout, 1970.

Concilia ævi Karolini I, MGH, Legum III, Concilia II, I.

Cook, A. S., ed. *The Christ of Cynewulf.* Boston, 1909.

Corpus Iuris Canonici, ed. Aemilius Ludwig Richter and Emil Albert Friedberg. 2 vols. Leipzig, 1879, rpt. Union, NJ, 2000.

Díaz y Díaz, M. C., ed. *Liber de ordine creaturarum.* Santiago de Compostela, 1972.

Dietenberger, Johann. *Phimostomos scripturariorum, Köln, 1532*, ed. Erwin Iserloh and Peter Fabisch. Corpus Catholicorum 38. Münster, 1985.

Dubois, Jacques, and Geneviève Renaud, eds. *Édition practique des martyrologes de Bède, de l'anonyme lyonnais et de Florus.* Paris, 1976.

Farmer, D. H., trans. *The Age of Bede.* London, 1983.

Fischer, Bonifatius, et al., eds. *Vetus Latina; die Reste der altlateinischen Bibel.* Freiburg, 1949– .

Fraipont, I., et al., eds. *Itineraria et alia geographica.* CCSL 175. Turnhout, 1965.

Frechulf of Lisieux. *Frechulfi Lexoviensis episcopi opera omnia*, ed. Michael I. Allen. CCCM 169, Text; CCCM 169A, Prolegomena and Indices. Turnhout, 2002.

Glossa ordinaria on the Song of Songs, trans. Mary Dove. Kalamazoo, 2004.

Gregory the Great, pope. *Homilia xl in Evangelia.* PL 76: 1131C.

———. Gregorii papae, *Registrum epistolarum*, ed. Dag Norberg. CCSL 140A. Turnhout, 1982.

Guido of Rechelles (de Orchellis). *Tractatus de Sacramentis ex eius summa de Sacramentis et officiis Ecclesiae*, ed. Damien and Odulphus van den Eynde. St. Bonaventure, NY, 1953.

Haddan, A. W., and W. Stubbs, eds. *Councils and Ecclesiastical Documents relating to Great Britain and Ireland.* 3 vols. Oxford, 1869–78.

Henry VIII. *Assertio Septem Sacramentorum adversus Martinum Lutherum*, ed. Pierre Fraenkel. Corpus Catholicorum 43. Münster, 1992.

Hieronymus Dungersheim. *Schriften gegen Luther*, ed. Theobald Freudenberger. Corpus Catholicorum 39. Münster, 1987.

Hieronymus Emser. *De disputatione Lipsicensi* (1519), ed. Franz Xavier Thurnhofer. Corpus Catholicorum 4. Münster, 1921.

_____. *Schriften zur Verteidigung der Messe*, ed. Theobald Freudenberger. Corpus Catholicorum 28. Münster, 1959.

Hincmar of Reims, *De praedestinatione dissertatio posterior.* PL 125: 353.

Isaiah 1–39, Joseph Blenkinsopp, ed. and trans. The Anchor Bible vol. 19. New York, 2000.

Isidore of Seville. *De natura rerum liber/ Traité de la nature.*, ed. and trans. J. Fontaine. Bordeaux, 1960.

Jacobus de Voragine. *Legenda Aurea*, ed. Giovanni Paolo Maggioni. 2nd rev. ed.

Società Internazionale per lo Studio del Medioevo Latino (SISMEL), Millennio Medievale (MM) 6. 2 vols. Florence, 1998.

Jerome (Hieronymus). *Commentaires de Jérôme sur le prophète Isaïe*, ed. Roger Gryson and V. Somers, Books 8–11. Freiburg, 1996.

_____. *Epistulae*, ed. I. Hilberg, CSEL 54. 3 vols. Vienna, 1996.

_____. *Liber interpretationis Hebraicorum nominum*, ed. P. de Lagarde. CCSL 72. Turnhout, 1959.

_____. *Selected Letters*, trans. F. A. Wright. Loeb edition. London, 1933.

Johann Dietenberger, *Phimostomus scripturariorum, Köln 1532*, ed. Erwin Iseloh and Peter Fabisch. Corpus Catholicorum 38. Münster 1985.

Johannes Eck. *Disputatio Viennae Pannoniae habita (1517)*, ed. Therese Virnich. Corpus Catholicorum 6. Münster, 1923.

_____. *Enchiridion locorum communium adversus Lutherum et alios hostes ecclesiae (1525–1543)*, ed. Pierre Fraenkel. Corpus Catholicorum 34. Münster, 1979.

John Calvin. *Opera omnia*, ed. Helmut Feld et al. 12 of 19 vols. to date. Geneva, 2001.

John Hus. *Tractatus de Ecclesia*, ed. Samuel Harrison Thomson. Boulder, 1956.

Keil, Heinrich, ed. *Grammatici latini*. 7 vols. and suppl. Leipzig, 1857–70.

Leo XIII, pope. *Bulla Urbis et Orbis. Acta Sanctae Sedis*, 1897. Pp. 338–39.

Lumby, J. Rawson, ed. *Be Domes Dæge, De die judicii*. Early English Text Society, Original Series 65. London. 1876.

Manuscripta medievalia. http://www.manuscripta-mediaevalia.de./

Marsilius of Padua. *Defensor pacis*, ed. Joannes de Janduno and Richard Scholz. Hanover, 1932.

Martin Luther. *D. Martin Luthers Werke*. Kritische Gesamtausgabe. 4 vols in multiple parts. Weimar, 1883–1999.

Matthew of Aquasparta. *Quaestiones disputatae de anima xiii*, ed. A. J. Gondras. Paris, 1961.

_____. *Quaestiones disputatae de anima separata, de anima beata, de ieiunio et de legibus*. Bibliotheca Franciscana scholastica medii aevi, vol. 18. Florence, 1959.

_____. *Quaestiones disputatae de fide et de cognitione*. Bibliotheca Franciscana scholastica Medii Aevi, vol. 1. Florence, 1957.

_____. *Quaestiones disputatae de incarnatione et de lapsu aliaeque selectae de Christo et de eucharistia*. 2nd ed. Bibliotheca Franciscana Scholastica medii aevi, vol. 2. Florence, 1957.

_____. *Quaestiones disputatae de productione rerum et de providentia*. Bibliotheca franciscana scholastica medii aevi, vol. 17. Florence, 1956.

Mittelalterliche Bibliothekskataloge Deutschlands und der Schweiz. Bayerische Akademie der Wissenschaften. 4 vols. in 8 with 3 supplements to date. Munich, 1969– .

Mittelalterliche Bibliothekskataloge Österreichs, vols. 1–5. Österreichische Akademie der Wissenschaften. 5 vols. with 1 suppl. Vienna, 1915; Aalen, 1974.

Monk of St. Gall. *De gestis Caroli magni*. PL 100: 121D–122A.

Nicholas of Cusa, *Opera omnia*, ed. Ernst Hoffmann, Raymond Klibansky, et al. 19 vols, in parts, to date. Hamburg, 1959– .

Nicholas Ellenbog. *Briefwechsel*, ed. Andreas Bigelmair and Friedrich Zoepfl. Corpus Catholicorum, 19/21. Münster, 1938.

Odericus Vitalis. *The Ecclesiastical History*, ed. Marjorie Chibnall. 6 vols. Oxford, 1969.

Works Cited: Classical and Medieval

Ólaf Saga Tryggsonar en Mesta, ed. Ólafur Halldórrson. Editiones Arnamagnæanæ. Series A, vol. 3. Copenhagen, 2000.

Oswald of Northumbria, ed. and trans. Marianne E. Kalinke. Medieval & Renaissance Texts & Studies, v. 297. Tempe, 2005.

Paschasius Radbertus. *Opera omnia.* PL 120.

Patrologia Latina, ed. J-P. Migne, 221 vols. Paris, 1844–64.

Peter Abelard. *Opera theologica*, ed. E. M. Buytaert et al. CCCM 11. Turnhout, 1969.

———. *Sic et non: A Critical Edition*, ed. Blanche B. Boyer and Richard McKeon. Chicago, 1977.

Peter Cantor. *Glossae super Genesim: Prologus et captula 1–3*, ed. Agneta Sylwan. Göteborg, 1992.

———. *Summa de Sacramentis et animae consiliis*, ed. Jean Albert Dugauquier. Louvain, 1954.

———. *Verbum abbreviatum: textus conflatus*, ed. Monique Boutry. CCCM 196. Turnhout, 2004.

Peter Comestor. *Historia scholastica.* PL 198: 1054–1721.

———. *Scholastica historia, Liber Genesis*, ed. Agneta Sylwan. CCCM 191. Turnhout, 2005.

Peter Lombard. *Sententiae in iv libris distinctae.* Spicilegium Bonaventurianum 4–5. 2 vols. in 3. Grottaferrata, 1971, 1981.

Petrus (Pierre) de Cava. *In librum primum Regum expositionum libri sex/ Commentaire sur le premier livre des Rois*, ed. Adalbert de Vogüé. 6 vols. Paris, 2003.

Pliny, *Naturalis historia/ Natural History*, ed. and trans. H. Rackham. 10 vols. Cambridge, MA, 1938–62.

Prepositinus. *Summa contra haereticos*, ed. Joseph N. Garvin and James A. Corbett. Notre Dame, 1958.

Pseudo-Augustine. *De mirabilibus Sacrae Scripturae.* PL 35: 2149–2200.

Pseudo-Isidore of Seville. *De Ordine Creaturarum.* PL 83: 913–54.

Quintilian. *Institutiones oratoriae*, ed. M. Winterbottom. Oxford Classical Texts. Oxford, 1970.

Robert Bellarmine, *Roberti Bellarmini Politiani Opera omnia*, ed. Justinus Fèvre. 12 vols. Paris, 1874; repr. Frankfurt, 1965.

Robert Grosseteste. *De cessatione legalium*, ed. Richard C. Dales and Edward B. King. London, 1986.

———. *De Decem Mandatis*, ed. Richard C. Dales and Edward B. King. London, 1987.

———. *Hexaëmeron*, ed. Richard C. Dales and Edward B. King. London, 1982.

———. *Die philosphischen Werke*, ed. Ludwig Baur. Münster, 1912.

Robert Kilwardby. *Quaestiones in libros Sententiarum*, ed. Gerhard Leibold et al. 5 vols. Bayerische Akademie der Wissenschaften 10, 12, 13, 16, 17. Munich, 1982–93.

Rodrigo Jiménez de Rada (Rodericus de Ximenes). *Historia de rebus Hispanie sive historia gothica*, part 1, ed. Juan Fernández Valverde. CCCM 72. Turnhout, 1987.

Roger Bacon. *Compotus Fratris Rogeri. Opera hactenus inedita Rogeri Baconi*, Fasciculus 6, ed. Robert Steele. Oxford, 1926.

Sabatier, P. *Bibliorum sacrorum latinae versiones antiquae seu Vetus Italica.* Reims, 1743; rpt. Turnhout, 1981.

Swanton, Michael, ed. *The Dream of the Rood.* Manchester and New York, 1970.

Symeon of Durham. *Libellus de exordio atque procursu istius, hoc est Dunhelmensis, Ecclesie/ Tract on the Origins and Progress of this the Church of Durham*. Ed. and trans. D. W. Rollason. Oxford Medieval Texts. Oxford; New York, 2000.

Thomas Aquinas. *Catena aurea in quatuor Evangelia*, ed. Angelico Guarienti. Turin, 1953.

_____. *Opera omnia*. Editio leonina. 50 vols. Rome, 1882–1976.

_____. *Scriptum super Sententiis: An Index of Authorities Cited*, ed. Charles H. Lohr. Avebury, 1980.

_____. *Super IV libros Sententiarum*, ed. Roberto Coggi. 10 vols. Bologna, 1999.

Thomas de Vio Caietanus, *De divina institutione pontificatus Romani Pontificis (1521)*, ed. Friedrich Lauchert. Corpus Catholicorum 10. Münster, 1925.

Tyconius. *The Book of Rules*, trans. William S. Babcock. Ithaca, 1989.

Ulrich (Huldreich) Zwingli. *Sämtliche Werke*, ed. Emil Egli, George Finsler, et al. In Corpus Reformatorum 97. Leipzig, 1929.

Walpole, A. S., ed. *Early Latin Hymns*. Cambridge, 1922, rpt. 1966.

Webb, J. F., ed. and trans. *Lives of the Saints: The Voyage of St. Brendan; Bede, Life of Cuthbert; Eddius Stephanus, Life of Wilfrid*. Harmondsworth, 1965, 1973.

William de la Mare, *Scriptum in primum librum Sententiarum*, ed. Hans Kraml. Texte aus der mittlelalterlichen Geisteswelt 15. Munich, 1989.

_____. *Scriptum in secundum librum Sententiarum*, ed. Hans Kraml. Texte aus der mittlelalterlichen Geisteswelt 18. Munich, 1995.

William of Auvergne, *De virtutibus et de moribus*. In *Opera de fide*, ed. Georg Stuchs. Nuremberg, 1497.

William of Auxerre. *Summa aurea*, ed. Jean Ribaillier. 4 vols. in 6. Paris and Rome, 1980.

William of Malmesbury. *The Deeds of the Bishops of England (Gesta pontificum Anglorum)*, trans. David Preest. Woodbridge, 2002.

_____. *Gesta regum Anglorum*, ed. R. A. B. Mynors, R. M. Thompson, and M. Winterbottom. 2 vols. Oxford, 1998.

William of Middleton, *Quaestiones de sacramentis*, ed. Caelestinus Pian and Gál Gedeon. Bibliotheca Franciscana scholastica medii aevi 22, 23. Florence, 1961.

SECONDARY LITERATURE

Aigrain, René. *L'hagiographie: ses sources, ses méthodes, son histoire*. Paris, 1953.

Albertson, Clinton, trans. *Anglo-Saxon Saints and Heroes*. New York, 1967.

Arnold, Johannes, Rainer Berndt, and Ralf M. W. Stammberger, eds. *Väter der Kirche: Ekklesiales Denken von den Anfängen bis in die Neuzeit*. Paderborn, 2004.

Astell, Ann W. *The Song of Songs in the Middle Ages*. Ithaca, 1990.

Beach, Alison I. *Women as Scribes: Book Production and Monastic Reform in Twelfth-Century Bavaria*. Cambridge, 2004.

Benedikz, Benedikt S. "Bede in the Uttermost North." In *Famulus Christi: Essays in Commemoration of the Thirteenth Centenary of the Birth of the Venerable Bede*, ed. Gerald Bonner. London, 1976. Ch. 18, pp. 334–41.

Bibliotheca Neerlandica Manuscripta. http://bnm.leidenuniv.nl.

Biggs, Frederick. Review of Graham Caie's edition of *De die iudicii*. *Modern Language Review* 98. 1 (2003): 153–54.

Bischoff, Bernhard. *Katalog der festländischen Handschriften des neunten Jahrhunderts (mit Ausnahme der wisigotischen).* 2 vols. to date. Wiesbaden, 1998– .

_____. *Mittelalterliche Studien.* 3 vols. Stuttgart, 1966.

_____. *Die südostdeutschen Schreibschule und Bibliotheken in der Karolingerzeit.* 2 vols. Wiesbaden, 1960.

_____ and Michael Lapidge, eds. *Biblical Commentaries from the Canterbury School of Theodore and Hadrian.* CSASE 10. Cambridge, 1994.

Blanton, Virginia. *Signs of Devotion: The Cult of St. Æthelthryth in Medieval England, 695–1615.* University Park, PA, 2007.

Bodarwé, Katrinette. *Sanctimoniales Litteratae: Schriftlichkeit und Bildung in den ottonischen Frauenkommunitäten Gandersheim, Essen und Quedlinburg.* Münster, 2004.

Bolton, Whitney F. *A History of Anglo-Latin Literature, 597–1066.* Vol. 1. Princeton, 1967.

Bonner, Gerald, ed. *Famulus Christi: Essays in Commemoration of the Thirteenth Centenary of the Birth of the Venerable Bede.* London, 1976.

_____. *Saint Bede in the Tradition of Western Apocalyptic Commentary.* Jarrow Lecture 1966. Jarrow, 1967. Reprinted in *Bede and his World: The Jarrow Lectures,* ed. Michael Lapidge. London, 1994. I: 153–73.

_____, David Rollason, and Clare Stancliffe, eds. *St Cuthbert, His Cult and His Community.* Woodbridge, 1989. Pp. 21–44.

Bonner, Stanley F. *Education in Ancient Rome.* Berkeley, 1977.

Bouhot, Jean-Paul. "Fragments attribués à Vigile de Thapse dans *l'Expositio Missae* de Florus de Lyon." *Revue des Études Augustiniennes* 21. 3–4 (1975): 302–16.

Bracken, Damian. "Virgil the Grammarian and Bede: A Preliminary Study." *ASE* 35 (2006): 7–21.

Brown, George Hardin. *The Bedan Legacy.* Publication of the *Journal of Medieval Latin* (in preparation).

_____. "Bede and the Cross." In *Sancta Crux/ Halige Rod: Cross and Culture in Anglo-Saxon England,* ed. Karen Louise Jolly, Catherine E. Karkov, and Sarah Larratt Keefer. Morgantown, 2008. Pp. 21–38.

_____. "Bede's Neglected Commentary on Samuel." In *Innovation and Tradition in the Writings of the Venerable Bede,* ed. Scott DeGregorio. Morgantown, 2006. Pp. 121–42.

_____. "Bede's Style in his Commentary on I Samuel." In *Text, Image, Interpretation: Studies in Anglo-Saxon Literature and its Insular Context in Honour of Éamonn Ó Carragáin,* ed. Alistair Minnis and Jane Roberts. Turnhout, 2007. Pp. 233–51.

_____. "The Descent-Ascent Motif in Christ II of Cynewulf." *JEGP* 73 (1974): 1–12.

_____. "Royal and Ecclesiastical Rivalries in Bede's *History.*" *Renascence* 52.1 (1999): 19–34.

Bullough, Donald A. *Alcuin: Achievement and Reputation.* Leiden, 2004.

———. "Hagiography as Patriotism: Alcuin's 'York Poem' and the Early Northumbrian 'Vitae sanctorum.'" *Hagiographie, Culture et Sociétés IVe–XIIe Siècles.* Paris, 1981. Pp. 339–59.

Burlin, Robert B., ed. *The Old English Advent: A Typological Commentary.* New Haven, 1968.

Byrne, Francis John. "*Ut Beda boat*: Cuanu's Signature?" In *Ireland and Europe in the Early Middle Ages: Texts and Transmission = Irland und Europa im früheren Mittelalter*, edited by Próinséas ní Chatháin and Michael Richter. Dublin; Portland, OR, 2002. Pp. 45–67.

Calder, Daniel G. *Cynewulf.* Twayne English Authors Series 327. Boston, 1981.

Campbell, James. "Bede" in *Latin Historians*, ed. T. A. Dorey. London, 1966. Pp. 159–89.

_____. "Some Considerations on Religion in Early England." In *Collectanea Antiqua: Essays in Memory of Sonia Chadwick Hawkes*, ed. Martin Henig and Tyler Jo Smith. Oxford, 2007. Pp. 67–73.

_____. "Some Twelfth-Century Views of the Anglo-Saxon Past." *Peritia* 3 (1984): 131–50.

Carroll, Sr. M. Thomas Aquinas. *The Venerable Bede: His Spiritual Teachings.* Catholic University of America Studies in Mediaeval History, New Series 9. Washington, DC, 1946.

Chazelle, Celia, and Burton Van Name Edwards, eds. *The Study of the Bible in the Carolingian Era.* Turnhout, 2003.

Coleman, Janet. *Ancient and Medieval Memories: Studies in the Reconstruction of the Past.* Cambridge, 1992.

Colish, Marcia. *Peter Lombard.* 2 vols. Leiden, 1994.

Contreni, John J. "John Scottus and Bede." In *History and Eschatology in John Scottus Eriugena and his Time*, ed. James McEvoy and Michael Dunne. Leuven, 2002. Pp. 91–140.

Cramp, Rosemary. *Wearmouth and Jarrow Monastic Sites.* English Heritage. Swindon, 2005.

Cubitt, Catherine. "Images of St Peter: The Clergy and the Religious Life in Anglo-Saxon England." In *The Christian Traditon in Anglo-Saxon England*, ed. Paul Cavill. Woodbridge, 2004. Pp. 41–54.

_____. "Memory and Narrative in the Cult of Early Anglo-Saxon Saints." In *The Uses of the Past in the Early Middle Ages*, ed. Y. Hen and M. Innes. Cambridge, 2000. Pp. 29–66.

_____. "Monastic Memory and Identity in Early Anglo-Saxon England." In *The Uses of the Past in the Early Middle Ages*, ed. Yitzhak Hen and Matthew Innes. Cambridge, 2000. Pp. 29–66.

Daniélou, Jean. *From Shadows to Reality: Studies in the Biblical Typology of the Fathers.* London, 1960.

Davidse, Jan. "The Sense of History in the Works of the Venerable Bede." *Studi Medievali* 23 (1982): 664–70.

Davis, R. H. C. "Bede after Bede." In *Studies in Medieval History Presented to R. Allen Brown*, edited by C. Harper-Bill, C. J. Holdsworth, and J. L. Nelson. Woodbridge, 1989. Pp. 103–116.

de Margerie, Bertrand. "Bède le Vénérable, Commentateur original du Nouveau Testament." In *Introduction à l'Histoire de l'Exégèse.* 4 vols. (Paris, 1980–90).

Declercq, George. *Anno Domini: The Origins of the Christian Era.* Turnhout, 2000.

DeGregorio, Scott. "Bede, the Monk, as Exegete: Evidence from the Commentary on Ezra-Nehemiah." *RB* 115 (2005): 343–69.

_____. "Bede's *In Ezram et Neemiam* and the Reform of the Northumbrian Church." *Speculum* 79 (2004): 1–25.

_____. "Literary Contexts: Cædmon's Hymn as a Center of Bede's World." In

Cædmon's Hymn and Material Culture in the World of Bede, ed. Allen J. Frantzen and John Hines. Morgantown, 2007. Pp. 51–79.

_____. " 'Nostrorum socordiam temporum': The Reforming Impulse of Bede's Later Exegesis." *Early Medieval Europe* 11 (2002): 107–22.

Dekker, Kees. "Pentecost and Linguistic Self-Consciousness in Anglo-Saxon England: Bede and Ælfric." *JEGP* 104 (2005): 345–72.

Delehaye, Hippolyte. *The Legends of the Saints*, trans. Donald Attwater. New York, 1962.

_____. *Les passions des martyrs et les genres littéraires*. 2nd ed. Brussels, 1966.

Dictionary of Scientific Biography, ed. Charles Coulston Gillispie. 18 vols. New York, 1970.

Dionisotti, Anna Carlotta. "On Bede, Grammars, and Greek." *RB* 92 (1982): 111–41.

Doyle, A. I. "Bede's Death Song in Durham Cathedral Library, MS. A. IV. 36." In *Symeon of Durham*, ed. David Rollason. (Stamford, 1998). Pp. 157–60.

Dumville, David N. "The Anglian Collection of Royal Genealogies and Regnal Lists." *Anglo-Saxon England* 5 (1976): 23–50.

_____. "The Local Rulers of England to AD 927." In *Handbook of British Chronology*, ed. E. B. Fryde, D. F. Greenway, S. Porter, I. Roy. London, 1986. Pp. 1–25.

_____. "The Two Earliest Manuscripts of Bede's Ecclesiastical History?" *Anglo-Saxon* 1 (2007): 55–108.

Dunn, Marilyn. *The Emergence of Monasticism: From the Desert Fathers to the Early Middle Ages*. Oxford, 2000.

Fletcher, Eric. *Benedict Biscop*. Jarrow Lecture 1981. Rpt. *Bede and his World*, ed. Michael Lapidge. Aldershot, 1994. II: 539–54.

Foley, W. Trent. "Bede's Exegesis of Passages Unique to the Gospel of Mark." In *Biblical Studies in the Early Middle Ages*, ed. Claudio Leonardi and Giovanni Orlandi. Florence, 2005. Pp. 105–24.

Foot, Sarah. *Monastic Life in Anglo-Saxon England, c. 600–900*. New York, 2006.

_____. *Veiled Women*. 2 vols. Aldershot, 2000.

Forbes, Charles, comte de Montalembert. *The Monks of the West, from St. Benedict to St. Bernard*. London, 1896.

Franklin, Carmela Vircillo. "Bilingual Philology in Bede's Exegesis." In *Medieval Cultures in Contact*, ed. Richard F. Gyug. New York, 2003. Pp. 3–17.

_____. "Grammar and Exegesis: Bede's *Liber de schematibus et tropis.*" In *Latin Grammar and Rhetoric from Classical Theory to Medieval Practice*, ed. Carol Dana Lanham. New York, 2002. Pp. 63–91.

Fryde, E. B., D. F. Greenway, S. Porter, I. Roy, eds. *Handbook of British Chronology*. London, 1986.

Fry, Donald K. "Bede Fortunate in his Translator: The Barking Nuns." *Studies in Earlier Old English Prose*, ed. Paul E. Szarmach. Albany, NY, 1986. Pp. 345–62.

Godman, Peter. "The Anglo-Latin *opus geminatum*: from Aldhelm to Alcuin," *Medium Aevum* 50.2 (1981): 215–29.

Goffart, Walter. "Bede's History in a Harsher Climate." In *Innovation and Tradition in the Writings of the Venerable Bede*, ed. Scott DeGregorio. Morgantown, 2006. Pp. 203–26.

_____. *The Narrators of Barbarian History (A.D. 550–800): Jordanes, Gregory of Tours, Bede, and Paul the Deacon* (Princeton, 1988).

Gorman, Michael. "Bede's *VIII Quaestiones* and Carolingian Biblical Scholarship."

RB 109 (1999): 32–74. Rpt. in *The Study of the Bible in the Early Middle Ages.* Florence, 2007. Pp. 299–345.

_____. "Bernhard Bischoff's Handlist of Carolingian Manuscripts." *Scrittura e Civiltà* 25 (2001): 89–112.

_____. "The Canon of Bede's Works and the World of Ps. Bede." *Révue Bénédictine* 111 (2001): 399–445.

_____. "Manuscript Books at Monte Amiata in the Eleventh Century." *Scriptorium* 56 (2002): 225–93.

Gransden, Antonia. "Bede's Reputation as an Historian in Medieval England." *Journal of Ecclesiastical History* 32 (1981): 397–425.

_____. *Legends, Traditions and History in Medieval England.* London and Rio Grande, OH, 1992.

Griffith, Mark. Review of Graham Caie's edition of *De die iudicii. Medium Ævum* 60.2 (2001): 322–23.

Gryson, Roger, ed. *Répertoire général des auteurs ecclésiastiques latins de l'antiquité et du haut Moyen Âge.* Freiburg, 2007.

Gulick, Michael. "The Hand of Symeon of Durham." In *Symeon of Durham*, ed. D. Rollason (Stamford, 1998). Pp. 14–31.

Hagendahl, Harald. *Latin Fathers and the Classics.* Göteborgs Universitets Årskrift 64: 2. Göteborg, 1958.

Handschriftencensus Rheinland: Erfassung mittelalterlicher Handschriften im rheinischen Landesteil von Nordrhein-Westfalen mit einem Inventar, ed. Günter Gattermann, Heinz Finger, et al. Wiesbaden, 1993.

Harris, Stephen, ed. Bede. http://bede.net/.

Heidenreich, Helmut. "Beda Venerabilis in Spain." *Modern Language Notes* 85:2 (1970): 120–37.

Higham, N. J. *(Re-)Reading Bede.* Abingdon, 2006.

Hill, Joyce. "Carolingian Perspectives on the Authority of Bede." In *Innovation and Tradition in the Writings of the Venerable Bede*, ed. Scott DeGregorio. Morgantown, 2006. Pp. 227–49.

Hill, V. "The Middle Irish Version of Bede's *De locis sanctis,*" *Zeitschrift für Celtische Philologie* 17 (1927): 225–40.

Holder, Arthur. "The Anti-Pelagian Character of Bede's *Commentary on the Song of Songs.*" In *Biblical Studies in the Early Middle Ages*, ed. Claudio Leonardi and Giovanni Orlandi. Florence, 2005. Pp. 91–103.

_____. "The Feminine Christ in Bede's Biblical Commentaries." In *Bède le Vénérable entre tradition et postérité*, ed. Stéphane Lebecq, Michel Perrin, Olivier Szerwiniack. Lille, 2005. Pp. 109–118.

_____. "The Patristic Sources of Bede's Commentary on the Song of Songs." *Studia Patristica* 34 (2001): 370–75.

_____. "(Un)Dating Bede's *De Arte Metrica.*" In *Northumbria's Golden Age*, ed. Jane Hawkes and Susan Mills. Stroud, 1999. Pp. 390–95.

Holdinger, Bruce. "The Parable of Caedmon's Hymn: Liturgical Invention and Literary Tradition." *JEGP* 106 (2007): 149–75.

Hollis, Stephanie. *Anglo-Saxon Women and the Church: Sharing a Common Fate.* Woodbridge, 1992.

Holtz, Louis. *Donat et la tradition de l'enseignement grammatical: étude sur l'Ars Donati et sa diffusion (IVe–IXe siècle) et édition critique.* Paris, 1981.

Houghton, John William. "Bede's Exegetical Theology: Ideas of the Church in the

Acts Commentaries of St. Bede the Venerable." Ph.D. dissertation. Notre Dame, 1994.

Houwen, L. A. J. R., and A. A. MacDonald, eds. *Beda venerabilis: Historian, Monk and Northumbrian*. Groningen, 1996.

Howlett, David. "Israelite Learning in Insular Latin." *Peritia* 11 (1997): 117–52.

Hughes, Kathleen. "The Church in Irish Society, 400–800." In *A New History of Ireland, I: Prehistoric and Early Ireland*, ed. Dáibhi Ó Cróinin. Oxford, 2005. Pp. 301–30.

Hunter Blair, Peter. *The World of Bede*. Cambridge, 1970, rev. 1990.

Huws, Daniel. *Medieval Welsh Manuscripts*. Aberystwyth, 2000.

Irvine, Martin. *The Making of Textual Culture: 'Grammatica' and Literary Theory 350–1100*. Cambridge, 1994.

Isola, Antonio. "Il *De schematibus et tropis* di Beda in rapporto al *De doctrina christiana* di Agostino." *Romanobarbarica* 1 (1976): 71–82.

James, Edward. "Bede and the Tonsure Question." *Peritia* 3 (1984): 85–98.

Jones, Charles W. "Bede's Place in Medieval Schools." In *Famulus Christi: Essays in Commemoration of the Thirteenth Centenary of the Birth of the Venerable Bede*, ed. Gerald Bonner. London, 1976. Pp. 271–77.

_____. "Some Introductory Remarks on Bede's Commentary on Genesis." *Sacris Erudiri* 19 (1969–70): 115–98.

_____. *Saints' Lives and Chronicles in Early England*. Ithaca, 1947.

J.S. "El llibre de les Homilies del venerabile Beda de Giron." *Vell i Nou* 5, no. 96 (1919): 287–89.

Kaczynski, Bernice M. "The Authority of the Fathers: Patristic Texts in Early Medieval Libraries and Scriptoria," *Journal of Medieval Latin* 16 (2006): 1–27.

_____. "Bede's Commentaries on Luke and Mark and the Formation of the Patristic Canon." In *Anglo-Latin and its Heritage: Essays in Honour of A.G. Rigg*, ed. Siân Echard and Gernot Wieland. Turnhout, 2001. Pp. 17–26.

Kelly, Joseph F. T. "The Venerable Bede and Hiberno-Latin Exegesis." In *Sources of Anglo-Saxon Literary Culture*, ed. Paul E. Szarmach. Kalamazoo, 1986. Pp. 65–75.

Kendall, Calvin B. "The Responsibility of *Auctoritas*: Method and Meaning in Bede's Commentary on Genesis." In *Innovation and Tradition in the Writings of the Venerable Bede*," ed. Scott DeGregorio. Morgantown, 2006. Pp. 101–19.

Ker, Neil R. *Medieval Manuscripts in British Libraries*, 5 vols. Vol. 5 with indexes and addenda ed. C. Cunningham and A. G. Watson. Oxford, 1969–2002.

_____. Review of M. L. W. Laistner with H. H. King, *Hand-List of Bede Manuscripts*. *Medium Aevum* 13 (1944): 36–40.

Killion, Steven B. "Bedan Historiography in the Irish Annals," *Medieval Perspectives* 6 (1991): 20–36.

Kirby, D. P. "The Genesis of a Cult: Cuthbert of Farne and Ecclesiastical Politics in Northumbria in the late Seventh and Early Eighth Centuries," *Journal of Ecclesiastical History* 46.3 (1995): 383–97.

Kitson, Peter. "Lapidary Traditions in Anglo-Saxon England, Part II: Bede's *Explanatio Apocalypsis* and Related Works." *Anglo-Saxon England* 12 (1983): 73–123.

Knappe, Gabriel. "Classical Rhetoric in Anglo-Saxon England." *ASE* 27 (1998): 5–29.

Ladner, Gerhard. "*Homo Viator*: Medieval Ideas on Alienation and Order." *Speculum* 42 (1967): 233–59.

Laistner, Max L. W. with H. H. King. *A Hand-List of Bede Manuscripts*. Ithaca, 1943.

_____, "The Latin Versions of Acts Known to the Venerable Bede." *Harvard Theological Review* 30 (1937): 37–50.

_____. "The Library of the Venerable Bede." In *Bede: His Life, Times and Writings*, ed. A. Hamilton Thompson. Oxford, 1935, rpt. 1969. Pp. 237–66.

_____. *Thought and Letters in Western Europe, AD 500 to 900*. Ithaca, 1957.

Lambert, Pierre-Yves. "Les commentaires celtiques à Bède le Vénérable." *Études Celtiques* 20 (1983): 119–43.

_____. "Gloses en vieux-breton, 1–5." *Études Celtiques* 26 (1990): 81–93.

Landes, Richard, "Lest the Millennium Be Fulfilled: Apocalyptic Expectations and the Pattern of Western Chronography 100–800 CE." In *The Use and Abuse of Eschatology in the Middle Ages*, ed. Werner Verbeke, Daniel Verhelst, and Andries Welkenhuysen. Leuven, 1988. Pp. 137–211.

Lapidge, Michael. "Acca of Hexham and the Origin of the *Old English Martyrology*." *Analecta Bollandiana* 123 (2005): 29–78.

_____. *Anglo-Latin Literature, 600–899*. 2 vols. London and Rio Grande, 1996.

_____. *The Anglo-Saxon Library*. Oxford, 2006.

_____, ed. *Archbishop Theodore: Commemorative Studies on his Life and Influence*. CSASE 11. Cambridge 1995.

_____, ed. *Bede and his World. The Jarrow Lectures, 1958–1973*. 2 vols. Aldershot, 1994.

_____. "Bede and the 'Versus de die iudicii.'" In *Nova de veteribus: Mittel- und neulateinische Studien für Gerhard Schmidt*, ed. Andreas Bihrer and Elisabeth Stein. Munich and Leipzig, 2004. Pp. 103–11.

_____, ed. *Blackwell Encyclopedia of Anglo-Saxon England*. Oxford, 1999.

_____. "Some Remnants of Bede's Lost *Liber epigrammatum*." *English Historical Review* 90 (1975): 798–820.

Law, Vivien. *The Insular Latin Grammarians*. Woodbridge, 1982.

Lawrence-Mathers, Anne. *Manuscripts in Northumbria in the Eleventh and Twelfth Centuries*. Woodbridge, 2003.

Lebecq, Stéphane, Michel Perrin, and Olivier Szerwiniack, eds. *Bède le Vénérable entre tradition et postérité*. Lille, 2005.

Leclercq, Jean. *The Love of Learning and the Desire for God*. New York, 1961.

Lees, Clare A., and Gillian R. Overing. "Birthing Bishops and Fathering Poets: Bede, Hild, and the Relations of Cultural Production." *Exemplaria* 6. 1 (Spring, 1994): 35–64.

Lendinara, Patricia, "Gregory and Damasus: Two Popes and Anglo-Saxon England." In *Rome and the North: The Early Reception of Gregory the Great in Germanic Europe*, ed. Rolf H. Bremmer, Jr., Kees Dekker, and David F. Johnson. Paris and Louvain, 2001. Pp. 137–56.

Levison, Wilhelm. "Bede as Historian." In *Bede: His Life, Times and Writings*, ed. A. Hamilton Thompson. Oxford, 1935, rpt. 1969. Pp. 111–51.

_____. "Modern Editions of Bede." *The Durham University Journal* 37, n.s. 6 (1945): 78–85.

Lowe, E. A., ed. *Codices latini antiquiores: A Palaeographical Guide to Latin Manuscripts Prior to the Ninth Century*. 12 vols. Oxford, 1934–71.

———, ed. *Codices latini antiquiores: A Palaeographical Guide to Latin Manuscripts*

Works Cited: Secondary

Prior to the Ninth Century. Part II: Great Britain and Ireland, Revised. Oxford, 1972.

Lubac, Henri de. *Exégèse médiévale: le quatre sens de l'Écriture*. 2 vols. in 4 parts. Lyons, 1960.

_____. *Medieval Exegesis: The Four Senses of Scripture*, trans. Mark Sebanc. 2 vols. Grand Rapids, 1998.

Lynch, Kevin M. "The Venerable Bede's Knowledge of Greek." *Traditio* 39 (1983): 432–39.

Mabillon, Jean. *Vetera Analecta, sive Collectio Veterum Aliquot Operum*. Paris, 1723, rpt. 1967.

Manitius, Max. *Geschichte der lateinischen Literatur des MIttelalters*. 3 vols. Munich, 1911–31.

Manuscripta-medievalia. www.manuscripta-medievalia.de. Handschriftendatenbank.

Markus, R. A. *Bede and the Tradition of Ecclesiastical Historiography*, Jarrow Lecture 1975. Rpt. in *Bede and his World*, ed. Michael Lapidge. London, 1994. I: 385–403.

Marrou, H. I. *A History of Education in Antiquity*, trans. George Lamb. Madison, 1982.

Marsden, Richard. *The Text of the Old Testament in Anglo-Saxon England*. Cambridge, 1995.

Matter, E. Ann. "The Bible in Early Medieval Saints' Lives." In *The Study of the Bible in the Carolingian Era*, ed. Celia Chazelle and Burton Van Name Edwards. Turnhout, 2003. Pp. 155–65.

_____. *The Voice of my Beloved: The Song of Songs in Western Medieval Christianity.* Philadelphia, 1990.

Mayr-Harting, Henry. *The Venerable Bede, the Rule of St Benedict, and Social Class*, Jarrow Lecture 1976. Jarrow, 1977.

Mazzatinti, G., et al. *Inventari dei Manoscritti delle Biblioteche d'Italia*, 111 vols. to date. Florence, 1890– .

McClure, Judith. "Bede and the Life of Ceolfrid." *Peritia* 3 (1984), 71–84.

McCready, William D. *Miracles and the Venerable Bede*. Toronto, 1994.

McKitterick, Rosamond. "Anglo-Saxon Missionaries in Germany: Reflections on the Manuscript Evidence." *Transactions of the Cambridge Bibliographic Society*, IX.4 (1989): 291–329.

_____. "Carolingian Book Production: Some Problems." *The Library*, 6th series 12 (1990): 1–33.

_____. "The Diffusion of Insular Culture in Neustria between 650 and 850: the Implications of the Manuscript Evidence." In *La Neustrie. Le pays au nord de la Loire de 650 à 850*, ed. Hartmut Atsma. Sigmaringen, 1989. Pp. 395–432.

_____. "Kulturelle Verbindungen zwischen England und den fränkischen Reichen in der Zeit der Karolinger: Kontexte und Implikationen." In *Deutschland und der Western Europas im Mittelalter*, ed. Joachim Ehlers. Stuttgart, 2002. Pp. 121–48.

McNally, Robert E., ed. *Scriptores Hiberniae minores*. Pars 1: *Commentarius in epistolas catholicas Scotti anonymi*. CCSL 108B. Turnhout, 1973.

Meyvaert, Paul. "Bede, Cassiodorus, and the Codex Amiatinus." *Speculum* 71 (1996): 827–83.

_____. "Bede and the Church Paintings at Wearmouth-Jarrow." *ASE* 8 (1979): 63–77.

_____. *Bede and Gregory the Great*, Jarrow Lecture 1964. Rpt. in *Benedict, Gregory, Bede and Others*. London, 1977. Selection VIII.

_____. "Bede the Scholar." In *Famulus Christi*, ed. Gerald Bonner. London, 1976. Pp. 48–51.

_____. "Bede's *Capitula Lectionum* for the Old and New Testaments." *RB* 105 (1995): 348–80.

_____. "Bede's Text of the *Libellus Responsionum* of Gregory the Great to Augustine of Canterbury." In *England before the Conquest: Studies in Primary Sources Presented to Dorothy Whitelock*, ed. P. Clemoes and K. Hughes. Cambridge, 1971. Pp. 15–73. Rpt. in *Benedict, Gregory, Bede and Others*. London, 1977. Selection X.

_____. "'In the Footsteps of the Fathers': The Date of Bede's *Thirty Questions on the Book of Kings to Nothelm*." In *The Limits of Ancient Christianity*, ed. William E. Klingshirn and Mark Vessey. Ann Arbor, 1999. Pp. 267–86.

_____. "Medieval Notions of Publication: The 'Upublished' *Opus Caroli Regis contra synodum* and the Council of Frankfort (794)." *Journal of Medieval Latin* 12 (2002): 78–89.

Mittelalterliche Bibliothekskataloge Deutschlands und der Schweiz, Bayerische Akademie der Wissenschaften, 4 vols. (vol. 3 in 4 parts, vol. 4 in 2 parts) with 3 supplements to date. Munich, 1969– .

Momigliano, Arnaldo. "Pagan and Christian Historiography in the Fourth Century AD." In *The Conflict between Paganism and Christianity in the Fourth Century*, ed. Momigliano. Oxford, 1963.

Murphy, Roland E. *The Song of Songs: A Commentary on the Book of Canticles or The Song of Songs*, ed. S. Dean McBride, Jr. Minneapolis, 1990. Pp. 11–41.

Mynors, R. A. B. *Durham Cathedral Manuscripts to the End of the Twelfth Century*. Oxford, 1939.

Napier, Arthur S., ed. *Old English Glosses, Chiefly Unpublished*. Oxford, 1900.

Newlands, Carole E. "Bede and Images of Saint Cuthbert." *Traditio* 52 (1997): 73–109

Ní Chatháin, Próinséas. "Bede's *Ecclesiastical History* in Irish." *Peritia* 3 (1984): 115–30.

Nicholson, Joan. "*Feminae gloriosae*: Women in the Age of Bede." In *Medieval Women*, ed. Derek Baker. Oxford, 1978. Pp. 15–29.

Norberg, Dag. *An Introduction to the Study of Medieval Latin Versification*, trans. Grant C. Roti and Jacqueline de la Chapelle Skubly. Washington, DC, 2004.

Nortier, Geneviève. *Les bibliothèques médiévales des abbayes bénédictines de Normandie. Fécamp, Le Bec, Mont St. Michel, St. Evroul, Lyre, Jumièges, Saint-Wandrille, St. Ouen*. Paris, 1971.

Ó Cróinín, Dáibhí, ed. *A New History of Ireland*. Vol. 1: *Prehistory and Early Ireland*. Oxford, 2005.

Ohly, Friedrich. *Sensus Spiritualis: Studies in Medieval Significs and the Philology of Culture*, ed. Samuel P. Jaffe, trans. Kenneth J. Northcott. Chicago, 2005.

O'Loughlin, Thomas. *Adomnán and the Holy Places: The Perceptions of an Insular Monk on the Locations of the Biblical Drama*. London and New York, 2007.

_____. *Teachers and Code-Breakers: The Latin Genesis Tradition, 430–800*. Turnhout, 1999.

O'Reilly, Jennifer, "Bede on Seeing the God of Gods in Zion." In *Text, Image, Interpretation: Studies in Anglo-Saxon Literature and its Insular Context in Honour of Éamonn Ó Carragáin*, ed. A. Minnis and J. Roberts. Turnhout, 2007. Pp. 3–29.

The Oxford Dictionary of the Christian Church, ed. F. L. Cross and E. A. Livingstone. 3rd ed. Oxford, 1997.

Oxford Dictionary of National Biography, ed. H. C. G. Matthew and Brian Harrison. 60 vols. Oxford, 2004; online, 2004.

Page, William, ed. *The Victoria History of the Counties of England: Durham*. 3 vols. London, 1905, rpt. 1968.

Palmer, Robert B. "Bede as Textbook Writer: A Study of his *De Arte Metrica*." *Speculum* 34 (1959): 573–84.

Parkes, Malcolm B. *The Scriptorium of Wearmouth-Jarrow*, Jarrow Lecture 1982. Rpt. in *Bede and his World*, ed. Michael Lapidge. Aldershot, 1994. II: 555–86.

Pelteret, David A. E. "Bede's Women." In *Women, Marriage and Family in Medieval Christendom*, ed. Constance M. Rousseau and Joel T. Rosenthal. Kalamazoo, 1998. Pp. 19–46.

Pfaff, Richard W. "Bede among the Fathers?" *Studia Patristica* 28 (1993): 225–29. Rpt. in Richard W. Pfaff, *Liturgical Calendars, Saints, and Services in Medieval England*. Aldershot, 1998. No. X.

Popoff, Michel. *Index général des manuscrits décrits dans le Catalogue général des manuscrits des bibliothèques publiques de France*. 3 vols. Paris, 1993.

Ray, Roger. "Bede, the Exegete, as Historian." In *Famulus Christi*, ed. Gerald Bonner. London, 1976. Pp. 125–40.

———. "Bede's *Vera lex historiae*." *Speculum* 55.1 (1980): 1–21.

Riché, Pierre. *Education and Culture in the Barbarian West, Sixth through Eighth Centuries*, trans. John J. Contreni. Columbia, 1976.

Richter, Michael. "Bede's *Angli*: Angles or English?" *Peritia* 3 (1984): 99–114.

Riedlinger, Helmut. *Die Makellosigkeit der Kirche in den lateinischen Hoheliedkommentaren des Mittelalters*. Münster, 1958.

Robins, R. H. *Ancient and Medieval Grammatical Theory in Europe*. London, 1951.

Roger, M. *L'Enseignement des lettres classiques d'Ausone à Alcuin*. Paris, 1905.

Rollason, David, ed. *Symeon of Durham: Historian of Durham and the North*. Stamford, 1998.

Rouse, Richard H., Mary A. Rouse, R. A. B. Mynors, eds. *Registrum anglie de libris doctorum et auctorum veterum*. Corpus of British Medieval Library Catalogues. London, 1991.

Ruff, Carin. "The Place of Metrics in Anglo-Saxon Latin Education: Aldhelm and Bede." *JEGP* 104.2 (2005): 149–70.

Schaller, Dietrich. "Bemerkungen zur Inschriften-Sylloge von Urbana," *Mittellateinisches Jahrbuch* 12 (1977): 9–21.

———. *Studien zur lateinischen Dichtung des Frühmittelalters*. Stuttgart, 1995.

Scheil, Andrew P. *The Footsteps of Israel: Understanding Jews in Anglo-Saxon England*. Ann Arbor, 2004.

Schindel, Ulrich. *Die lateinischen Figurenlehren des 5. bis 7. Jahrhunderts und Donats Vergilkommentar (mit zwei Editionen)*. Abhandlungen der Akademie der Wissenschaften in Göttingen, Philosophisch-historische Klasse, dritte Folge. Göttingen, 1975.

Schipke, Renate. *Scriptorium und Bibliothek des Benediktinerklosters Bosau bei Zeitz: die Bosauer Handschriften in Schulpforte.* Wiesbaden, 2000.

Scully, Diarmuid. "Bede's *Chronica Maiora*: Early Insular History in a Universal Context." In *Anglo-Saxon/Irish Relations before the Vikings, Proceedings of the*

Works Cited: Secondary

Royal Irish Academy/ British Academy Symposium, London, 12th–14th October 2005. London, forthcoming. Pp. 1–29.

Sharpe, Richard. *British Medieval Library Catalogues* online, List of Identifications, http://www.history.ox.ac.uk/sharpe/index.htm#catalogues. Pp. 133–40.

Silvestre, Hubert. "À propos de quelques manuscrits de Bède." *Scriptorium* 17 (1963): 110–13.

_____. *Les manuscrits de Bède à la Bibliothèque Royale de Bruxelles*, Studia Universitatis "Lovanium," Faculté de philosophie et lettres 6. Leopoldville, 1959.

Sims-Williams, Patrick. "Milred of Worcester's Collection of Latin Epigrams and its Continental Counterparts." *ASE* 10 (1982): 21–28.

_____. *Religion and Literature in Western England, 600–800*. Cambridge, 1990.

Sirat, Colette. *Hebrew Manuscripts of the Middle Ages*. Cambridge, 2002.

Smalley, Beryl. *The Study of the Bible in the Middle Ages*. Oxford, 1962.

Smyth, Marina. *Understanding the Universe in Seventh-Century Ireland*. Woodbridge, 1996.

Southern, R. W. *Robert Grosseteste*. Oxford, 1986.

Stancliffe, Clare. "St Cuthbert and the Polarity between Pastor and Solitary." In *St Cuthbert, his Cult and his Community to AD 1200*, ed. Gerald Bonner, David Rollason, and Clare Stancliffe. Woodbridge, 1989. Pp. 21–44.

Stegmüller, Friedrich, ed. *Repertorium biblicum medii aevi*. 11 vols. Matriti, 1950–80.

Stenton, Frank. *Anglo-Saxon England*. 3rd ed. Oxford, 1968, reissued 2001.

Strachan, John. "The Vienna Fragments of Bede." *Revue Celtique* 23 (1902): 40–49.

Strubel, Armand. "'Allegoria in factis' et 'Allegoria in verbis'." *Poétique* 23 (1975): 351–53.

Szerwiniack, Olivier. "Frères et sœurs dans *l'Histoire ecclésiastique dur peuple anglais* de Bède le Vénérable: De la fratrie biologique à la fratrie spirituelle," *RB* 118.2 (2008): 239–61.

Thacker, Alan. "Bede and the Ordering of Understanding." In *Innovations and Tradition in the Writings of the Venerable Bede*, ed. Scott DeGregorio. Morgantown, 2006. Pp. 37–63.

_____. "Bede's Ideal of Reform." In *Ideal and Reality in Frankish and Anglo-Saxon Society*, ed. Patrick Wormald, Donald Bullough, and Roger Collins. Oxford, 1983. Pp. 130–53.

Thesaurus Palaeohibernicus, ed. Whitley Stokes and John Strachan. 2 vols. Cambridge, 1901–03.

Thompson, A. Hamilton, ed. *Bede: His Life, Times and Writings*. Oxford, 1935, rpt. 1969.

Wallace-Hadrill, J. M. *Bede's Ecclesiastical History of the English People: A Historical Commentary*. Oxford, 1988.

_____. *Bede's Europe*. Jarrow Lecture 1962. Rpt. *Bede and his World: The Jarrow Lectures*, ed. Michael Lapidge. Aldershot, 1994. I: 73–85.

_____. *Early Medieval History*. Oxford, 1975.

Wallach, Luitpold. "The Urbana Anglo-Saxon Sylloge of Latin Inscriptions." In *Poetry and Poetics from Ancient Greece to the Renaissance: Studies in Honor of James Hutton*, ed. G. M. Kirkwood. Cornell Studies in Classical Philology 38. Ithaca, NY 1975. Pp. 134–151.

Ward, Benedicta. "Beda Venerabilis: *Doctor Anglorum*." In *Väter der Kirche: Ekklesiales Denken von den Anfängen bis in die Neuzeit, Festgabe für Josef Sieben,* ed. Johannes Arnold, Rainer Berndt, and Ralf M. W. Stammberger. Paderborn, 2004. Pp. 533–42.

————. *Bede and the Psalter*, Jarrow Lecture. Jarrow, 1991. Rpt. in *Bede and his World*, ed. Michael Lapidge. Aldershot, 1994. II: 869–902.

————. *Miracles and the Medieval Mind*. Philadelphia, 1982.

————. "'To my dearest Sister': Bede and the Educated Woman.'" In *Women, the Book, and the Godly: Selected Proceedings of the St. Hilda's Conference, 1993*, ed. Lesley Smith and Jane H. M. Taylor. Woodbridge, 1995. Pp. 105–11.

————. *The Venerable Bede*. Harrisburg, 1990.

West, Philip J. "Ruminations in Bede's Account of Cædmon." *Monastic Studies* 12 (1976): 217–36.

Westgard, Joshua. "Bede and the Continent in the Carolingian Age and Beyond." In *The Cambridge Companion to Bede*, ed. Scott DeGregorio. Cambridge, forthcoming 2010.

————. "Dissemination and Reception of Bede's *Historia ecclesiastica gentis anglorum* in Germay, c. 731–1500: The Manuscript Evidence." Ph.D. dissertation. University of North Carolina, Chapel Hill. 2005.

Wetherbee, W. "Some Implications of Bede's Latin Style." In *Bede and Anglo-Saxon England: Papers in Honour of the 1300th Anniversary of the Birth of Bede, Given at Cornell University in 1973 and 1974*, ed. R. T. Farrell. British Archaeological Reports 46. Oxford, 1978. Pp. 23–31.

Whitbread, Leslie. "After Bede: The Influence and Dissemination of his Doomsday Verses." *Archiv für das Studium der neueren Sprachen* 204 (1967): 250–66.

————. "Bede's Verses on Doomsday: A Supplementary Note." *Philological Quarterly* 51 (1972): 485–86.

————. "The Old English Poem *Judgment Day II* and its Latin Source." *Philological Quarterly* 45 (1966): 635–56.

————, ed. "A Study of Bede's *Versus de die iudicii*." *Philological Quarterly* 23 (1944): 193–221.

————. "Text-Notes on the Old English Poem Judgment Day II." *English Studies* 48 (1967): 531–33.

Whitelock, Dorothy. *After Bede*. Jarrow Lecture 1960. Rpt. in *Bede and his World: The Jarrow Lectures*, ed. Michael Lapidge. Aldershot, 1994. I: 37–49.

————, ed. *English Historical Documents.*Vol. 1: *c. 500–1042*. 2nd ed. Oxford, 1979.

Wieland, Gernot. "Caedmon, the Clean Animal." *American Benedictine Review*, 35 (1984): 194–203.

————. "*Geminus Stilus*: Studies in Anglo-Latin Hagiography." In *Insular Latin Studies*, ed. Michael Herren. Toronto, 1981. Pp.113–33.

Wilmart, André. "La collection de Bède le Vénérable sur l'Apôtre." *RB* 38 (1926): 16–52.

Wilson, David R. *Anglo-Saxon Paganism*. London and New York, 1992.

Wormald, Patrick. "Bede and Benedict Biscop." In *Famulus Christi*, ed. Gerald Bonner. London, 1976. Pp. 3–29.

————. *Bede and the Conversion of England: The Charter Evidence*. Jarrow Lecture, 1984. Rpt. *Bede and his World*, ed. Michael Lapidge. Aldershot, 1994. II: 631–35.

————. "*Engla Lond*: The Making of an Allegiance." *Journal of Historical Sociology* 7: 1 (March 1994): 1–24.

————. *The Times of Bede: Studies in Early English Christian Society and its Historian*, ed. Stephen David Baxter. Malden, 2006.

Works Cited: Secondary

Wright, Robert, *A Companion to Bede: A Reader's Commentary on The Ecclesiastical History of the English People*. Grand Rapids, 2008.

Yorke, Barbara. "Anglo-Saxon Origin Legends." In *Myth, Rulership, Church and Charters: Essays in Honour of Nicholas Brooks*, ed. Julia Barrow and Andrew Wareham. Aldershot, 2008. Pp. 15–29.

_____. *The Kings and Kingdoms of Early Anglo-Saxon England*. London, 1990, rpt. 1992.

_____. *Nunneries and the Anglo-Saxon Royal Houses*. London, 2003.

Index of Bede's Works

General Index

ANGLO-SAXON STUDIES